# OLD MAN LOGAN

## DAYS OF ANGER

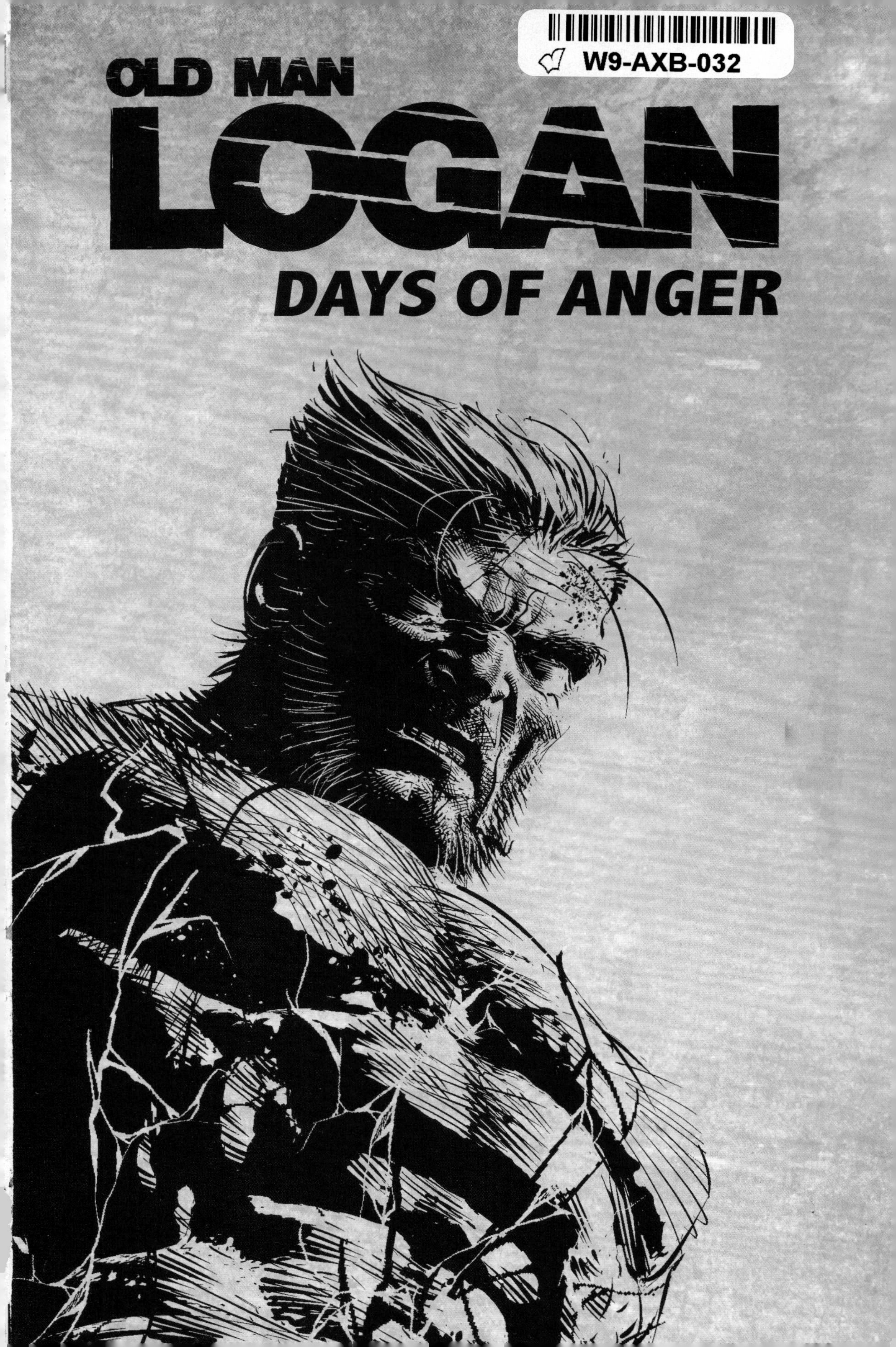

# OLD MAN LOGAN

## DAYS OF ANGER

WRITER **ED BRISSON**

ARTIST **MIKE DEODATO JR.**

COLOR ARTIST **FRANK MARTIN**

COVER ART **MIKE DEODATO JR. & FRANK MARTIN**

LETTERER **VC's CORY PETIT**

ASSOCIATE EDITOR **MARK BASSO**

EDITOR **MARK PANICCIA**

COLLECTION EDITOR **MARK D. BEAZLEY**
ASSISTANT EDITOR **CAITLIN O'CONNELL**
ASSOCIATE MANAGING EDITOR **KATERI WOODY**
SENIOR EDITOR, SPECIAL PROJECTS **JENNIFER GRÜNWALD**
VP PRODUCTION & SPECIAL PROJECTS **JEFF YOUNGQUIST**
SVP PRINT, SALES & MARKETING **DAVID GABRIEL**
BOOK DESIGNER **ADAM DEL RE**

EDITOR IN CHIEF **C.B. CEBULSKI**
CHIEF CREATIVE OFFICER **JOE QUESADA**
PRESIDENT **DAN BUCKLEY**
EXECUTIVE PRODUCER **ALAN FINE**

**WOLVERINE: OLD MAN LOGAN VOL. 6 — DAYS OF ANGER.** Contains material originally published in magazine form as OLD MAN LOGAN #25-30. First printing 2018. ISBN 978-1-302-90575-0. Published by MARVEL WORLDWIDE, INC., a subsidiary of MARVEL ENTERTAINMENT, LLC. OFFICE OF PUBLICATION: 135 West 50th Street, New York, NY 10020.  **Printed in Canada.** DAN BUCKLEY, President, Marvel Entertainment; JOE QUESADA, Chief Creative Officer; TOM BREVOORT, SVP of Publishing; DAVID BOGART, SVP of Business Affairs & Operations, Publishing & Partnership; DAVID GABRIEL, SVP of Sales & Marketing, Publishing; JEFF YOUNGQUIST, VP of Production & Special Projects; DAN CARR, Executive Director of Publishing Technology; ALEX MORALES, Director of Publishing Operations; SUSAN CRESPI, Production Manager; STAN LEE, Chairman Emeritus. For information regarding advertising in Marvel Comics or on Marvel.com, please contact Jonathan Parkhideh, VP of Digital Media & Marketing Solutions, at jparkhideh@marvel.com. For Marvel subscription inquiries, please call 888-511-5480. **Manufactured between 12/1/2017 and 1/2/2018 by SOLISCO PRINTERS, SCOTT, QC, CANADA.**

10 9 8 7 6 5 4 3 2 1

Surviving a future known as the wastelands, where everything good in the world, including his family, was destroyed, Old Man Logan awoke in the present determined to prevent this catastrophic reality from ever coming to pass. Now, Logan tries to find his place in a world not quite his own.

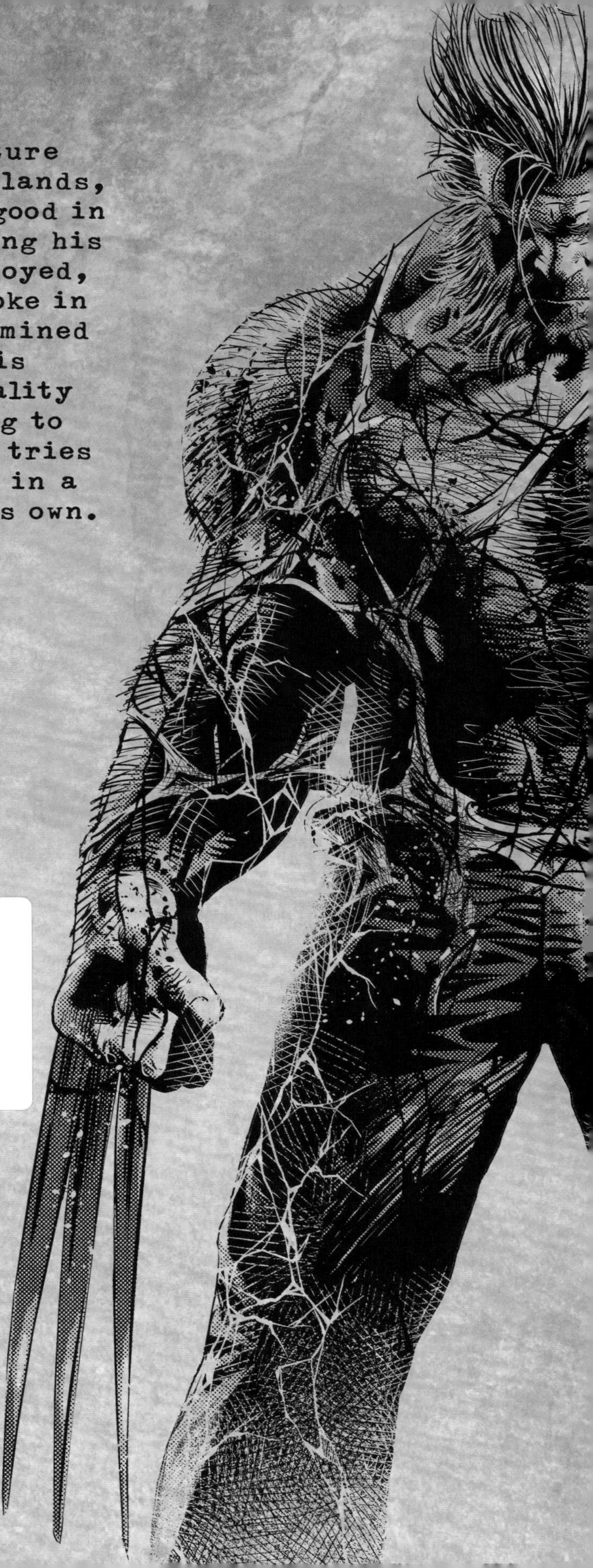

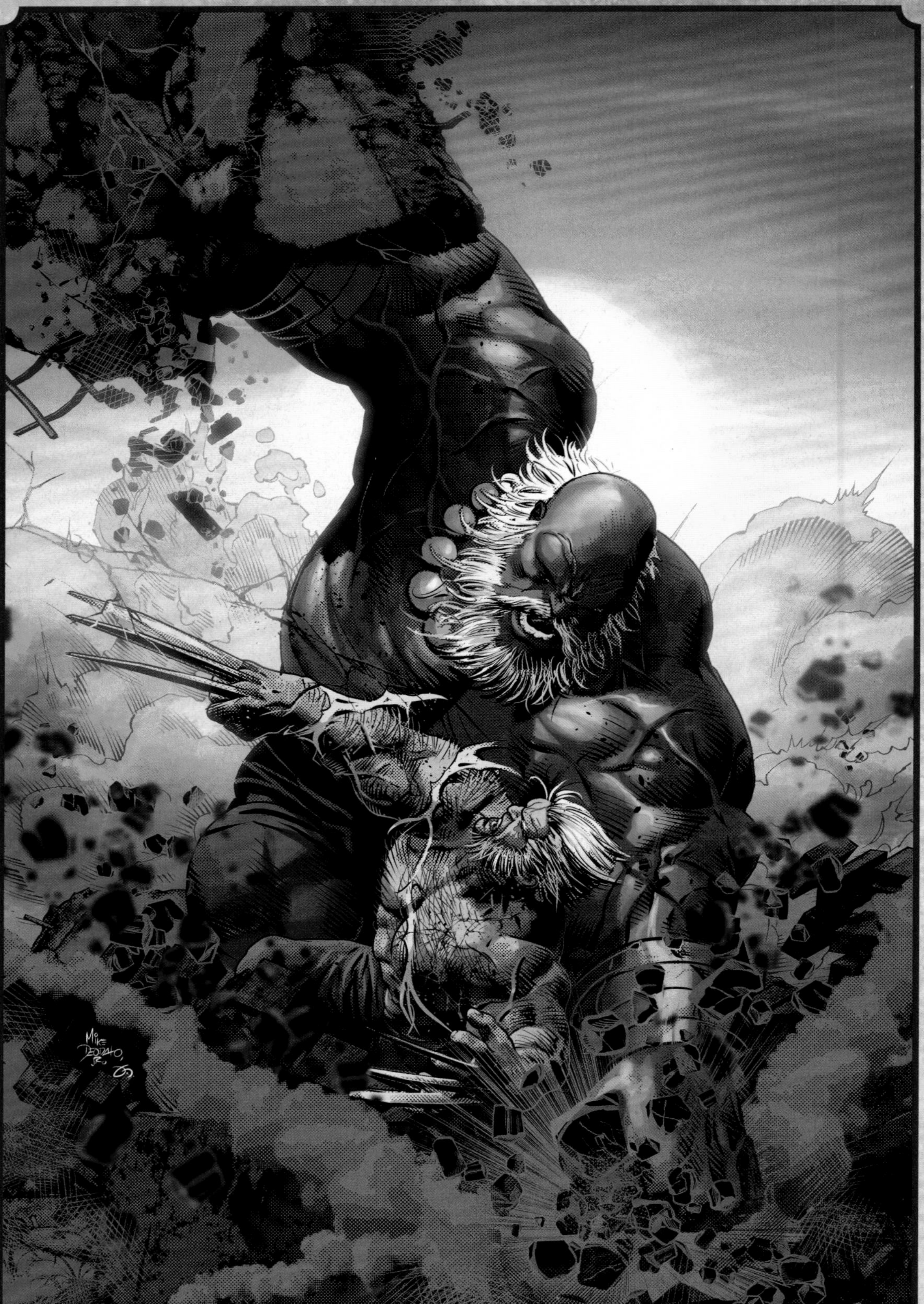

25

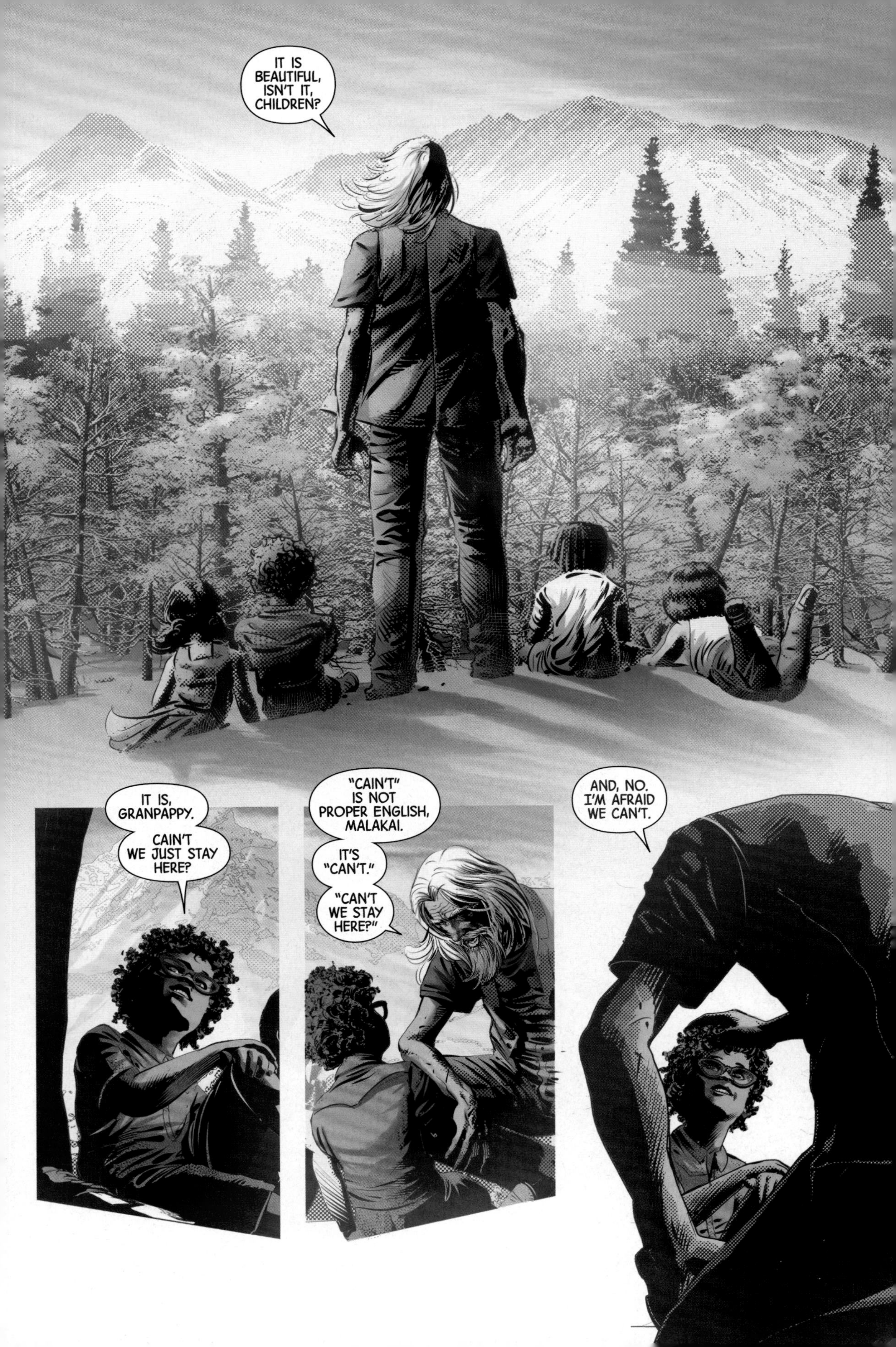
IT IS BEAUTIFUL, ISN'T IT, CHILDREN?
IT IS, GRANPAPPY.
CAIN'T WE JUST STAY HERE?
"CAIN'T" IS NOT PROPER ENGLISH, MALAKAI.
IT'S "CAN'T."
"CAN'T WE STAY HERE?"
AND, NO. I'M AFRAID WE CAN'T.

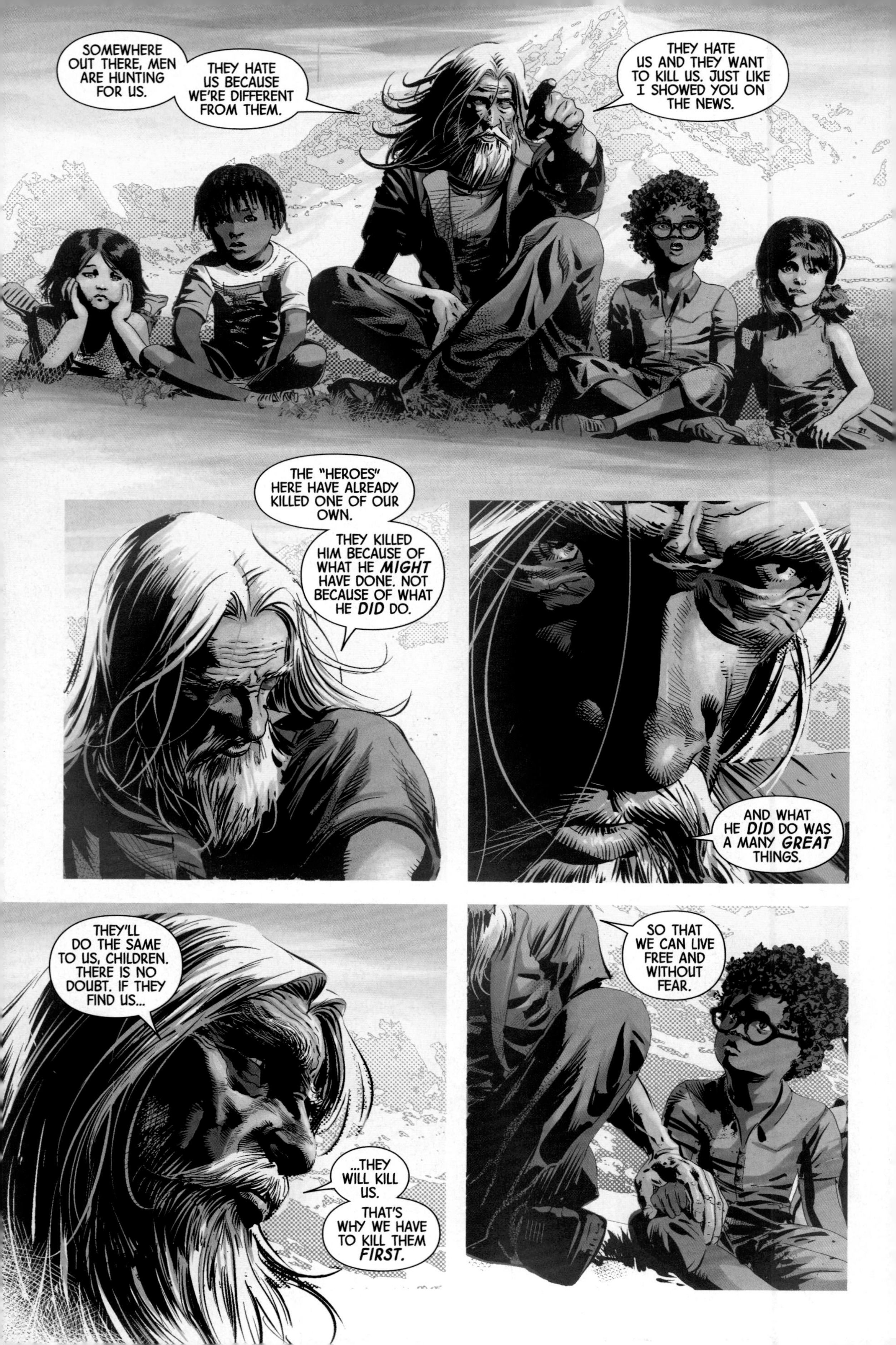
SOMEWHERE OUT THERE, MEN ARE HUNTING FOR US.
THEY HATE US BECAUSE WE'RE DIFFERENT FROM THEM.
THEY HATE US AND THEY WANT TO KILL US. JUST LIKE I SHOWED YOU ON THE NEWS.
THE "HEROES" HERE HAVE ALREADY KILLED ONE OF OUR OWN.
THEY KILLED HIM BECAUSE OF WHAT HE *MIGHT* HAVE DONE. NOT BECAUSE OF WHAT HE *DID* DO.
AND WHAT HE *DID* DO WAS A MANY *GREAT* THINGS.
THEY'LL DO THE SAME TO US, CHILDREN. THERE IS NO DOUBT. IF THEY FIND US...
...THEY WILL KILL US.
THAT'S WHY WE HAVE TO KILL THEM *FIRST.*
SO THAT WE CAN LIVE FREE AND WITHOUT FEAR.

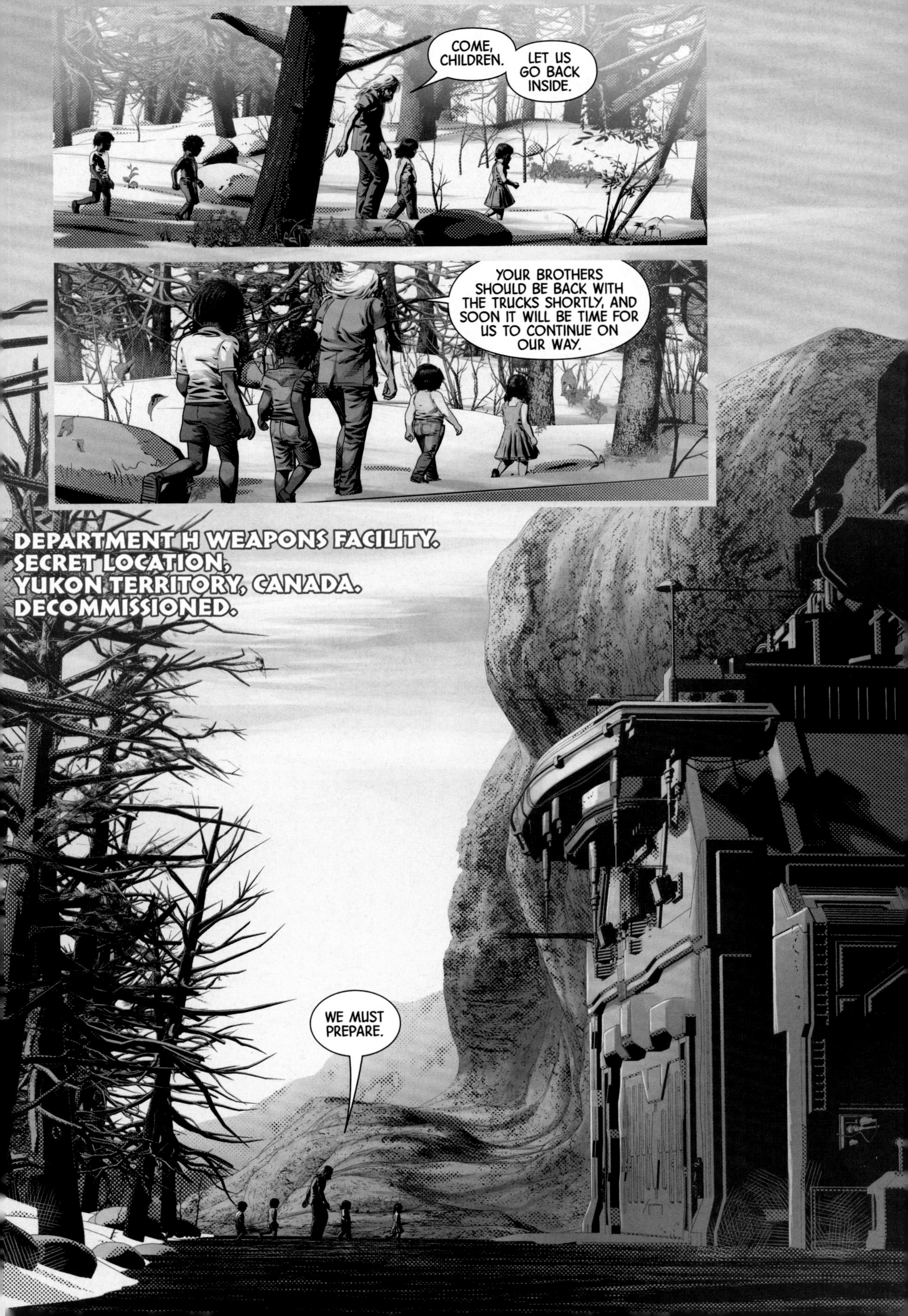
COME, CHILDREN.
LET US GO BACK INSIDE.
YOUR BROTHERS SHOULD BE BACK WITH THE TRUCKS SHORTLY, AND SOON IT WILL BE TIME FOR US TO CONTINUE ON OUR WAY.
DEPARTMENT H WEAPONS FACILITY. SECRET LOCATION, YUKON TERRITORY, CANADA. DECOMMISSIONED.
WE MUST PREPARE.

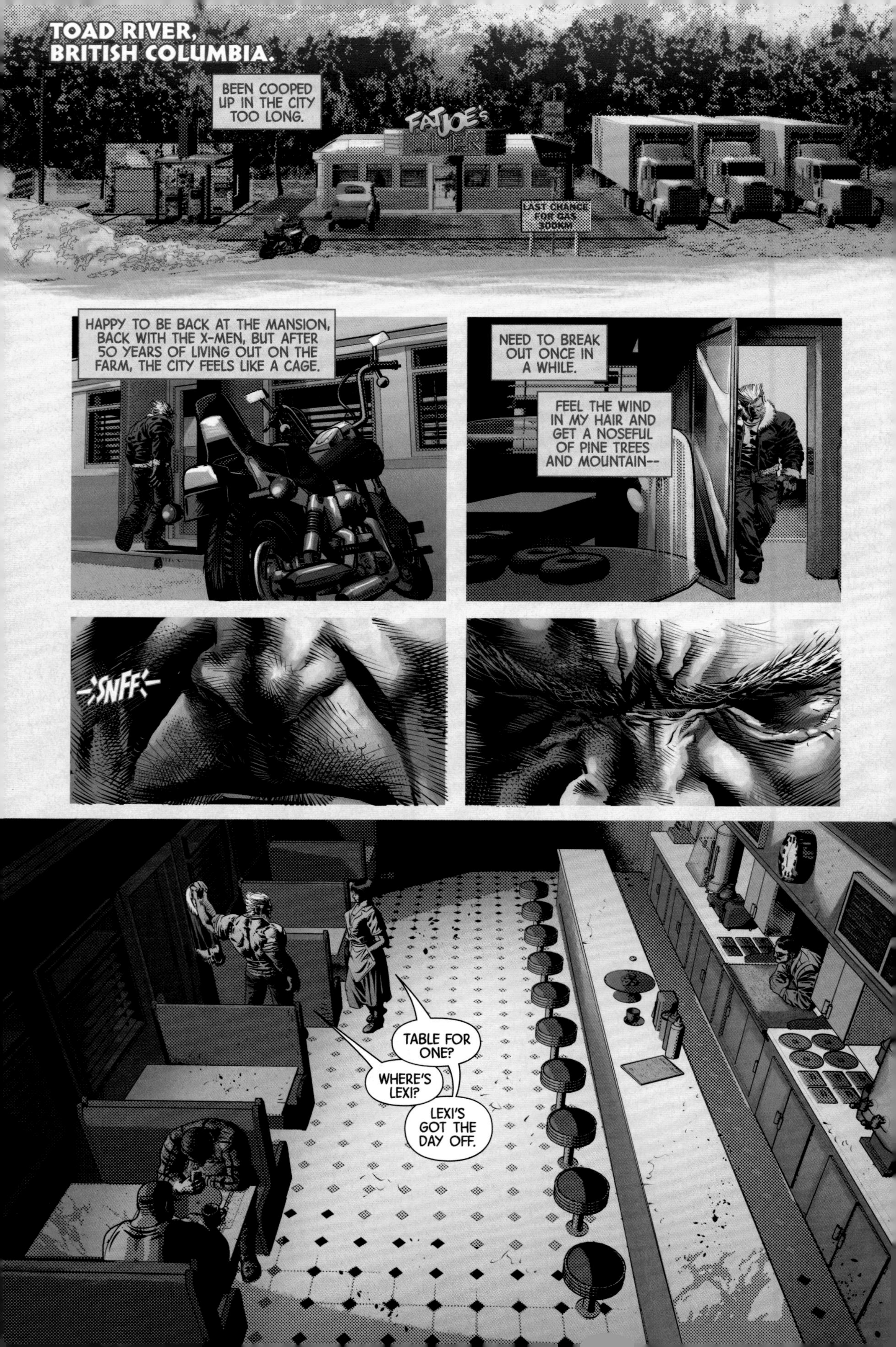

TOAD RIVER, BRITISH COLUMBIA.
BEEN COOPED UP IN THE CITY TOO LONG.
FAT JOE's
LAST CHANCE FOR GAS 300KM
HAPPY TO BE BACK AT THE MANSION, BACK WITH THE X-MEN, BUT AFTER 50 YEARS OF LIVING OUT ON THE FARM, THE CITY FEELS LIKE A CAGE.
NEED TO BREAK OUT ONCE IN A WHILE.
FEEL THE WIND IN MY HAIR AND GET A NOSEFUL OF PINE TREES AND MOUNTAIN--
SNFF
TABLE FOR ONE?
WHERE'S LEXI?
LEXI'S GOT THE DAY OFF.

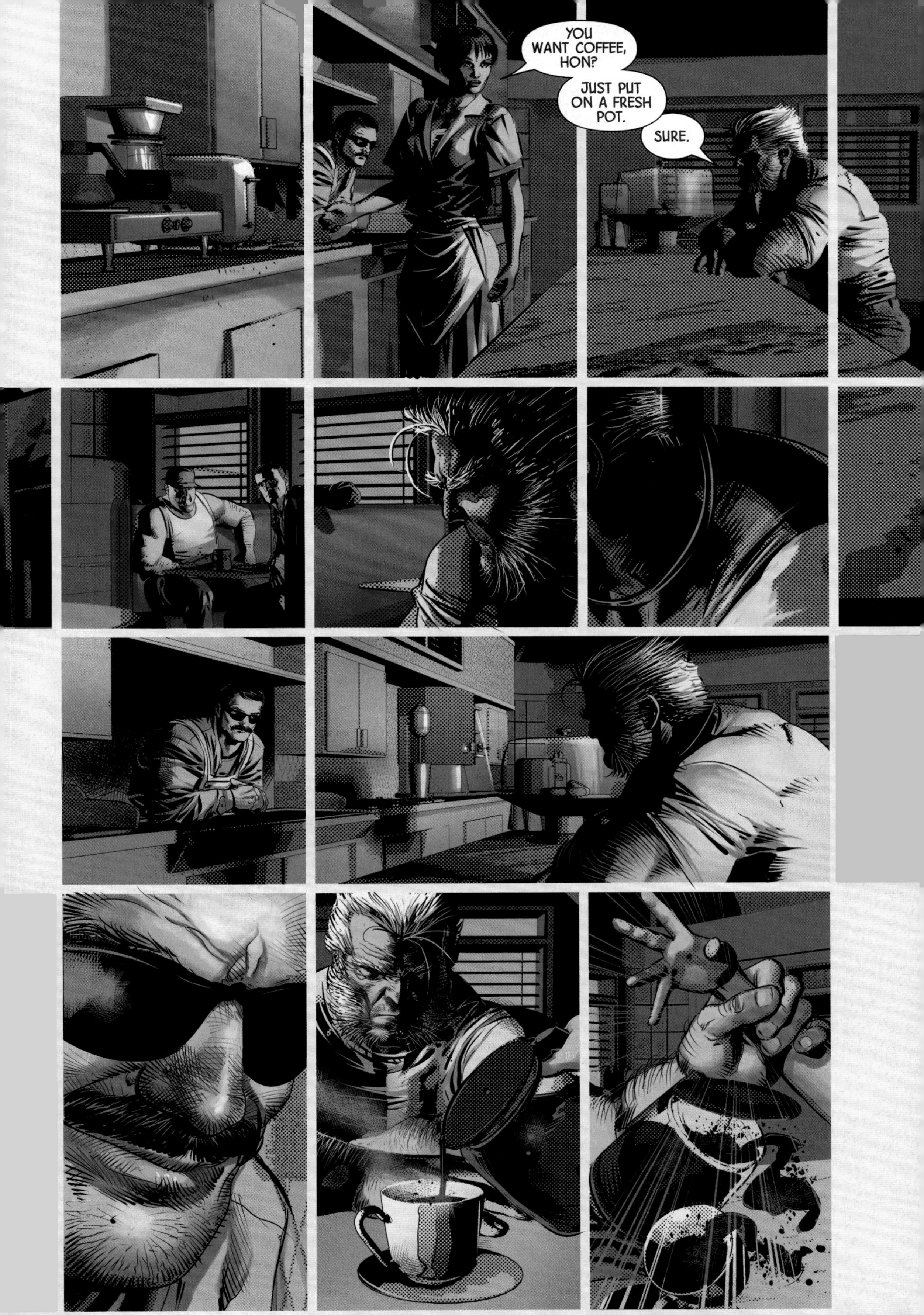
YOU WANT COFFEE, HON?
JUST PUT ON A FRESH POT.
SURE.

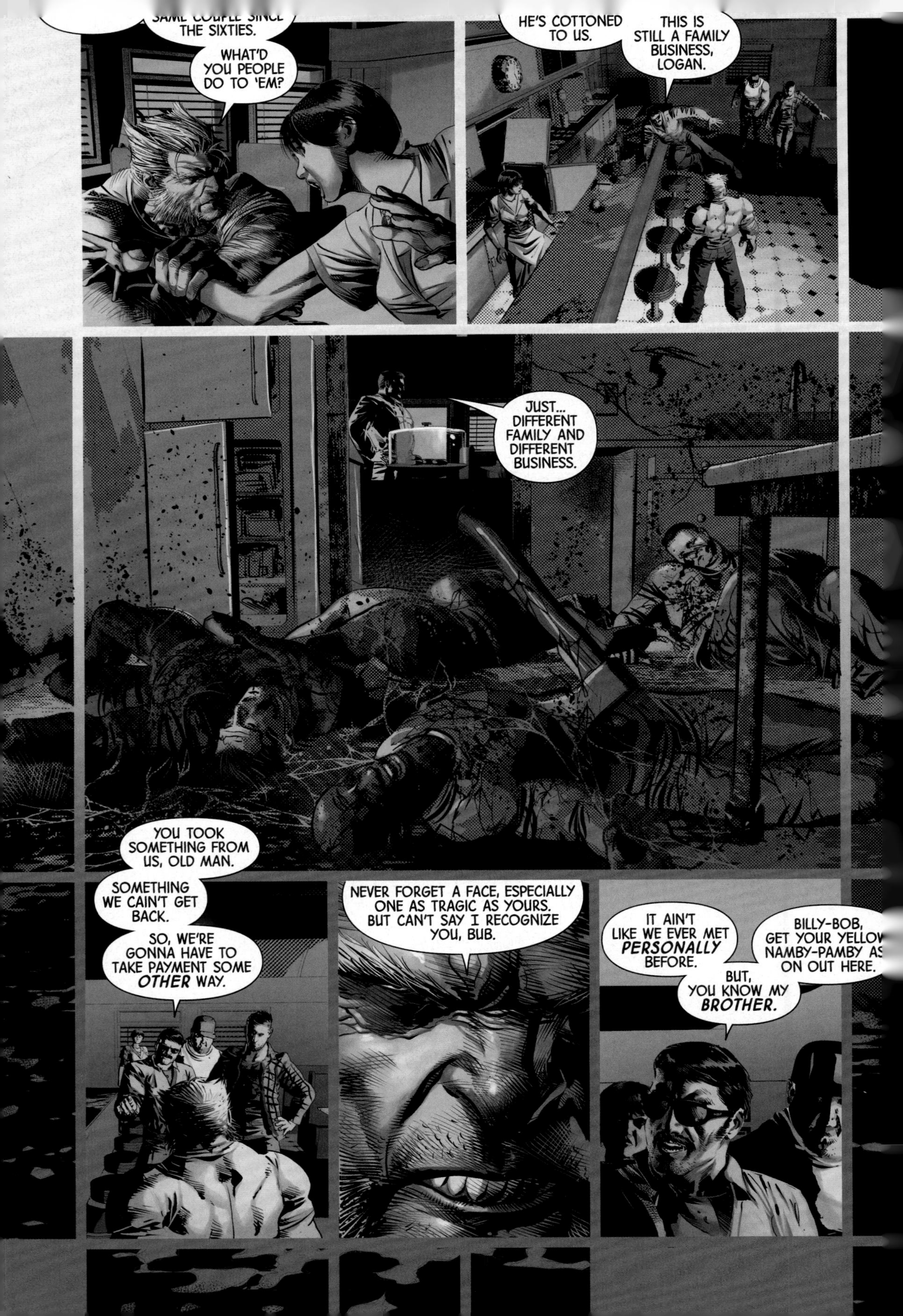
SAME COUPLE SINCE THE SIXTIES.
WHAT'D YOU PEOPLE DO TO 'EM?
HE'S COTTONED TO US.
THIS IS STILL A FAMILY BUSINESS, LOGAN.
JUST... DIFFERENT FAMILY AND DIFFERENT BUSINESS.
YOU TOOK SOMETHING FROM US, OLD MAN.
SOMETHING WE CAIN'T GET BACK.
SO, WE'RE GONNA HAVE TO TAKE PAYMENT SOME *OTHER* WAY.
NEVER FORGET A FACE, ESPECIALLY ONE AS TRAGIC AS YOURS. BUT CAN'T SAY I RECOGNIZE YOU, BUB.
IT AIN'T LIKE WE EVER MET *PERSONALLY* BEFORE.
BUT, YOU KNOW MY *BROTHER.*
BILLY-BOB, GET YOUR YELLOW NAMBY-PAMBY AS ON OUT HERE.

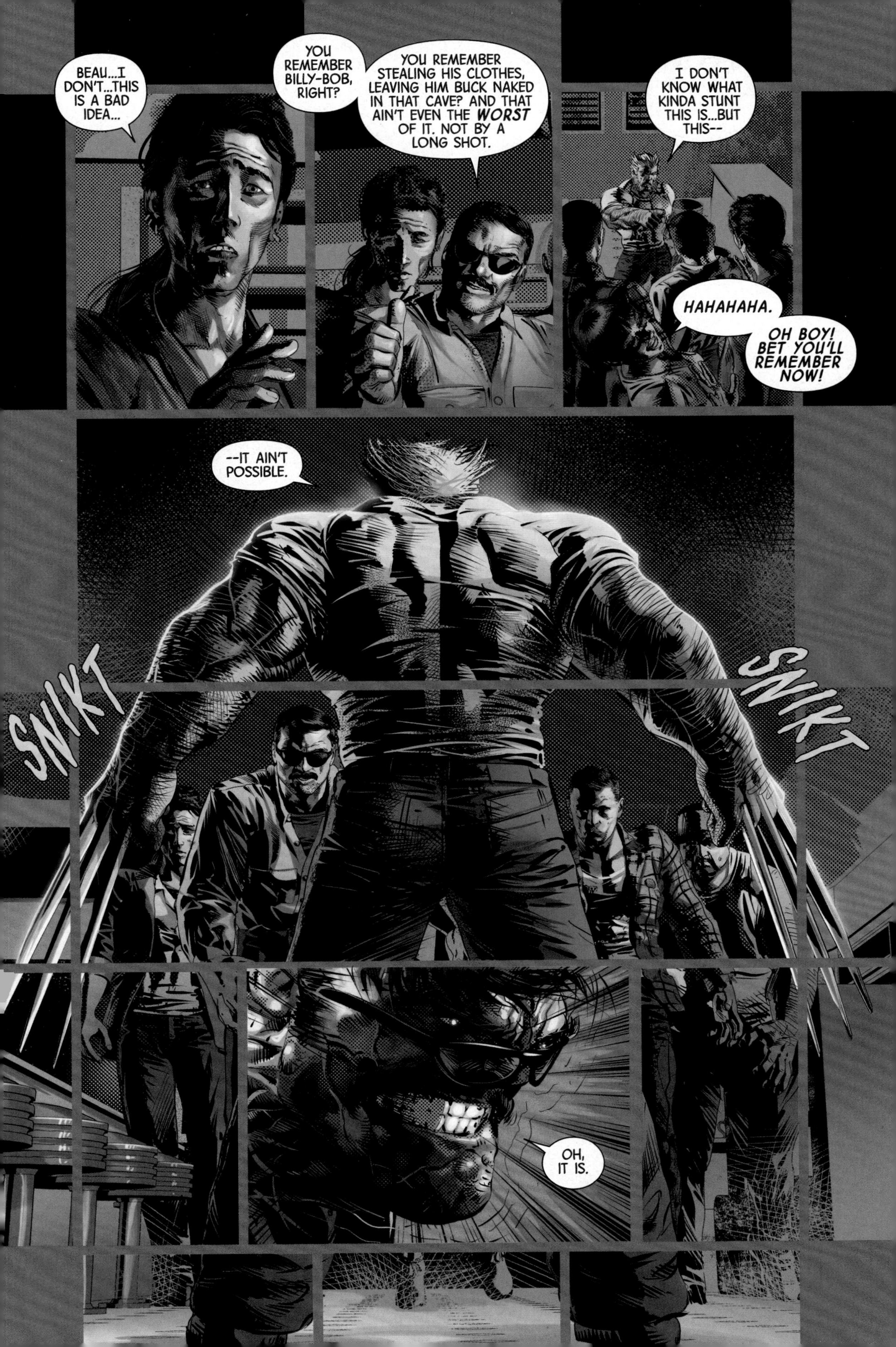
BEAU...I DON'T...THIS IS A BAD IDEA...
YOU REMEMBER BILLY-BOB, RIGHT?
YOU REMEMBER STEALING HIS CLOTHES, LEAVING HIM BUCK NAKED IN THAT CAVE? AND THAT AIN'T EVEN THE WORST OF IT. NOT BY A LONG SHOT.
I DON'T KNOW WHAT KINDA STUNT THIS IS...BUT THIS--
HAHAHAHA.
OH BOY! BET YOU'LL REMEMBER NOW!
--IT AIN'T POSSIBLE.
SNIKT
SNIKT
OH, IT IS.

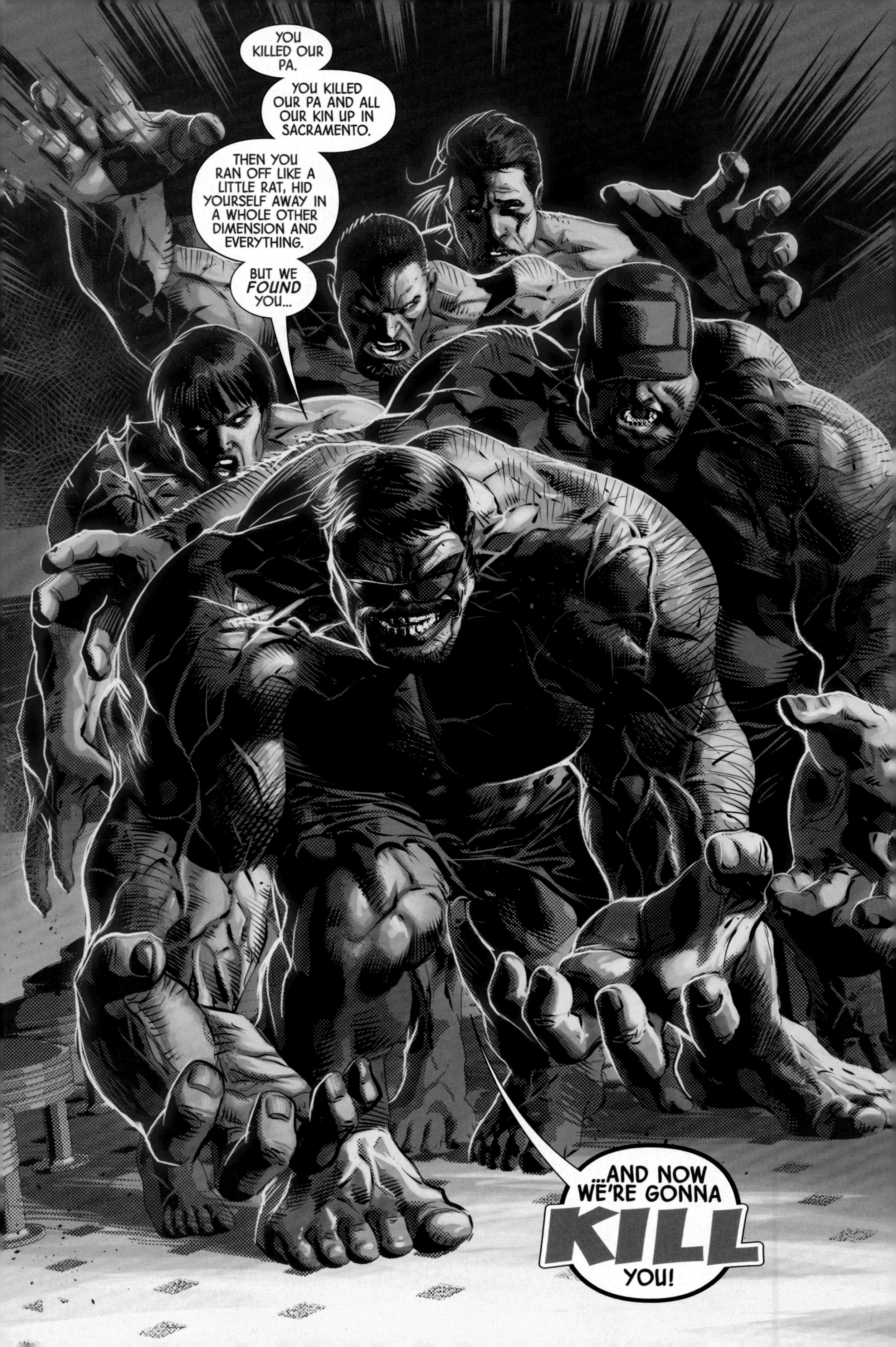
YOU KILLED OUR PA.
YOU KILLED OUR PA AND ALL OUR KIN UP IN SACRAMENTO.
THEN YOU RAN OFF LIKE A LITTLE RAT, HID YOURSELF AWAY IN A WHOLE OTHER DIMENSION AND EVERYTHING.
BUT WE *FOUND* YOU...
...AND NOW WE'RE GONNA KILL YOU!

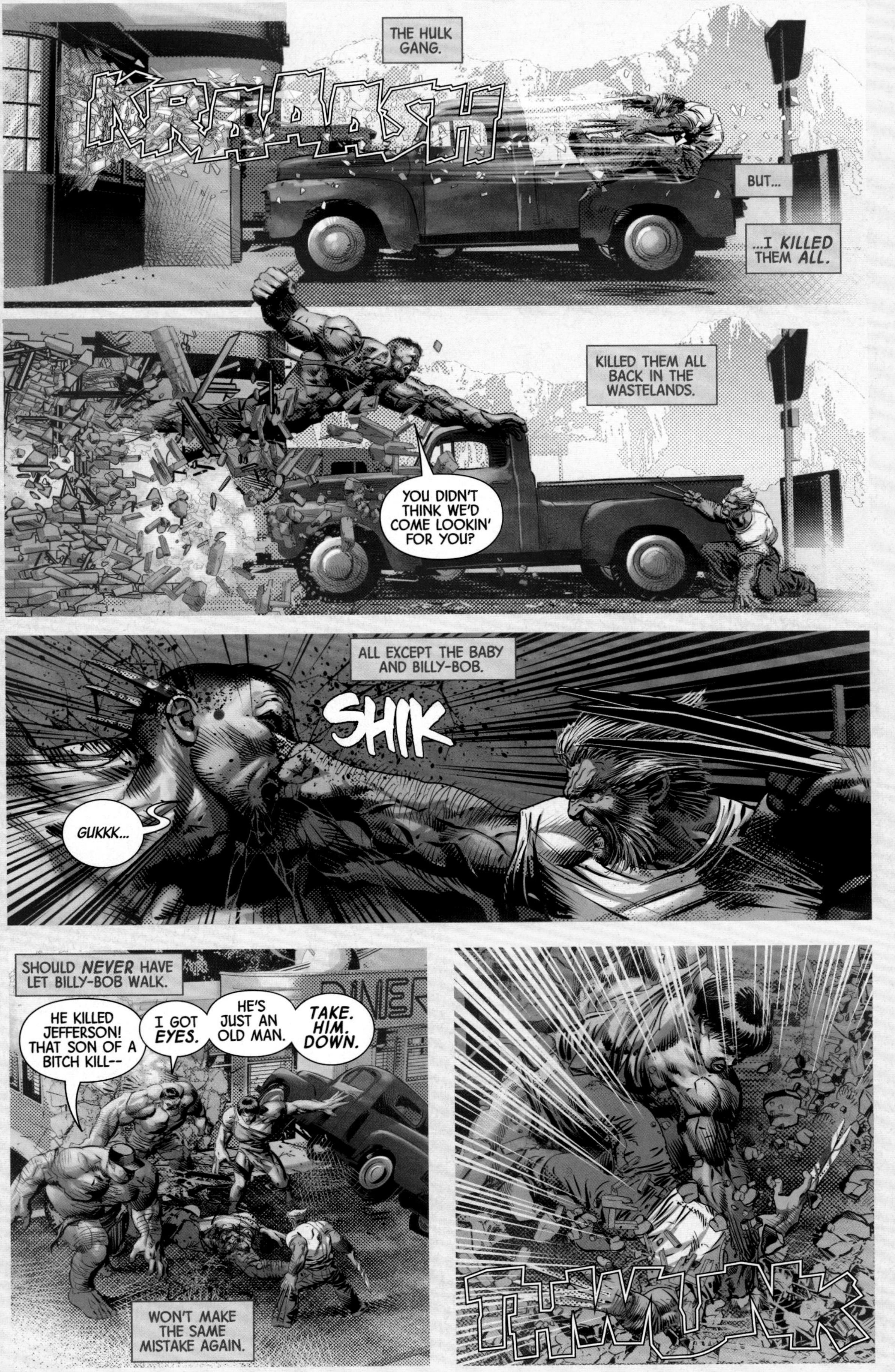
THE HULK GANG.
KRRAASH
BUT...
...I KILLED THEM ALL.
KILLED THEM ALL BACK IN THE WASTELANDS.
YOU DIDN'T THINK WE'D COME LOOKIN' FOR YOU?
ALL EXCEPT THE BABY AND BILLY-BOB.
SHIK
GUKKK...
SHOULD NEVER HAVE LET BILLY-BOB WALK.
HE KILLED JEFFERSON! THAT SON OF A BITCH KILL--
I GOT EYES.
HE'S JUST AN OLD MAN.
TAKE. HIM. DOWN.
DINER
WON'T MAKE THE SAME MISTAKE AGAIN.
THWUNK

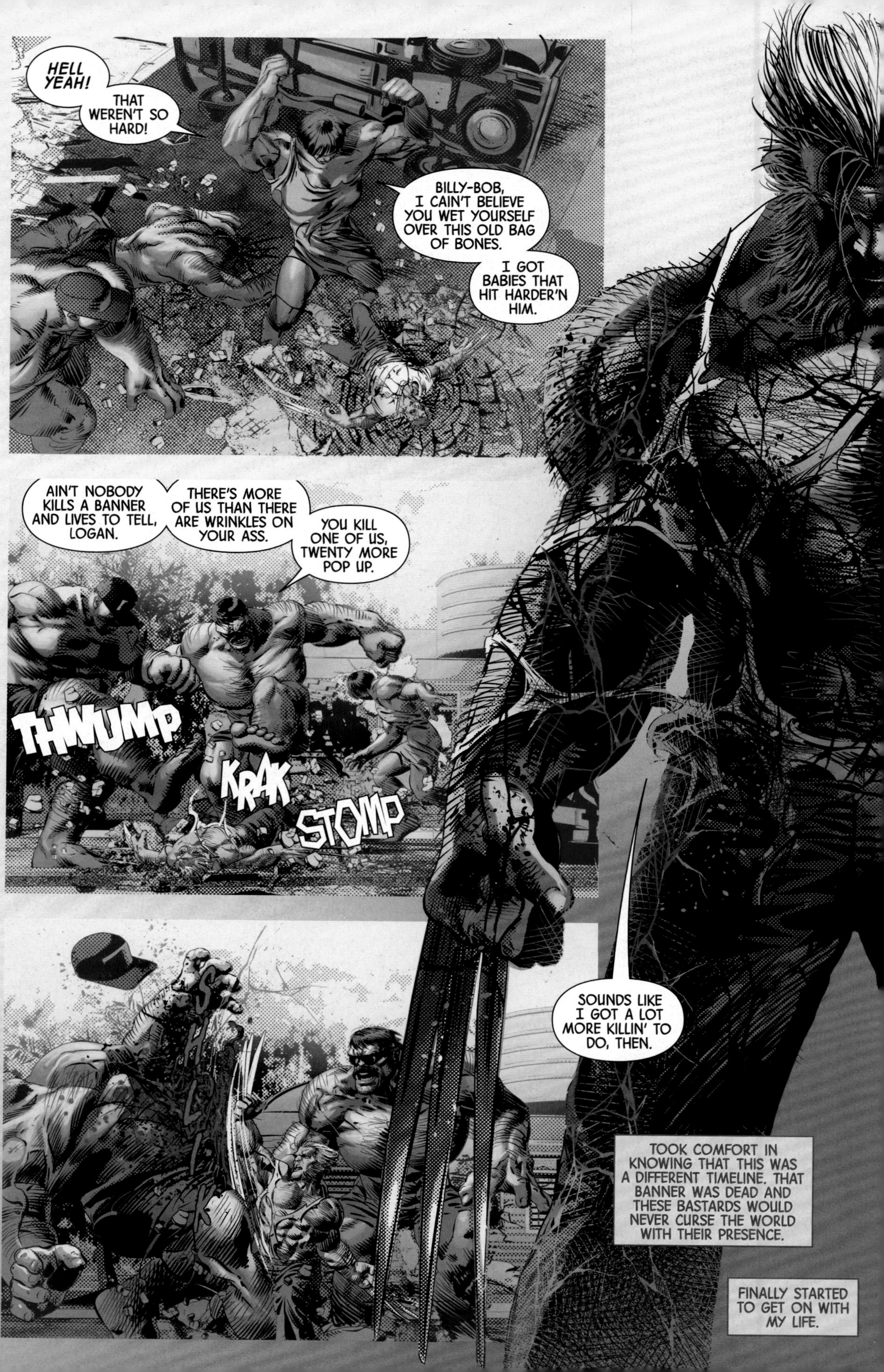

HELL YEAH!
THAT WEREN'T SO HARD!
BILLY-BOB, I CAIN'T BELIEVE YOU WET YOURSELF OVER THIS OLD BAG OF BONES.
I GOT BABIES THAT HIT HARDER'N HIM.
AIN'T NOBODY KILLS A BANNER AND LIVES TO TELL, LOGAN.
THERE'S MORE OF US THAN THERE ARE WRINKLES ON YOUR ASS.
YOU KILL ONE OF US, TWENTY MORE POP UP.
THWUMP
KRAK
STOMP
SOUNDS LIKE I GOT A LOT MORE KILLIN' TO DO, THEN.
TOOK COMFORT IN KNOWING THAT THIS WAS A DIFFERENT TIMELINE. THAT BANNER WAS DEAD AND THESE BASTARDS WOULD NEVER CURSE THE WORLD WITH THEIR PRESENCE.
FINALLY STARTED TO GET ON WITH MY LIFE.

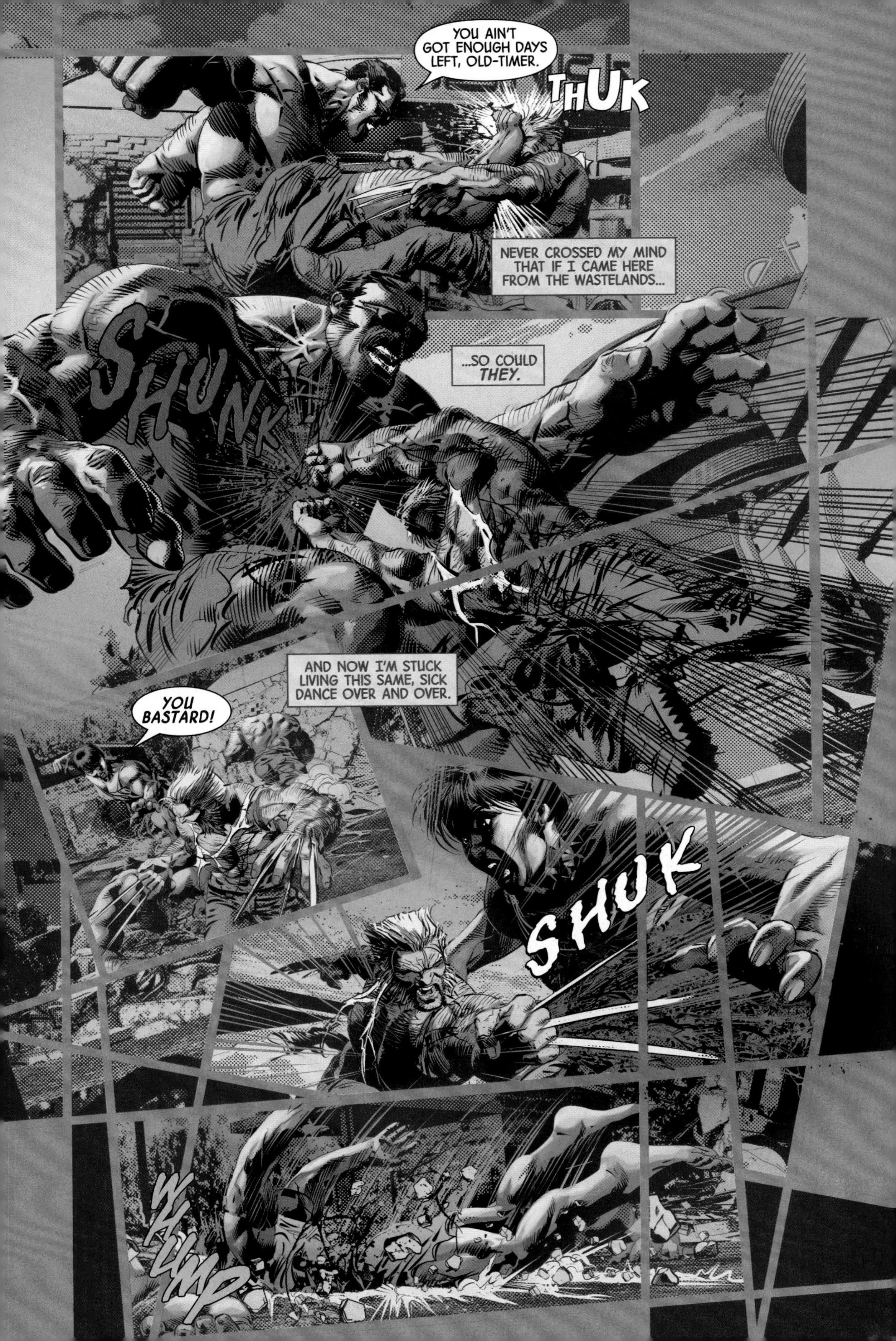
YOU AIN'T GOT ENOUGH DAYS LEFT, OLD-TIMER.
THUK
NEVER CROSSED MY MIND THAT IF I CAME HERE FROM THE WASTELANDS...
SHUNK
...SO COULD THEY.
AND NOW I'M STUCK LIVING THIS SAME, SICK DANCE OVER AND OVER.
YOU BASTARD!
SHUK
WHUMP

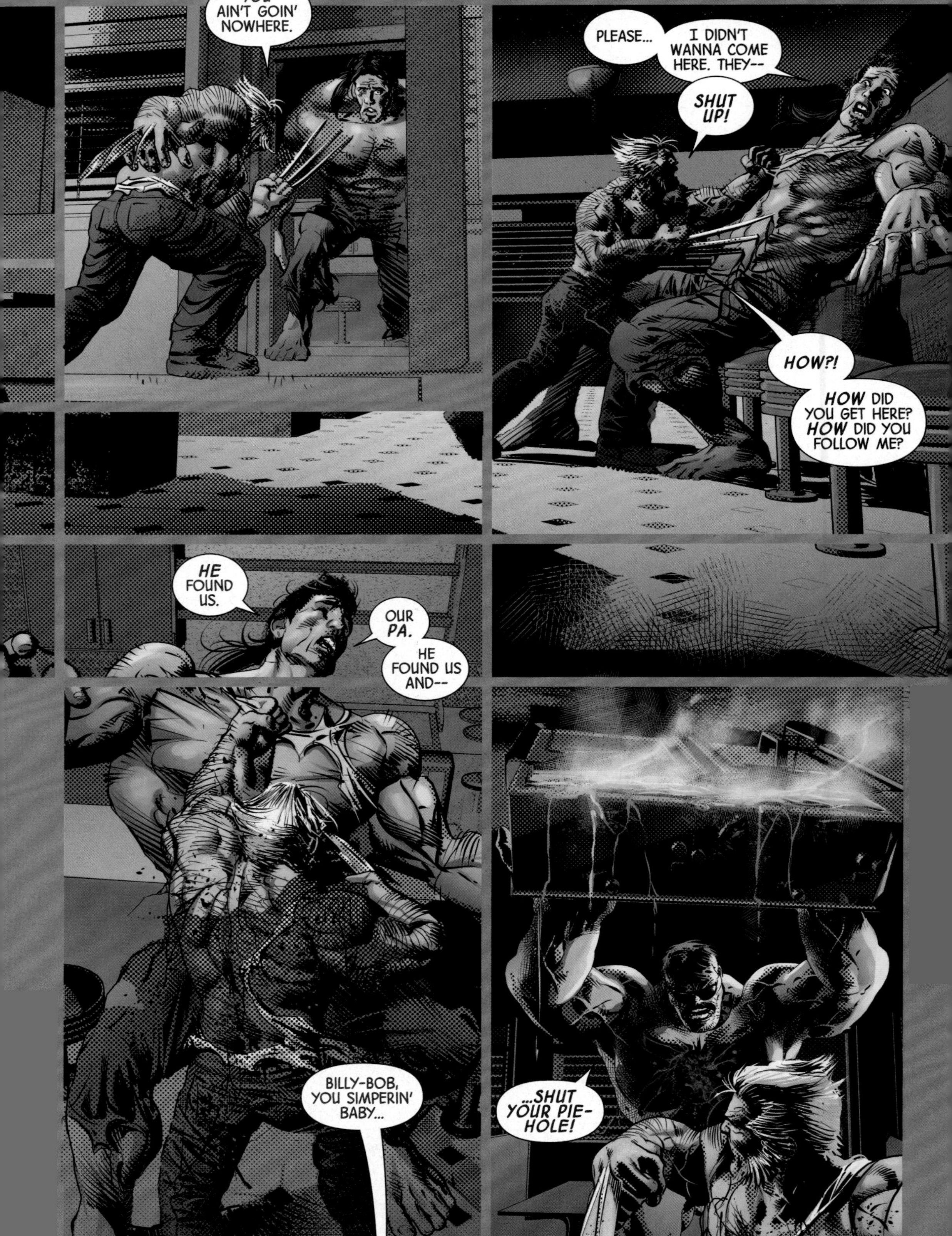
AIN'T GOIN' NOWHERE.
PLEASE...
I DIDN'T WANNA COME HERE. THEY--
SHUT UP!
HOW?!
HOW DID YOU GET HERE? HOW DID YOU FOLLOW ME?
HE FOUND US.
OUR PA.
HE FOUND US AND--
BILLY-BOB, YOU SIMPERIN' BABY...
...SHUT YOUR PIE-HOLE!

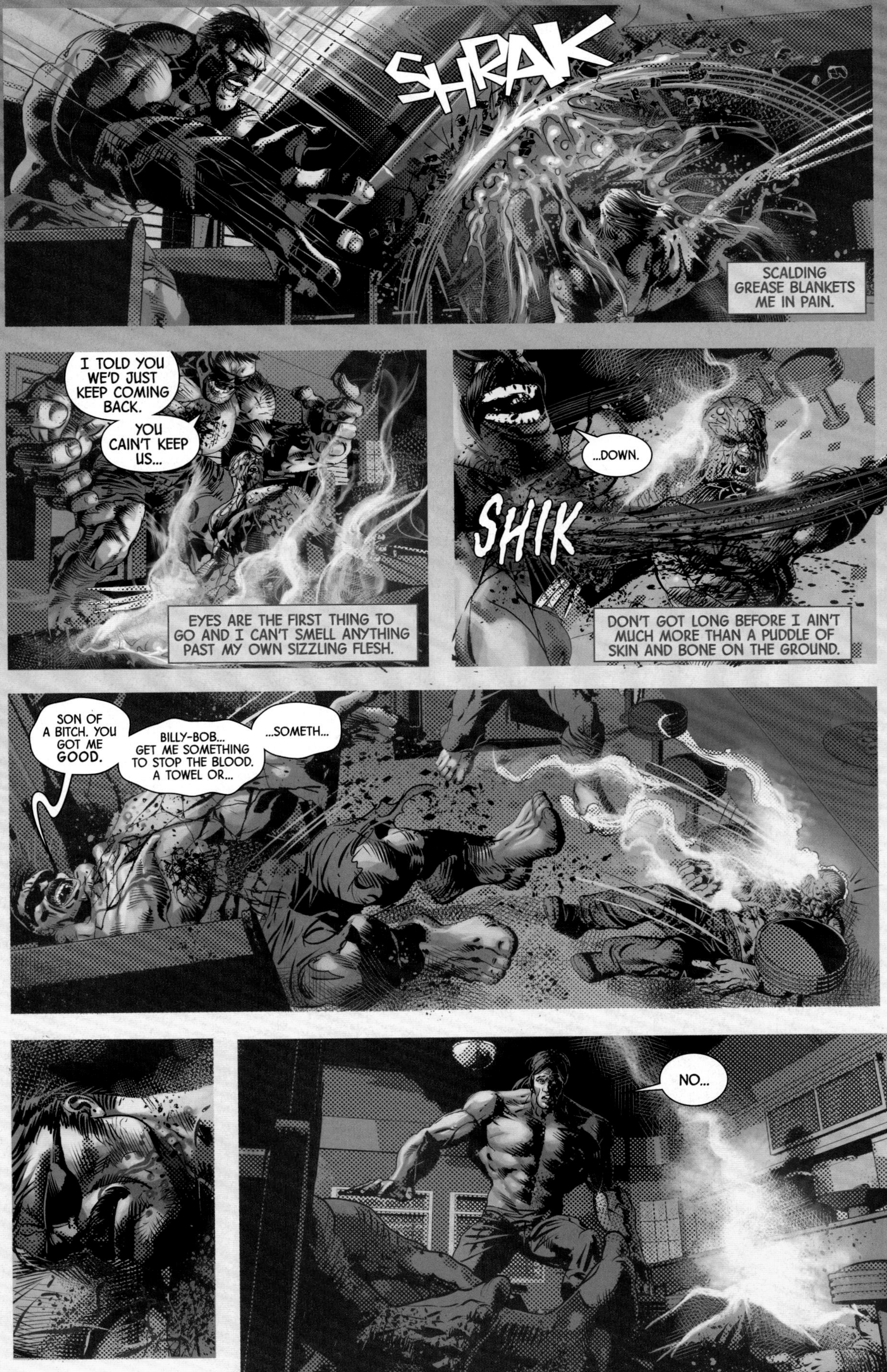
SHRAK
SCALDING GREASE BLANKETS ME IN PAIN.
I TOLD YOU WE'D JUST KEEP COMING BACK.
YOU CAIN'T KEEP US...
EYES ARE THE FIRST THING TO GO AND I CAN'T SMELL ANYTHING PAST MY OWN SIZZLING FLESH.
...DOWN.
SHIK
DON'T GOT LONG BEFORE I AIN'T MUCH MORE THAN A PUDDLE OF SKIN AND BONE ON THE GROUND.
SON OF A BITCH. YOU GOT ME GOOD.
BILLY-BOB... GET ME SOMETHING TO STOP THE BLOOD. A TOWEL OR...
...SOMETH...
NO...

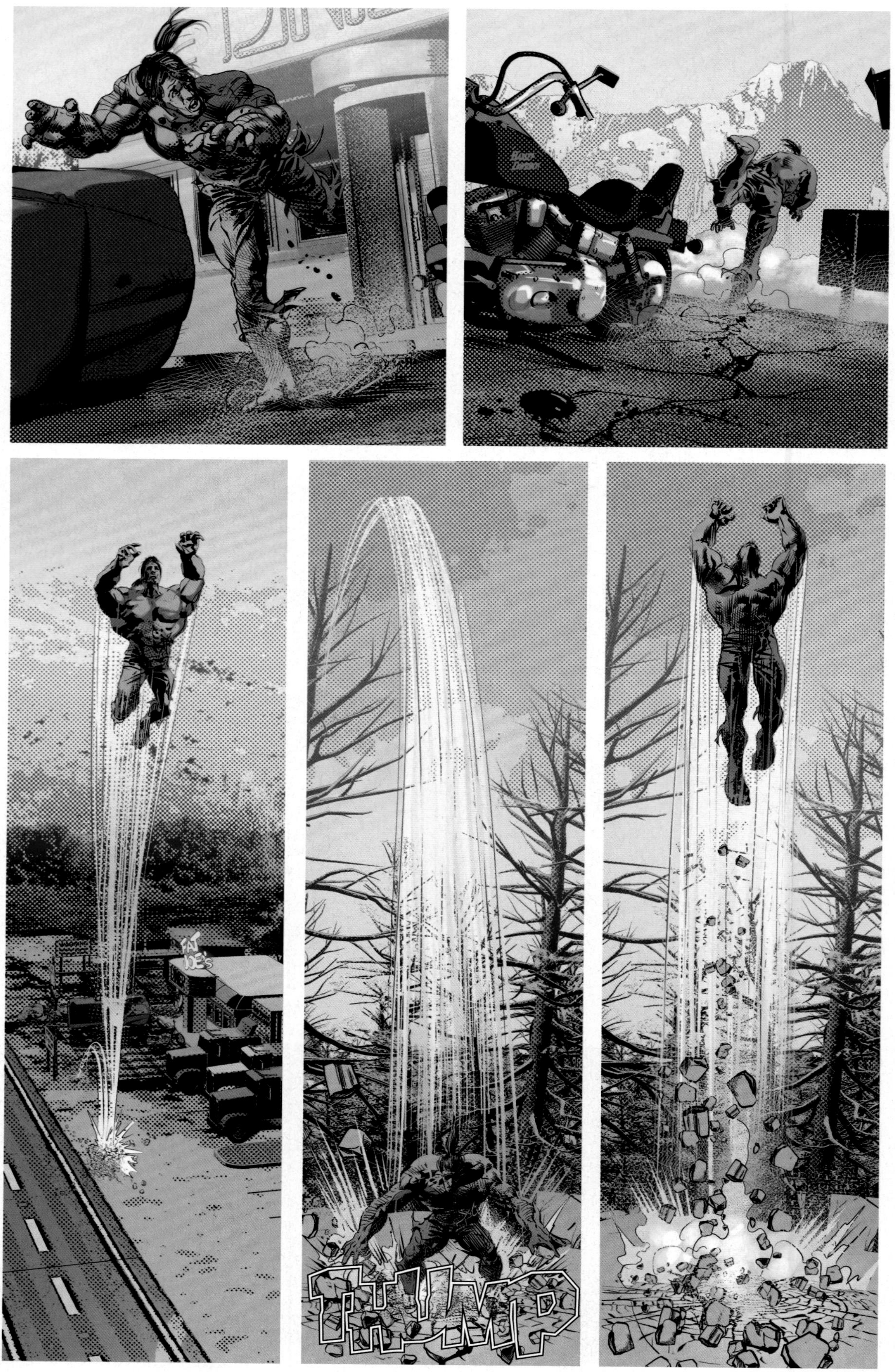
FAT JOE'S
THUMP

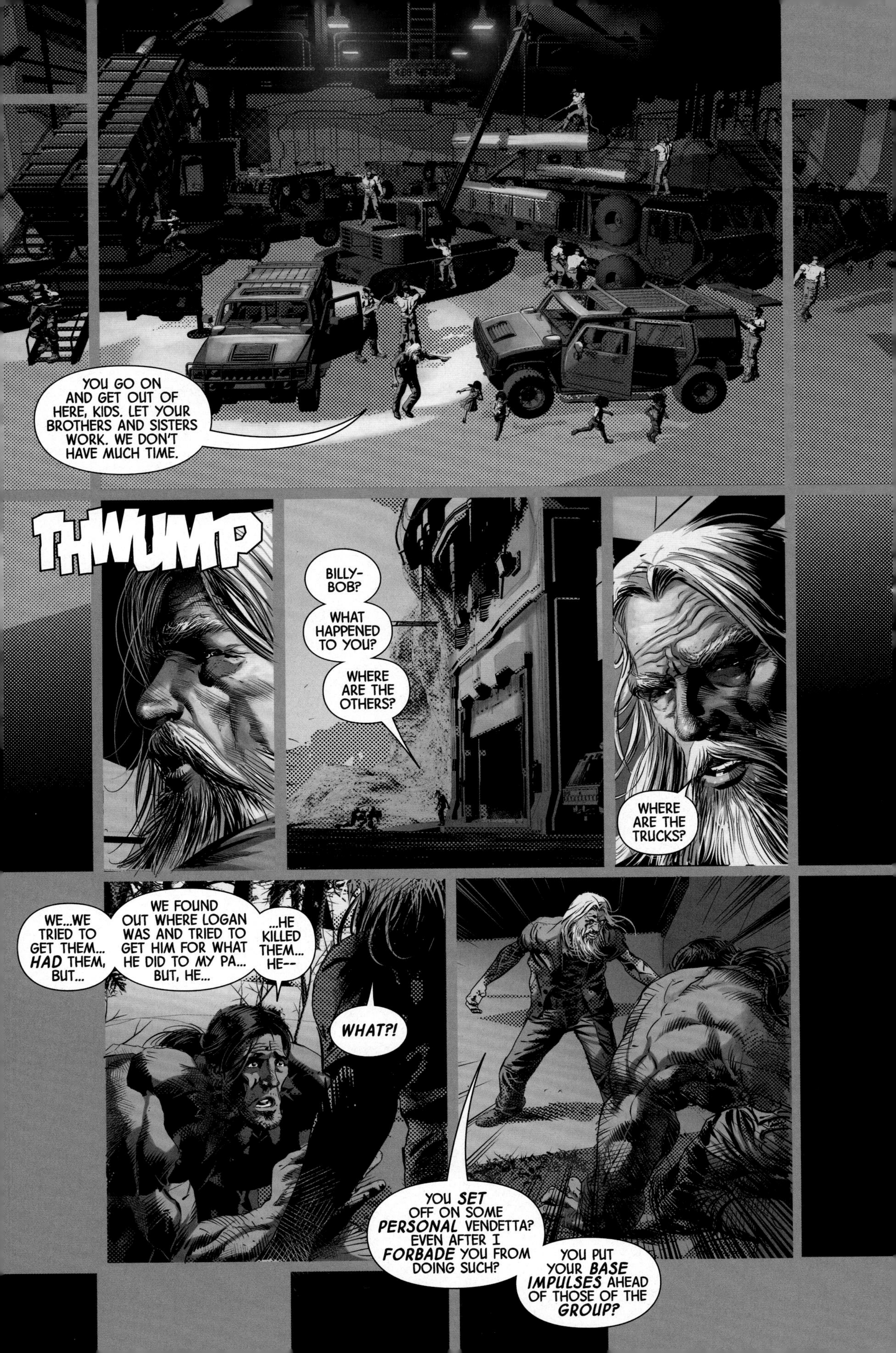
YOU GO ON AND GET OUT OF HERE, KIDS. LET YOUR BROTHERS AND SISTERS WORK. WE DON'T HAVE MUCH TIME.
THWUMP
BILLY-BOB?
WHAT HAPPENED TO YOU?
WHERE ARE THE OTHERS?
WHERE ARE THE TRUCKS?
WE...WE TRIED TO GET THEM... HAD THEM, BUT...
WE FOUND OUT WHERE LOGAN WAS AND TRIED TO GET HIM FOR WHAT HE DID TO MY PA... BUT, HE...
...HE KILLED THEM... HE--
WHAT?!
YOU SET OFF ON SOME PERSONAL VENDETTA? EVEN AFTER I FORBADE YOU FROM DOING SUCH?
YOU PUT YOUR BASE IMPULSES AHEAD OF THOSE OF THE GROUP?

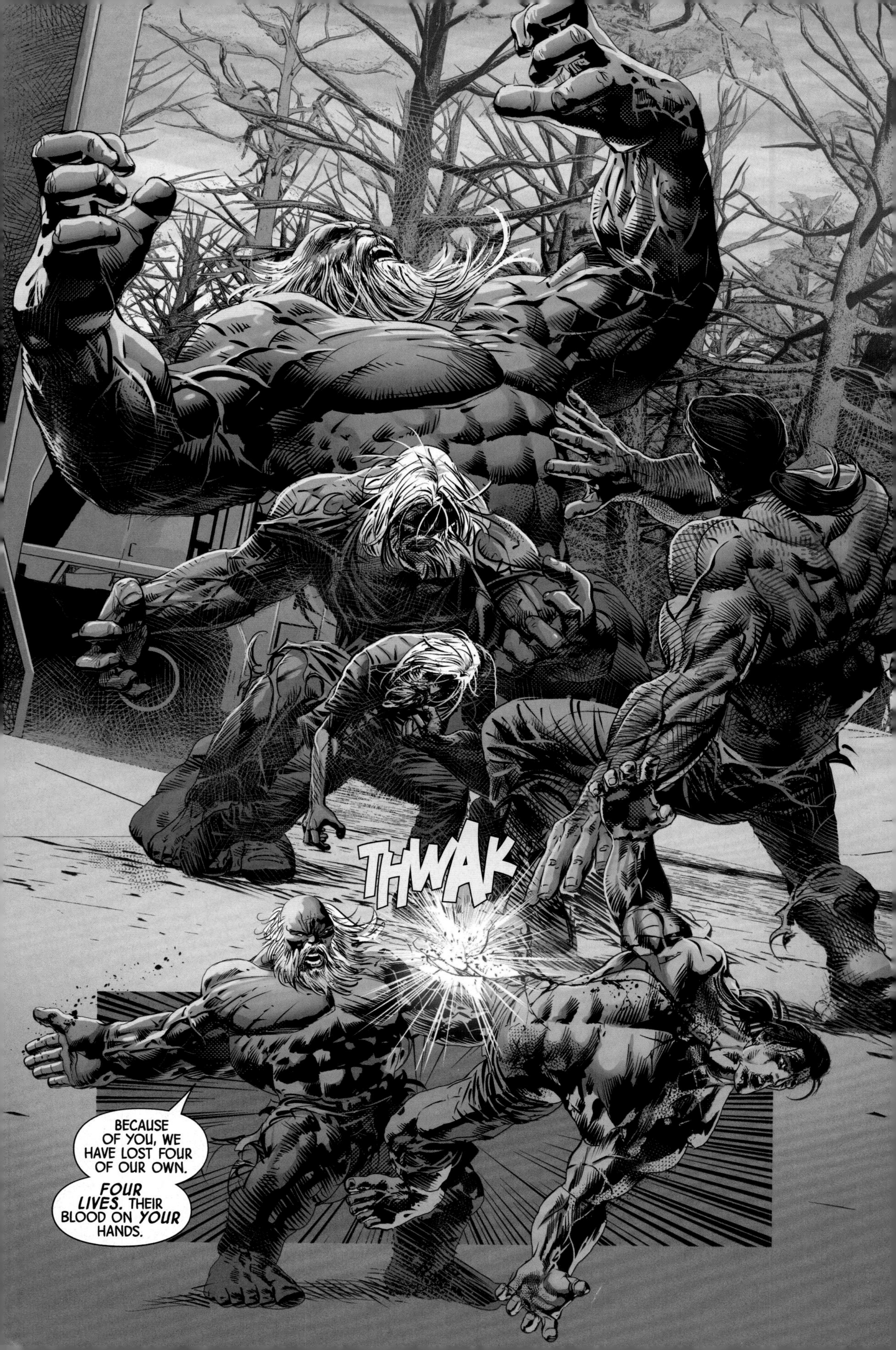
THWAK
BECAUSE OF YOU, WE HAVE LOST FOUR OF OUR OWN.
FOUR LIVES. THEIR BLOOD ON YOUR HANDS.

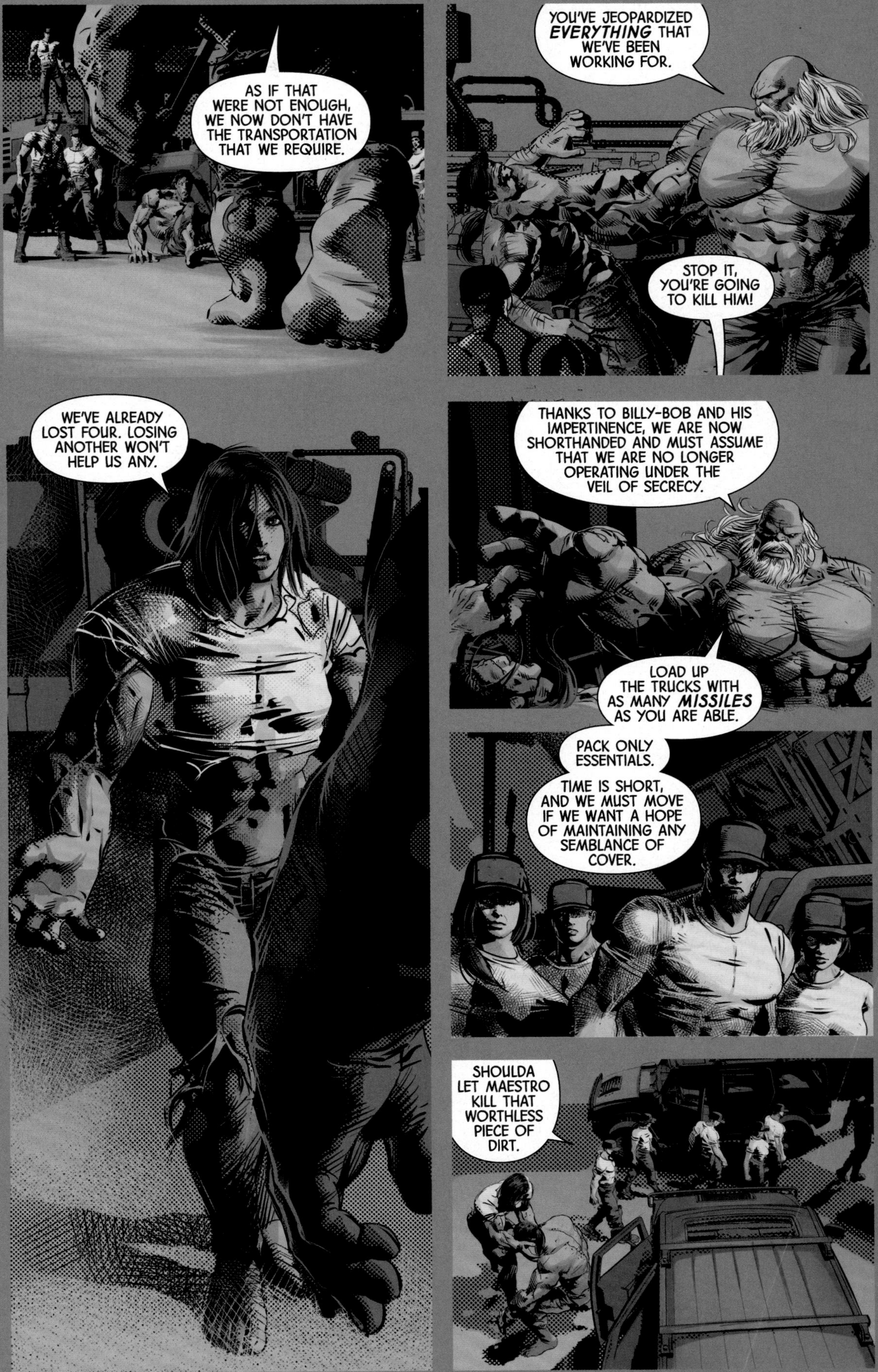

AS IF THAT WERE NOT ENOUGH, WE NOW DON'T HAVE THE TRANSPORTATION THAT WE REQUIRE.
YOU'VE JEOPARDIZED *EVERYTHING* THAT WE'VE BEEN WORKING FOR.
STOP IT, YOU'RE GOING TO KILL HIM!
WE'VE ALREADY LOST FOUR. LOSING ANOTHER WON'T HELP US ANY.
THANKS TO BILLY-BOB AND HIS IMPERTINENCE, WE ARE NOW SHORTHANDED AND MUST ASSUME THAT WE ARE NO LONGER OPERATING UNDER THE VEIL OF SECRECY.
LOAD UP THE TRUCKS WITH AS MANY *MISSILES* AS YOU ARE ABLE.
PACK ONLY ESSENTIALS.
TIME IS SHORT, AND WE MUST MOVE IF WE WANT A HOPE OF MAINTAINING ANY SEMBLANCE OF COVER.
SHOULDA LET MAESTRO KILL THAT WORTHLESS PIECE OF DIRT.

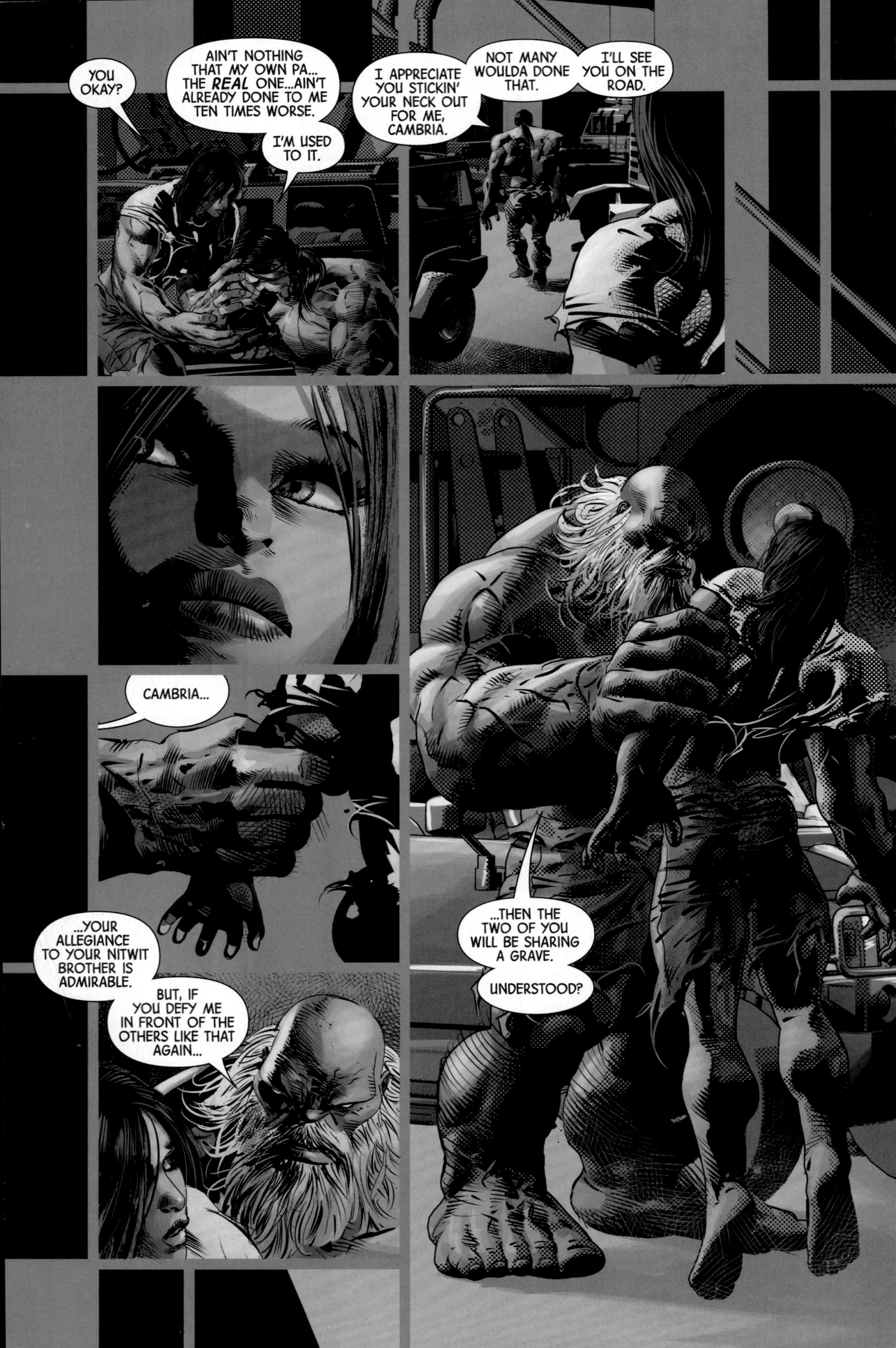
YOU OKAY?
AIN'T NOTHING THAT MY OWN PA... THE *REAL* ONE...AIN'T ALREADY DONE TO ME TEN TIMES WORSE.
I'M USED TO IT.
I APPRECIATE YOU STICKIN' YOUR NECK OUT FOR ME, CAMBRIA.
NOT MANY WOULDA DONE THAT.
I'LL SEE YOU ON THE ROAD.
CAMBRIA...
...YOUR ALLEGIANCE TO YOUR NITWIT BROTHER IS ADMIRABLE.
BUT, IF YOU DEFY ME IN FRONT OF THE OTHERS LIKE THAT AGAIN...
...THEN THE TWO OF YOU WILL BE SHARING A GRAVE.
UNDERSTOOD?

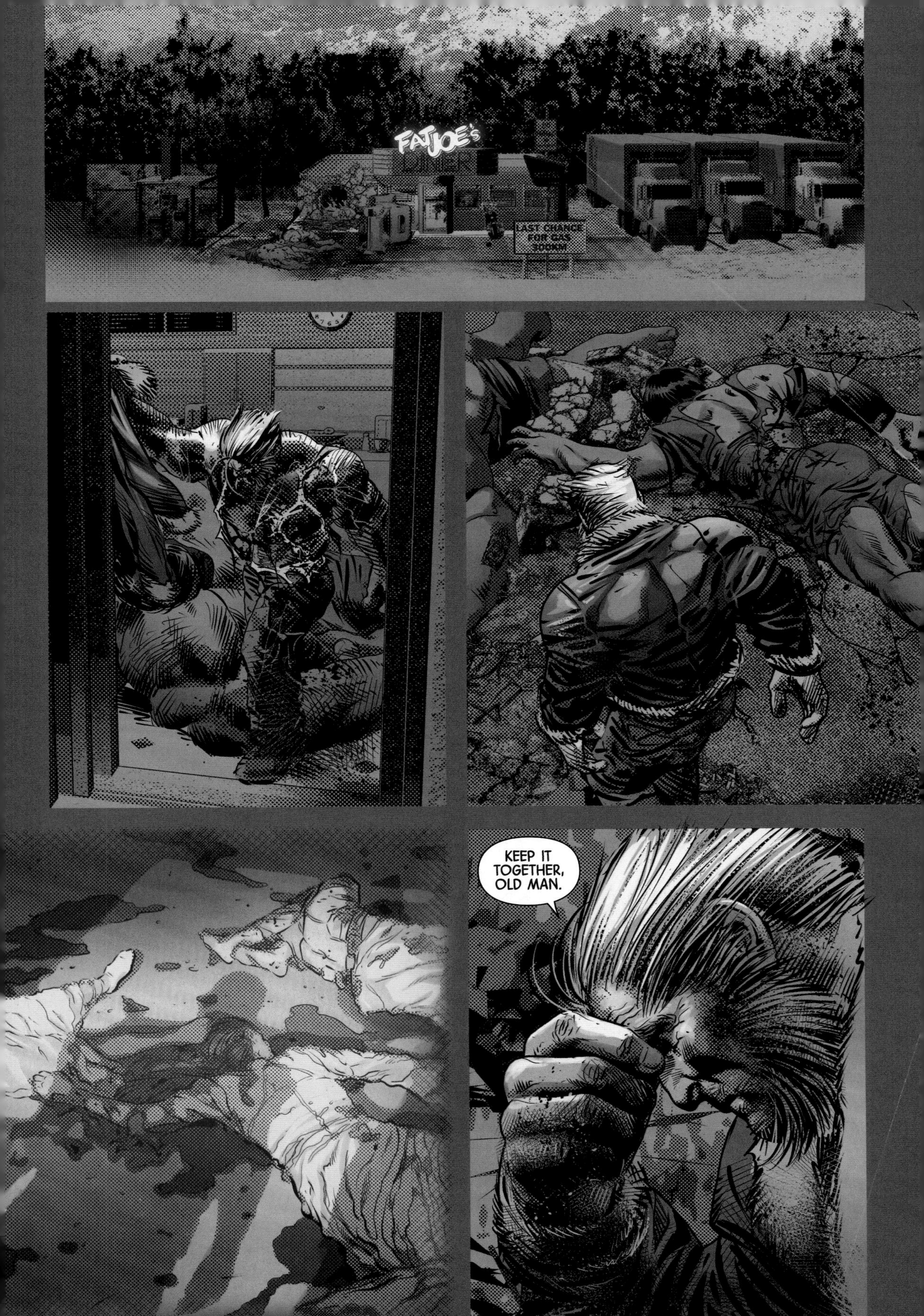
FAT JOE's
DINER
LAST CHANCE FOR GAS 300KM
KEEP IT TOGETHER, OLD MAN.

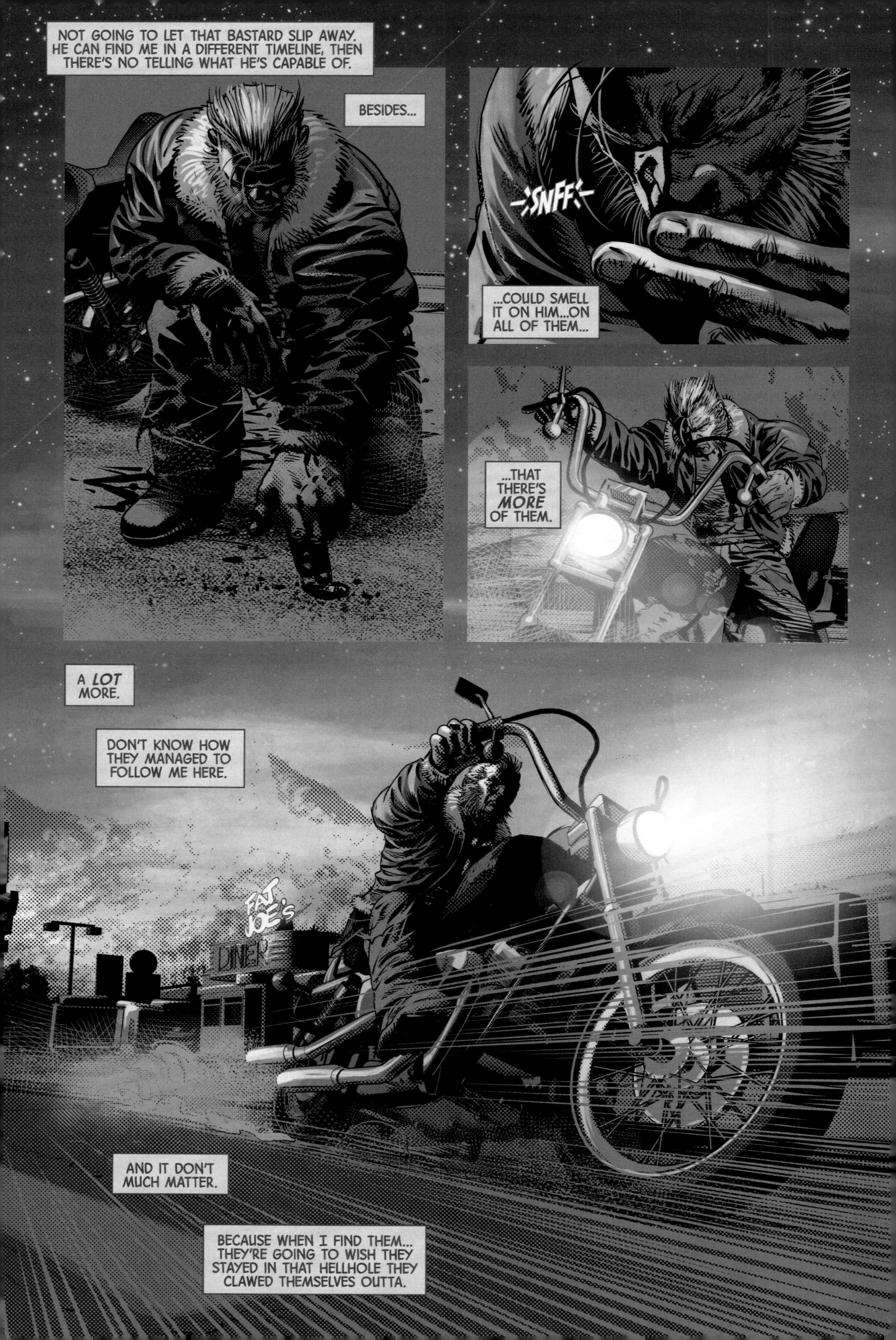
NOT GOING TO LET THAT BASTARD SLIP AWAY. HE CAN FIND ME IN A DIFFERENT TIMELINE, THEN THERE'S NO TELLING WHAT HE'S CAPABLE OF.
BESIDES...
SNFF
...COULD SMELL IT ON HIM...ON ALL OF THEM...
...THAT THERE'S *MORE* OF THEM.
A *LOT* MORE.
DON'T KNOW HOW THEY MANAGED TO FOLLOW ME HERE.
FAT JOE'S
DINER
AND IT DON'T MUCH MATTER.
BECAUSE WHEN I FIND THEM... THEY'RE GOING TO WISH THEY STAYED IN THAT HELLHOLE THEY CLAWED THEMSELVES OUTTA.

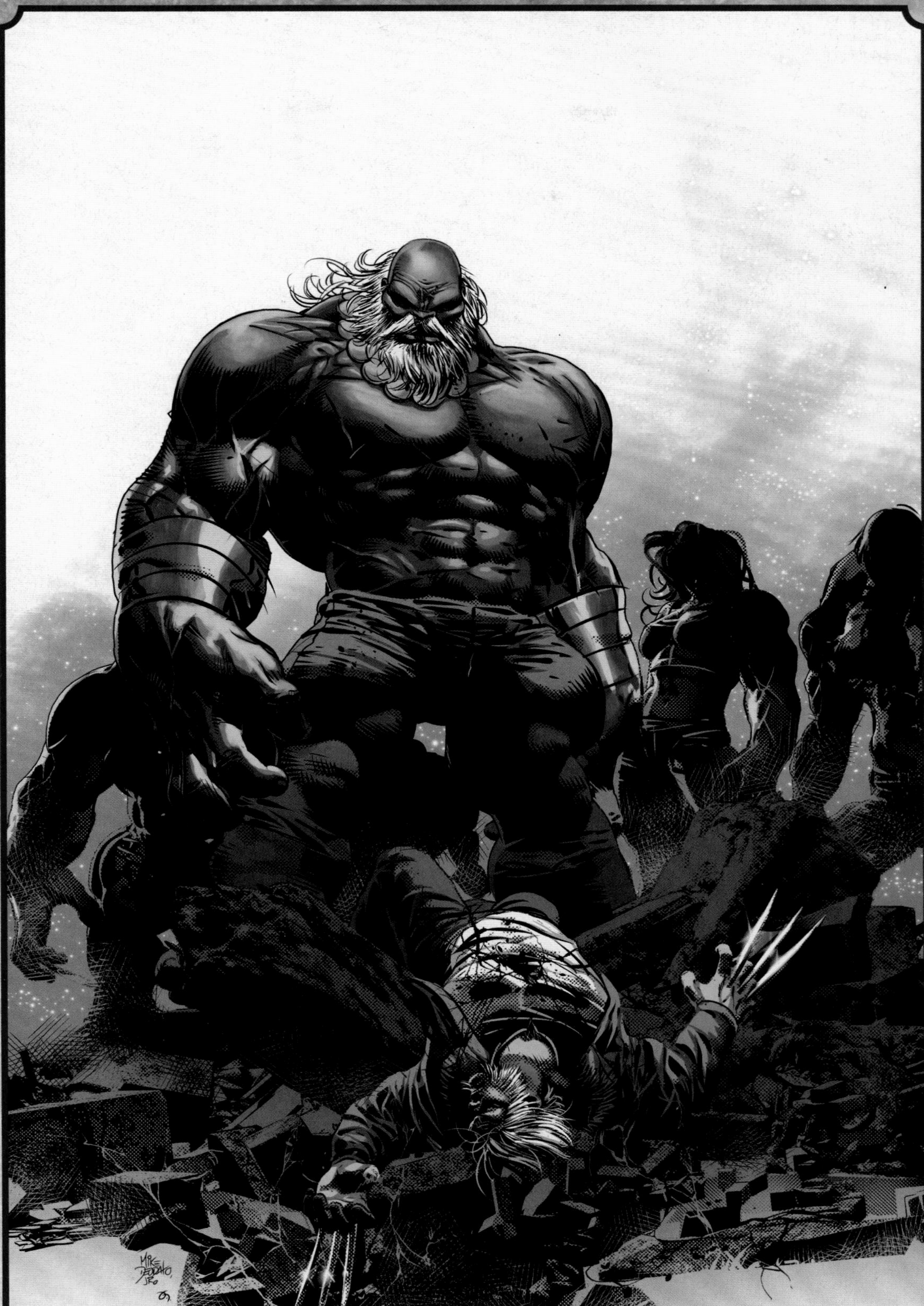

26

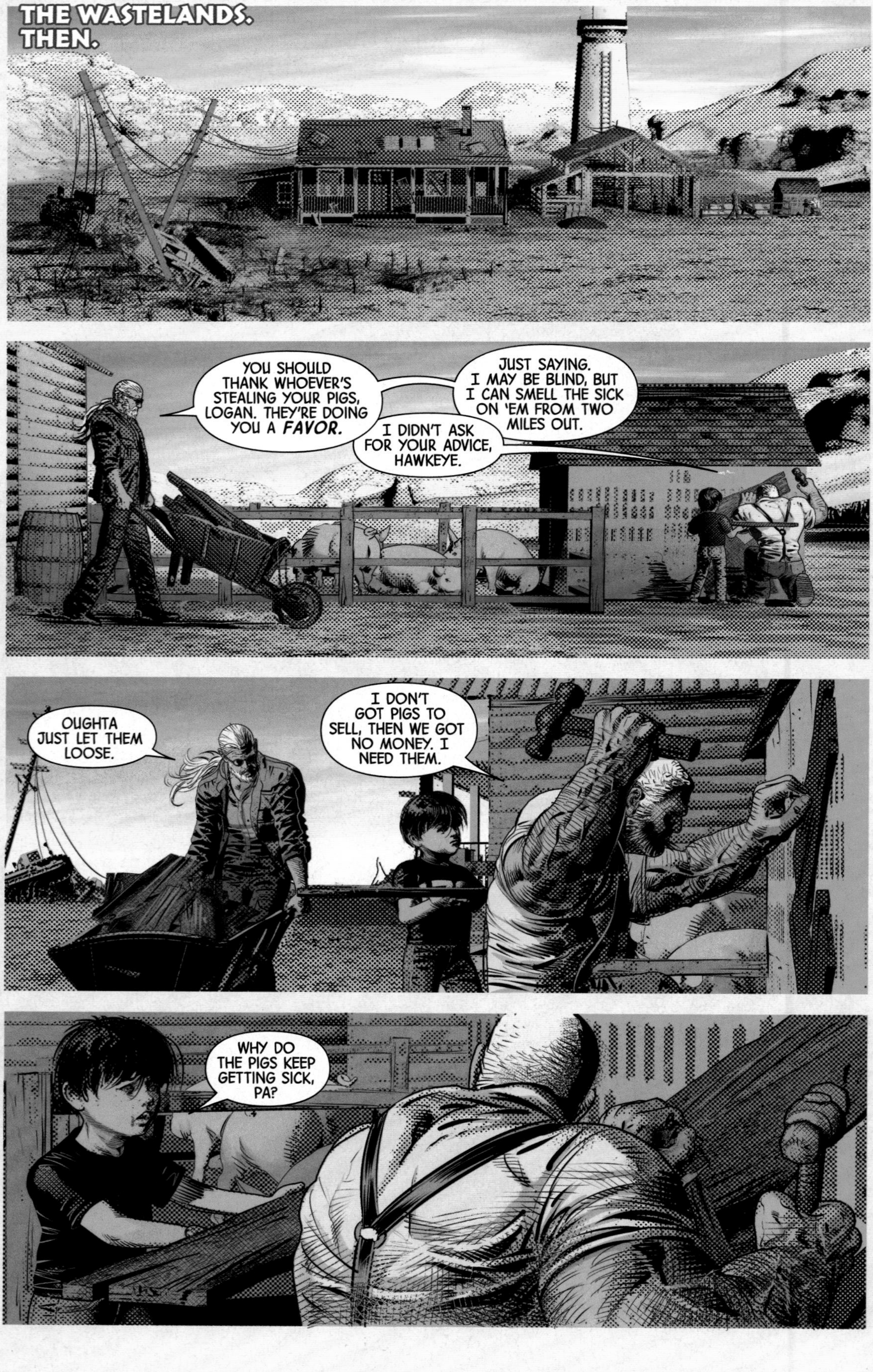
THE WASTELANDS.
THEN.
YOU SHOULD THANK WHOEVER'S STEALING YOUR PIGS, LOGAN. THEY'RE DOING YOU A *FAVOR.*
JUST SAYING. I MAY BE BLIND, BUT I CAN SMELL THE SICK ON 'EM FROM TWO MILES OUT.
I DIDN'T ASK FOR YOUR ADVICE, HAWKEYE.
OUGHTA JUST LET THEM LOOSE.
I DON'T GOT PIGS TO SELL, THEN WE GOT NO MONEY. I NEED THEM.
WHY DO THE PIGS KEEP GETTING SICK, PA?

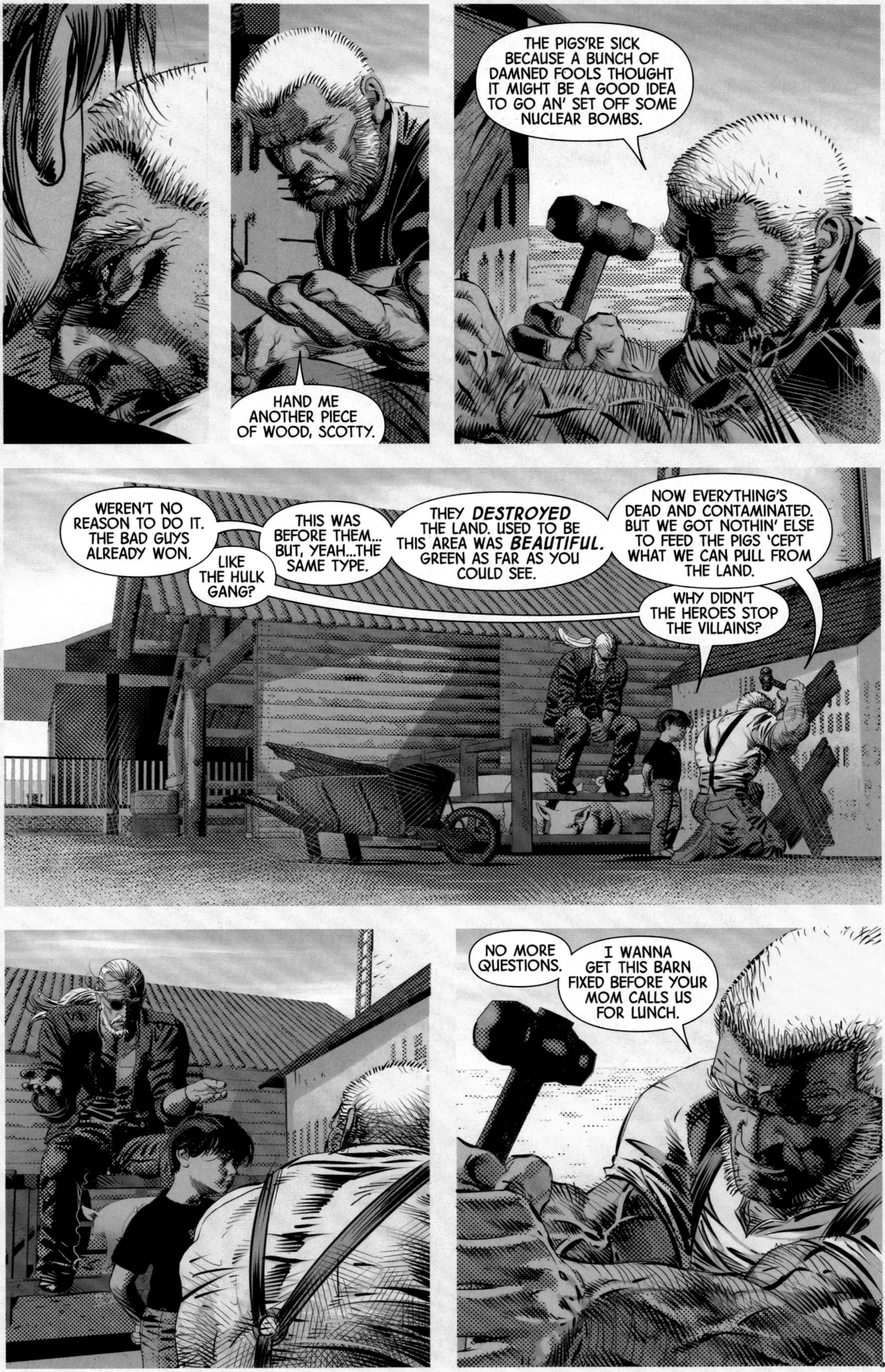
HAND ME ANOTHER PIECE OF WOOD, SCOTTY.
THE PIGS'RE SICK BECAUSE A BUNCH OF DAMNED FOOLS THOUGHT IT MIGHT BE A GOOD IDEA TO GO AN' SET OFF SOME NUCLEAR BOMBS.
WEREN'T NO REASON TO DO IT. THE BAD GUYS ALREADY WON.
LIKE THE HULK GANG?
THIS WAS BEFORE THEM... BUT, YEAH...THE SAME TYPE.
THEY *DESTROYED* THE LAND. USED TO BE THIS AREA WAS *BEAUTIFUL*. GREEN AS FAR AS YOU COULD SEE.
NOW EVERYTHING'S DEAD AND CONTAMINATED. BUT WE GOT NOTHIN' ELSE TO FEED THE PIGS 'CEPT WHAT WE CAN PULL FROM THE LAND.
WHY DIDN'T THE HEROES STOP THE VILLAINS?
NO MORE QUESTIONS.
I WANNA GET THIS BARN FIXED BEFORE YOUR MOM CALLS US FOR LUNCH.

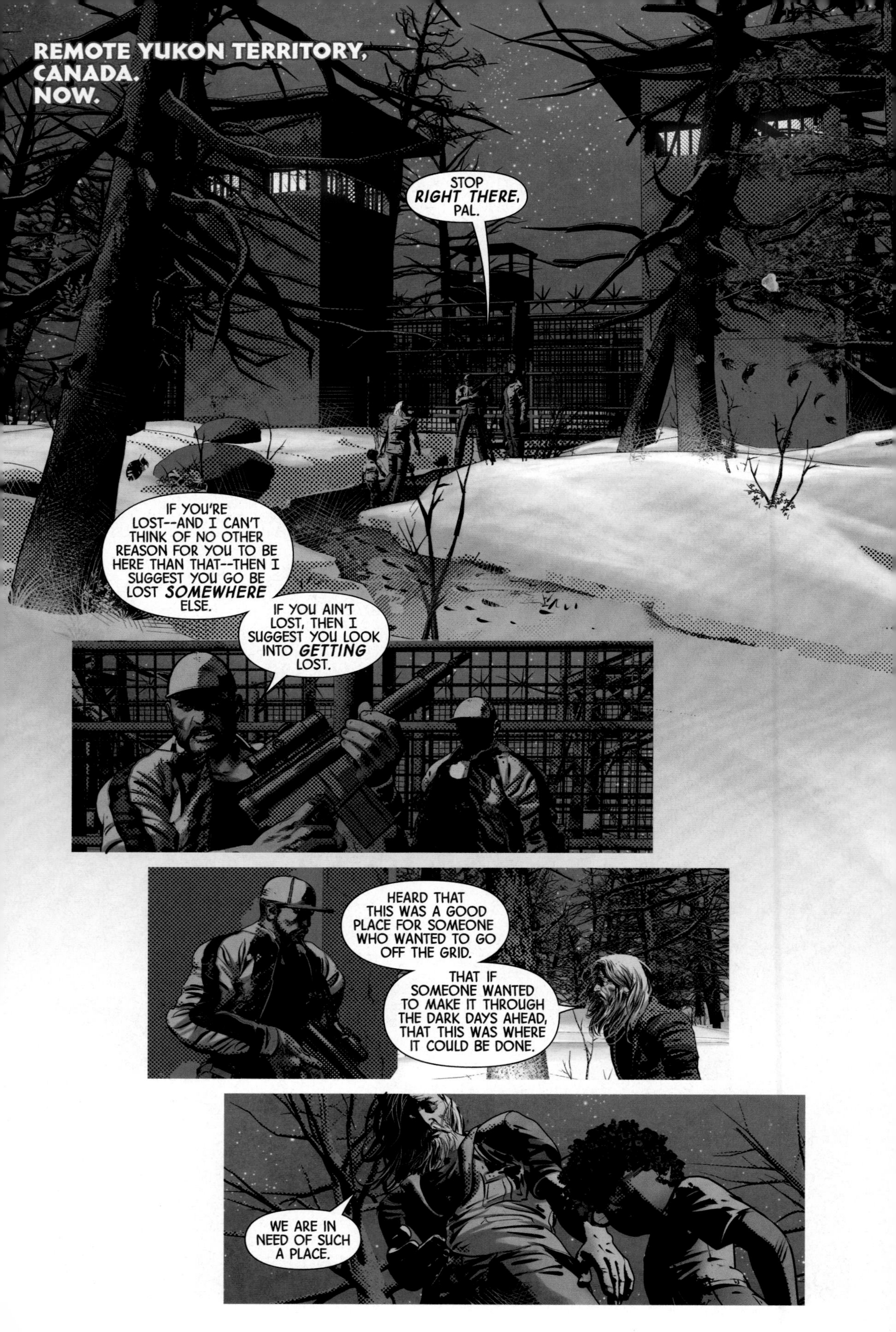
REMOTE YUKON TERRITORY, CANADA. NOW.
STOP RIGHT THERE, PAL.
IF YOU'RE LOST--AND I CAN'T THINK OF NO OTHER REASON FOR YOU TO BE HERE THAN THAT--THEN I SUGGEST YOU GO BE LOST SOMEWHERE ELSE.
IF YOU AIN'T LOST, THEN I SUGGEST YOU LOOK INTO GETTING LOST.
HEARD THAT THIS WAS A GOOD PLACE FOR SOMEONE WHO WANTED TO GO OFF THE GRID.
THAT IF SOMEONE WANTED TO MAKE IT THROUGH THE DARK DAYS AHEAD, THAT THIS WAS WHERE IT COULD BE DONE.
WE ARE IN NEED OF SUCH A PLACE.

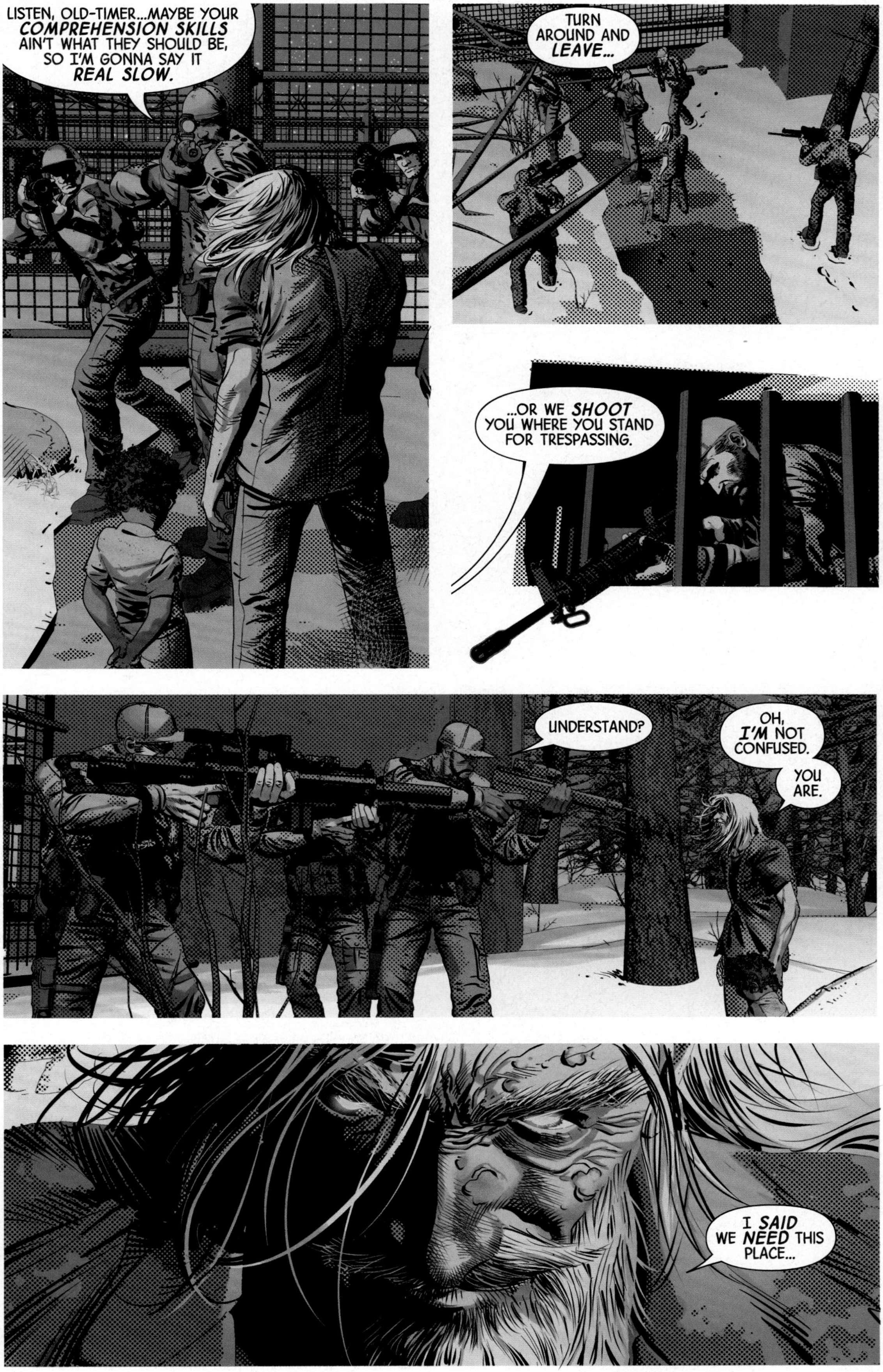
LISTEN, OLD-TIMER...MAYBE YOUR COMPREHENSION SKILLS AIN'T WHAT THEY SHOULD BE, SO I'M GONNA SAY IT REAL SLOW.
TURN AROUND AND LEAVE...
...OR WE SHOOT YOU WHERE YOU STAND FOR TRESPASSING.
UNDERSTAND?
OH, I'M NOT CONFUSED.
YOU ARE.
I SAID WE NEED THIS PLACE...

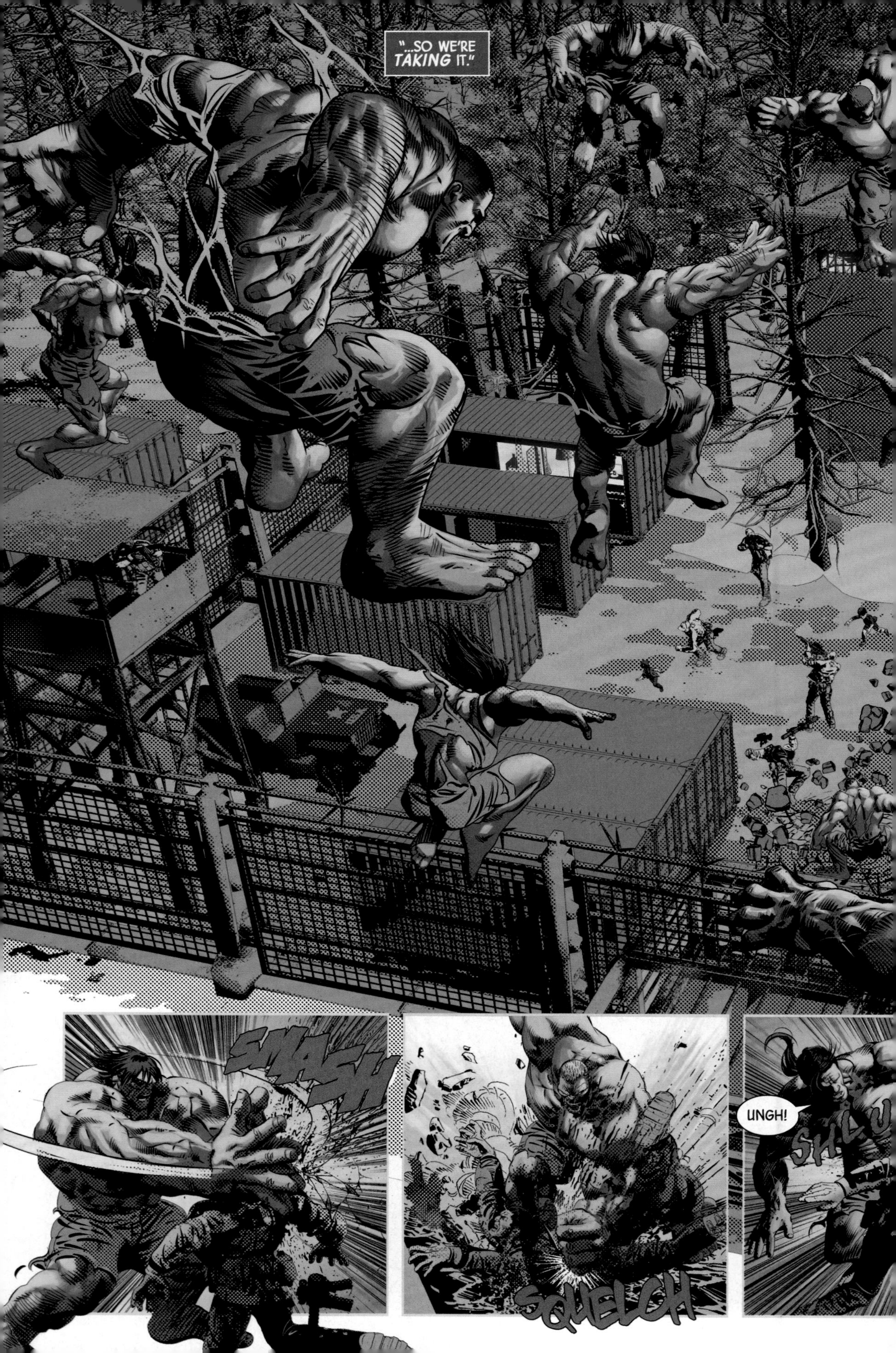
"...SO WE'RE TAKING IT."
SMASH
SQUELCH
UNGH!
SHLU

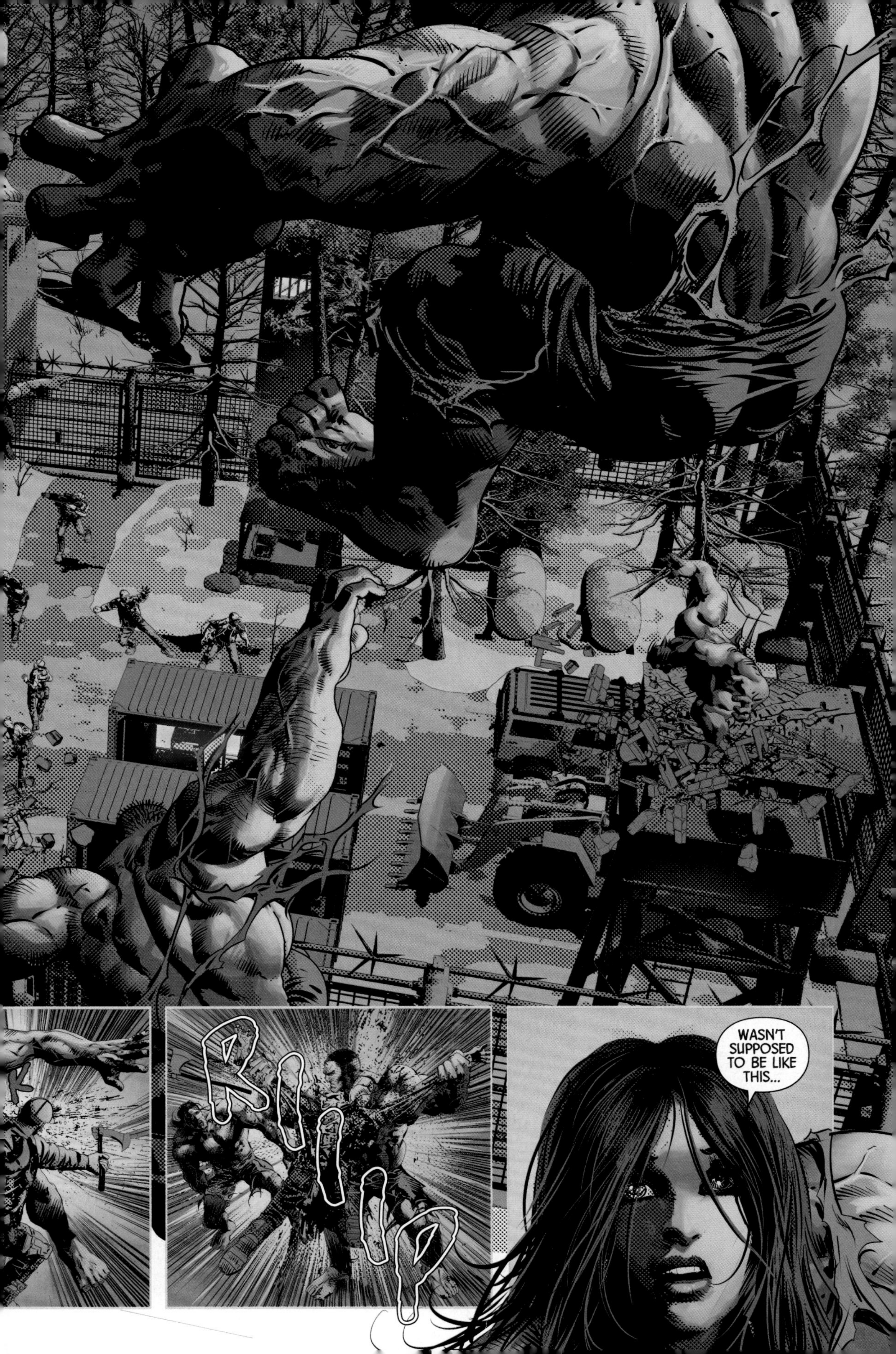
RIIIP
WASN'T SUPPOSED TO BE LIKE THIS...

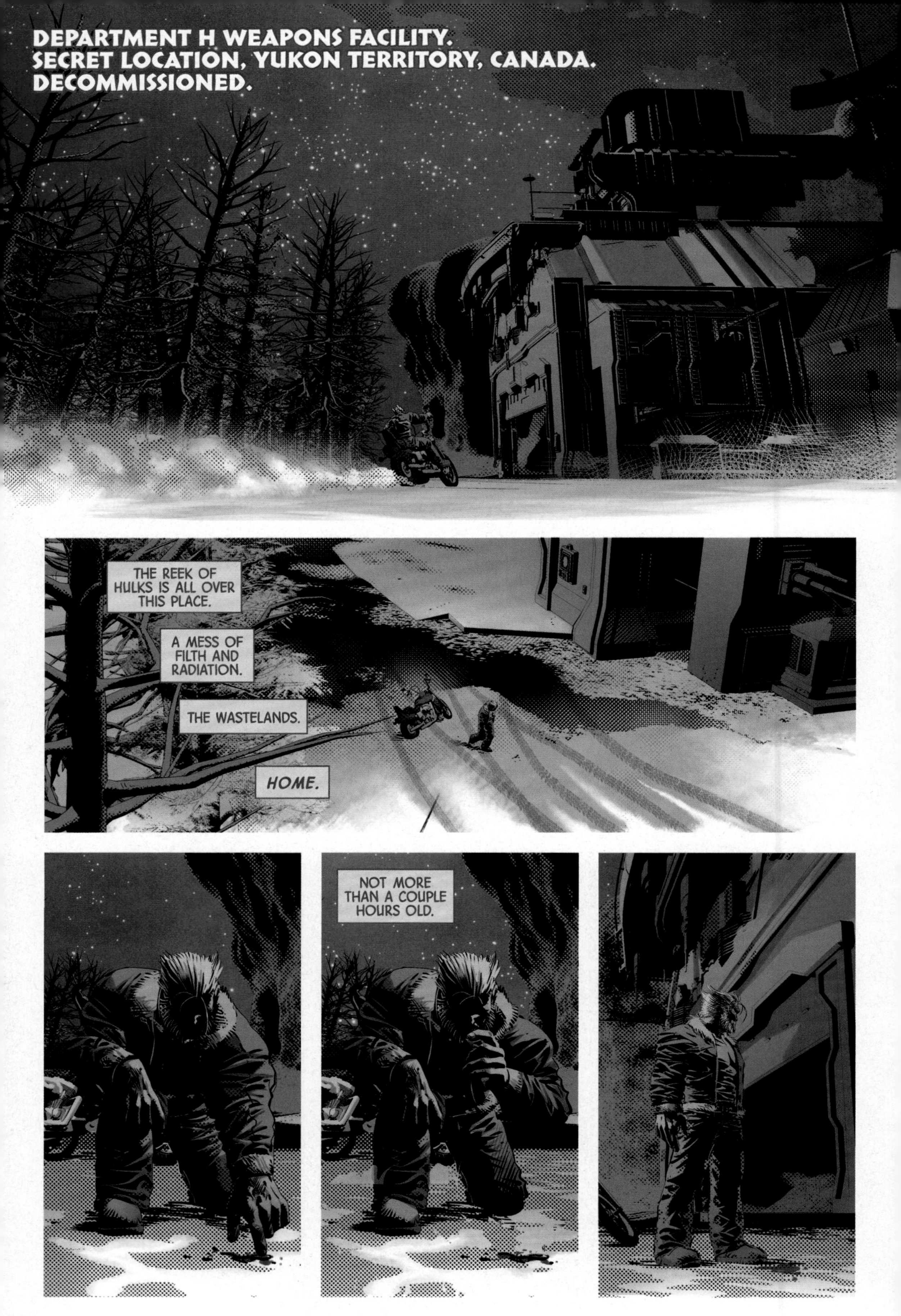
DEPARTMENT H WEAPONS FACILITY.
SECRET LOCATION, YUKON TERRITORY, CANADA.
DECOMMISSIONED.
THE REEK OF HULKS IS ALL OVER THIS PLACE.
A MESS OF FILTH AND RADIATION.
THE WASTELANDS.
HOME.
NOT MORE THAN A COUPLE HOURS OLD.

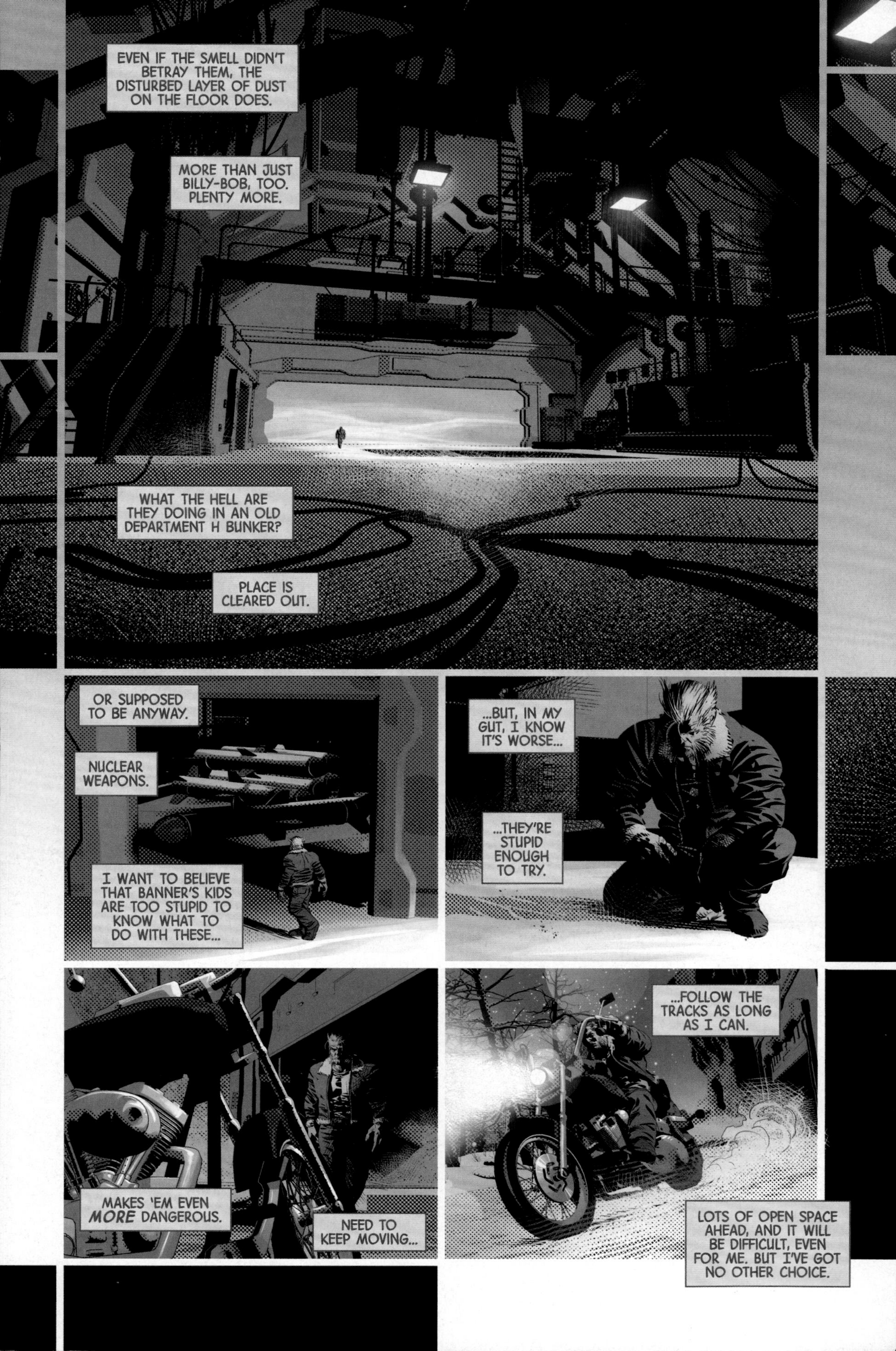

EVEN IF THE SMELL DIDN'T BETRAY THEM, THE DISTURBED LAYER OF DUST ON THE FLOOR DOES.
MORE THAN JUST BILLY-BOB, TOO. PLENTY MORE.
WHAT THE HELL ARE THEY DOING IN AN OLD DEPARTMENT H BUNKER?
PLACE IS CLEARED OUT.
OR SUPPOSED TO BE ANYWAY.
NUCLEAR WEAPONS.
I WANT TO BELIEVE THAT BANNER'S KIDS ARE TOO STUPID TO KNOW WHAT TO DO WITH THESE...
...BUT, IN MY GUT, I KNOW IT'S WORSE...
...THEY'RE STUPID ENOUGH TO TRY.
MAKES 'EM EVEN *MORE* DANGEROUS.
NEED TO KEEP MOVING...
...FOLLOW THE TRACKS AS LONG AS I CAN.
LOTS OF OPEN SPACE AHEAD, AND IT WILL BE DIFFICULT, EVEN FOR ME. BUT I'VE GOT NO OTHER CHOICE.

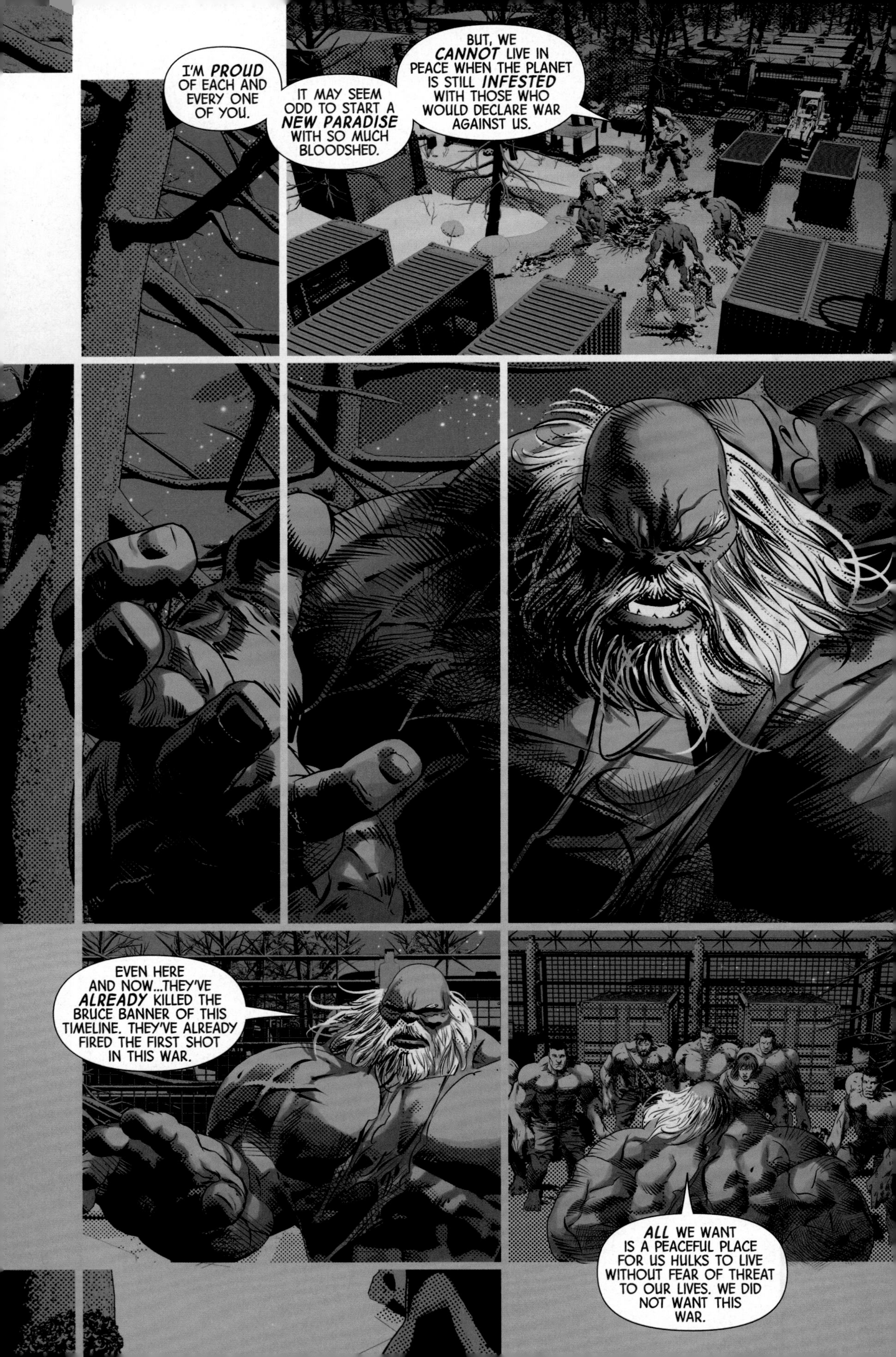
I'M PROUD OF EACH AND EVERY ONE OF YOU.
IT MAY SEEM ODD TO START A NEW PARADISE WITH SO MUCH BLOODSHED.
BUT, WE CANNOT LIVE IN PEACE WHEN THE PLANET IS STILL INFESTED WITH THOSE WHO WOULD DECLARE WAR AGAINST US.
EVEN HERE AND NOW...THEY'VE ALREADY KILLED THE BRUCE BANNER OF THIS TIMELINE. THEY'VE ALREADY FIRED THE FIRST SHOT IN THIS WAR.
ALL WE WANT IS A PEACEFUL PLACE FOR US HULKS TO LIVE WITHOUT FEAR OF THREAT TO OUR LIVES. WE DID NOT WANT THIS WAR.

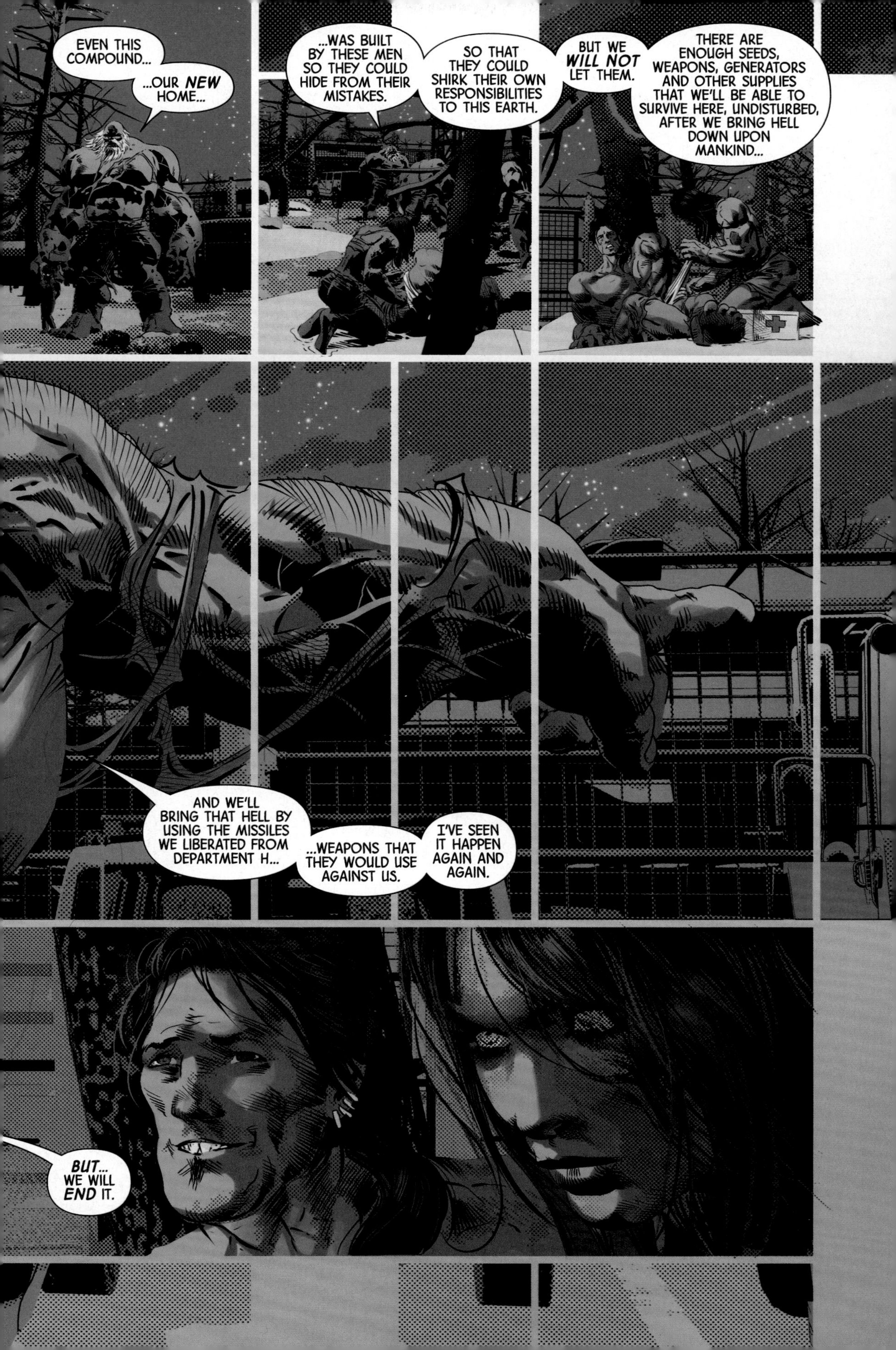
EVEN THIS COMPOUND...
...OUR NEW HOME...
...WAS BUILT BY THESE MEN SO THEY COULD HIDE FROM THEIR MISTAKES.
SO THAT THEY COULD SHIRK THEIR OWN RESPONSIBILITIES TO THIS EARTH.
BUT WE WILL NOT LET THEM.
THERE ARE ENOUGH SEEDS, WEAPONS, GENERATORS AND OTHER SUPPLIES THAT WE'LL BE ABLE TO SURVIVE HERE, UNDISTURBED, AFTER WE BRING HELL DOWN UPON MANKIND...
AND WE'LL BRING THAT HELL BY USING THE MISSILES WE LIBERATED FROM DEPARTMENT H...
...WEAPONS THAT THEY WOULD USE AGAINST US.
I'VE SEEN IT HAPPEN AGAIN AND AGAIN.
BUT... WE WILL END IT.

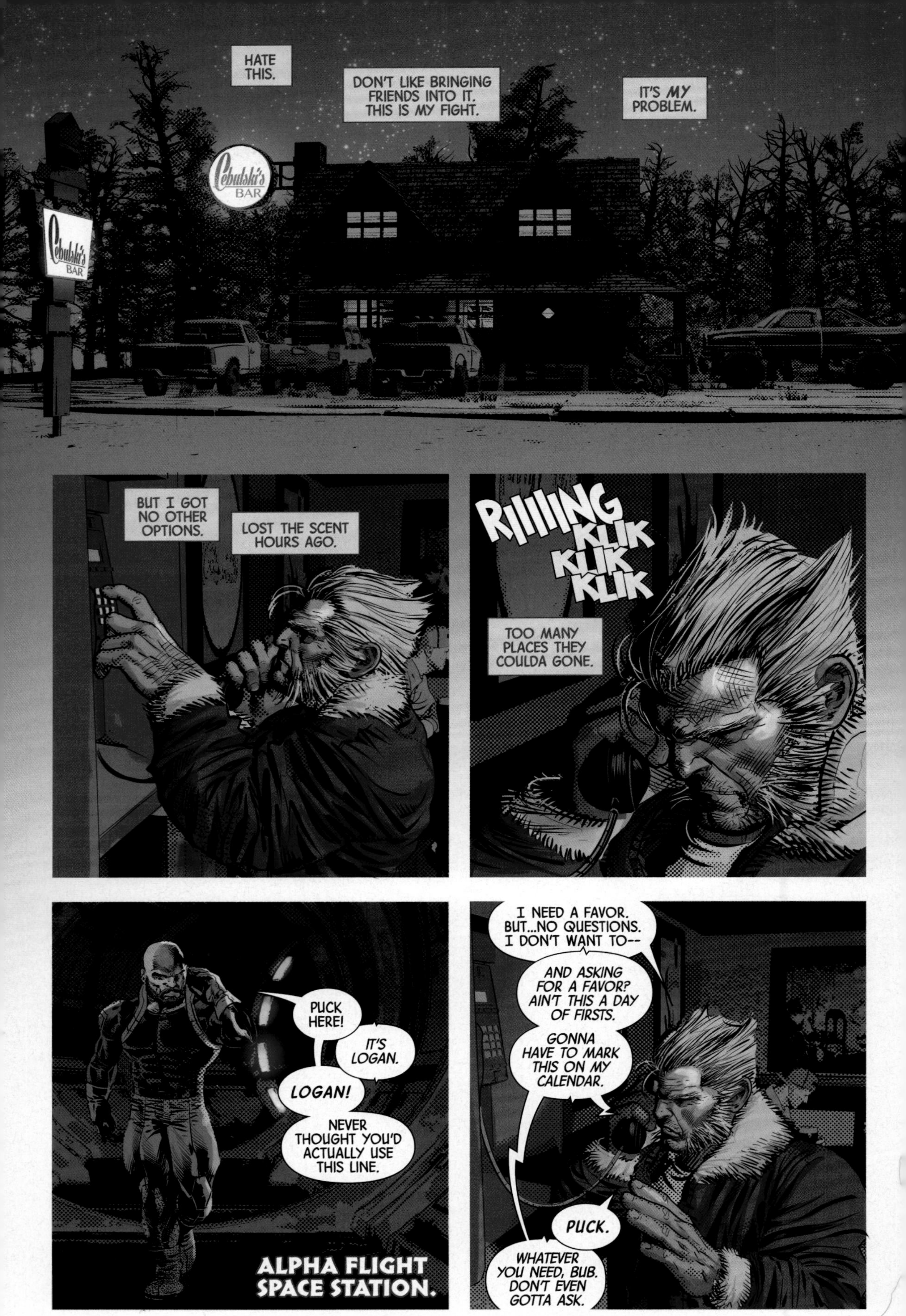
HATE THIS.
DON'T LIKE BRINGING FRIENDS INTO IT. THIS IS MY FIGHT.
IT'S *MY* PROBLEM.
Cebulski's BAR
Cebulski's BAR
BUT I GOT NO OTHER OPTIONS.
LOST THE SCENT HOURS AGO.
RIIIIING
KLIK KLIK KLIK
TOO MANY PLACES THEY COULDA GONE.
PUCK HERE!
IT'S LOGAN.
*LOGAN!*
NEVER THOUGHT YOU'D ACTUALLY USE THIS LINE.
ALPHA FLIGHT SPACE STATION.
I NEED A FAVOR. BUT...NO QUESTIONS. I DON'T WANT TO--
*AND ASKING FOR A FAVOR? AIN'T THIS A DAY OF FIRSTS.*
*GONNA HAVE TO MARK THIS ON MY CALENDAR.*
PUCK.
*WHATEVER YOU NEED, BUB. DON'T EVEN GOTTA ASK.*

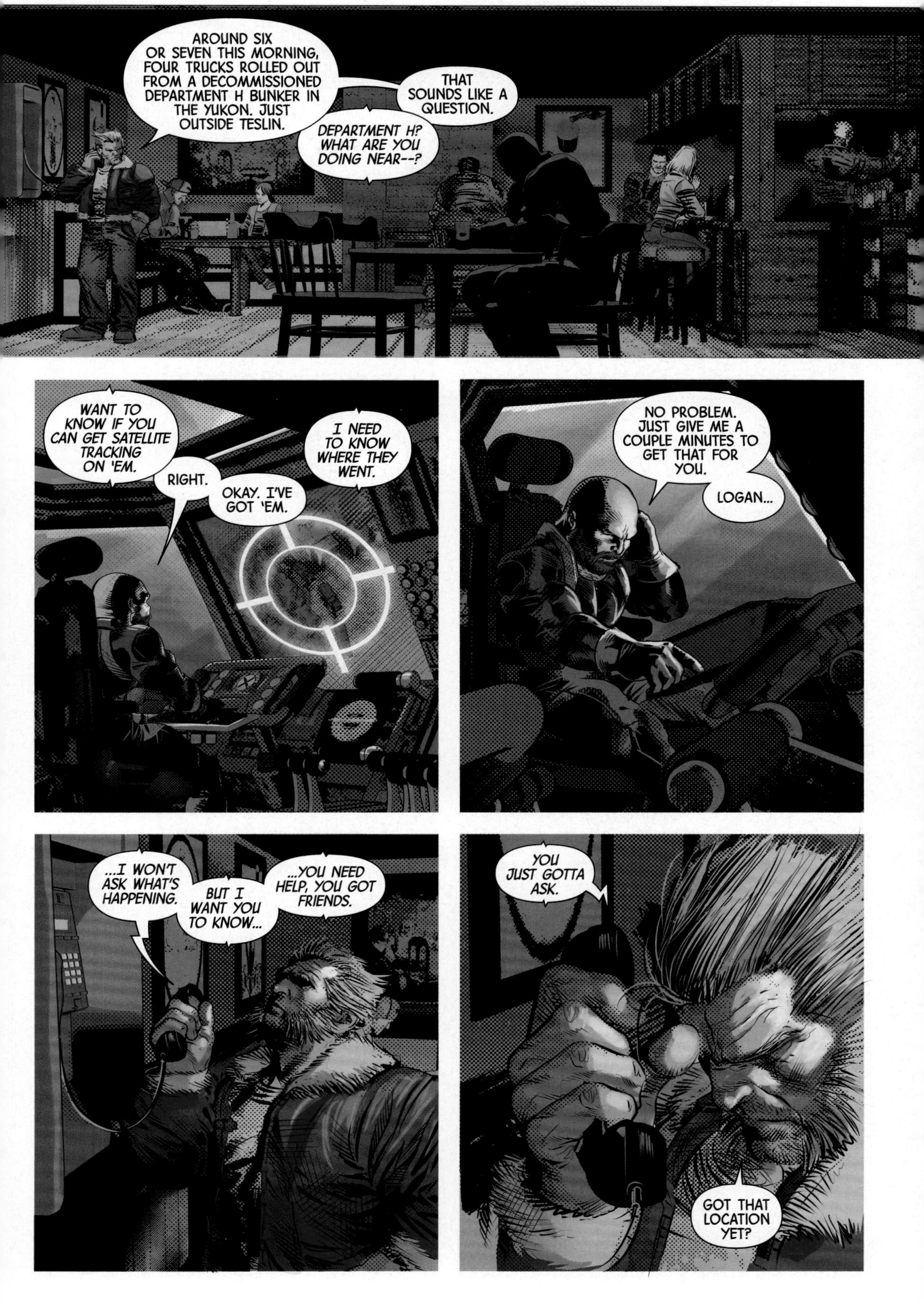
AROUND SIX OR SEVEN THIS MORNING, FOUR TRUCKS ROLLED OUT FROM A DECOMMISSIONED DEPARTMENT H BUNKER IN THE YUKON. JUST OUTSIDE TESLIN.
DEPARTMENT H? WHAT ARE YOU DOING NEAR--?
THAT SOUNDS LIKE A QUESTION.
WANT TO KNOW IF YOU CAN GET SATELLITE TRACKING ON 'EM.
RIGHT.
OKAY. I'VE GOT 'EM.
I NEED TO KNOW WHERE THEY WENT.
NO PROBLEM. JUST GIVE ME A COUPLE MINUTES TO GET THAT FOR YOU.
LOGAN...
...I WON'T ASK WHAT'S HAPPENING.
BUT I WANT YOU TO KNOW...
...YOU NEED HELP, YOU GOT FRIENDS.
YOU JUST GOTTA ASK.
GOT THAT LOCATION YET?

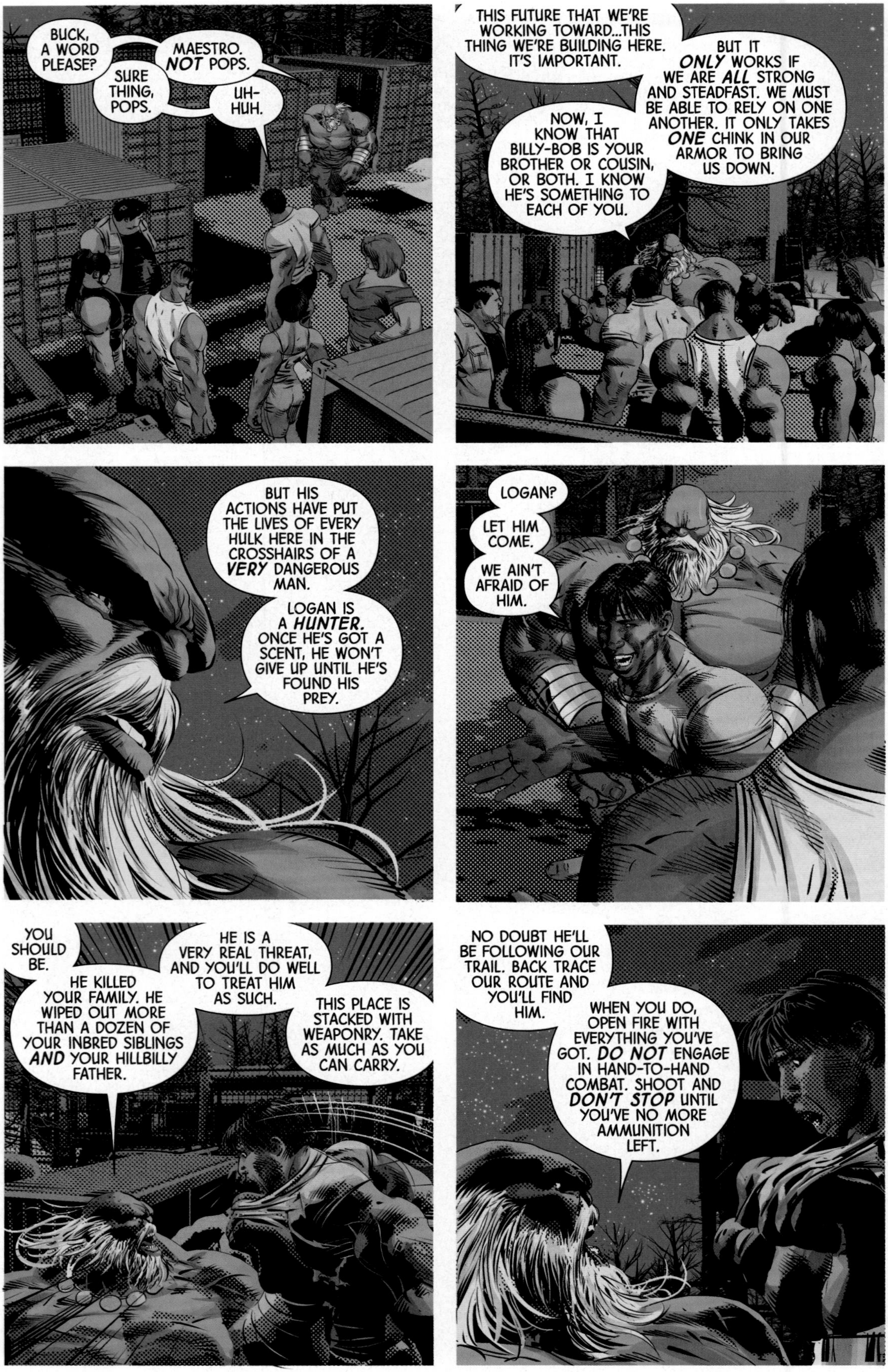
BUCK, A WORD PLEASE?
SURE THING, POPS.
MAESTRO. NOT POPS.
UH-HUH.
THIS FUTURE THAT WE'RE WORKING TOWARD...THIS THING WE'RE BUILDING HERE. IT'S IMPORTANT.
BUT IT ONLY WORKS IF WE ARE ALL STRONG AND STEADFAST. WE MUST BE ABLE TO RELY ON ONE ANOTHER. IT ONLY TAKES ONE CHINK IN OUR ARMOR TO BRING US DOWN.
NOW, I KNOW THAT BILLY-BOB IS YOUR BROTHER OR COUSIN, OR BOTH. I KNOW HE'S SOMETHING TO EACH OF YOU.
BUT HIS ACTIONS HAVE PUT THE LIVES OF EVERY HULK HERE IN THE CROSSHAIRS OF A VERY DANGEROUS MAN.
LOGAN IS A HUNTER. ONCE HE'S GOT A SCENT, HE WON'T GIVE UP UNTIL HE'S FOUND HIS PREY.
LOGAN?
LET HIM COME.
WE AIN'T AFRAID OF HIM.
YOU SHOULD BE.
HE KILLED YOUR FAMILY. HE WIPED OUT MORE THAN A DOZEN OF YOUR INBRED SIBLINGS AND YOUR HILLBILLY FATHER.
HE IS A VERY REAL THREAT, AND YOU'LL DO WELL TO TREAT HIM AS SUCH.
THIS PLACE IS STACKED WITH WEAPONRY. TAKE AS MUCH AS YOU CAN CARRY.
NO DOUBT HE'LL BE FOLLOWING OUR TRAIL. BACK TRACE OUR ROUTE AND YOU'LL FIND HIM.
WHEN YOU DO, OPEN FIRE WITH EVERYTHING YOU'VE GOT. DO NOT ENGAGE IN HAND-TO-HAND COMBAT. SHOOT AND DON'T STOP UNTIL YOU'VE NO MORE AMMUNITION LEFT.

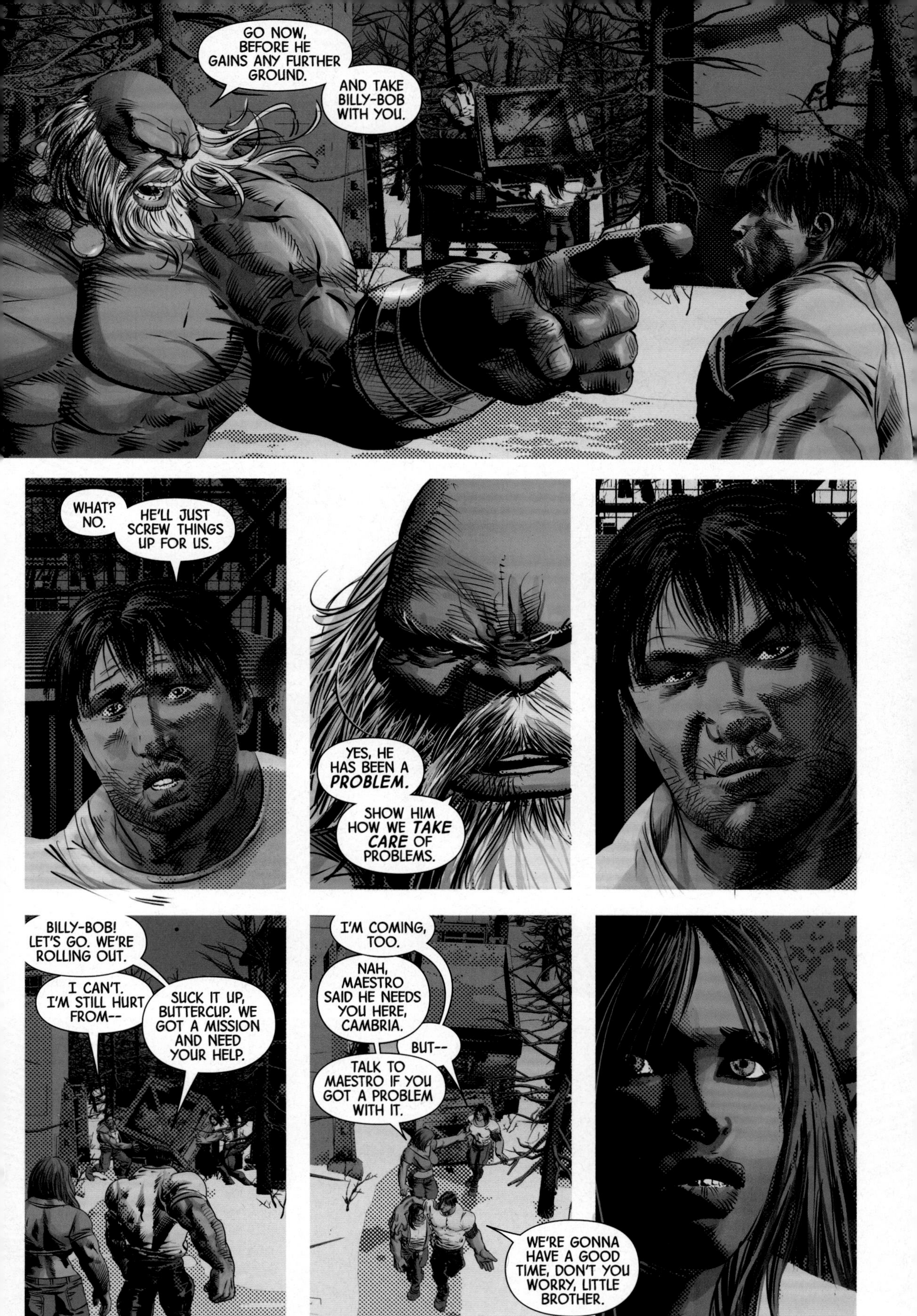
GO NOW, BEFORE HE GAINS ANY FURTHER GROUND.
AND TAKE BILLY-BOB WITH YOU.
WHAT? NO.
HE'LL JUST SCREW THINGS UP FOR US.
YES, HE HAS BEEN A PROBLEM.
SHOW HIM HOW WE TAKE CARE OF PROBLEMS.
BILLY-BOB! LET'S GO. WE'RE ROLLING OUT.
I CAN'T. I'M STILL HURT FROM--
SUCK IT UP, BUTTERCUP. WE GOT A MISSION AND NEED YOUR HELP.
I'M COMING, TOO.
NAH, MAESTRO SAID HE NEEDS YOU HERE, CAMBRIA.
BUT--
TALK TO MAESTRO IF YOU GOT A PROBLEM WITH IT.
WE'RE GONNA HAVE A GOOD TIME, DON'T YOU WORRY, LITTLE BROTHER.

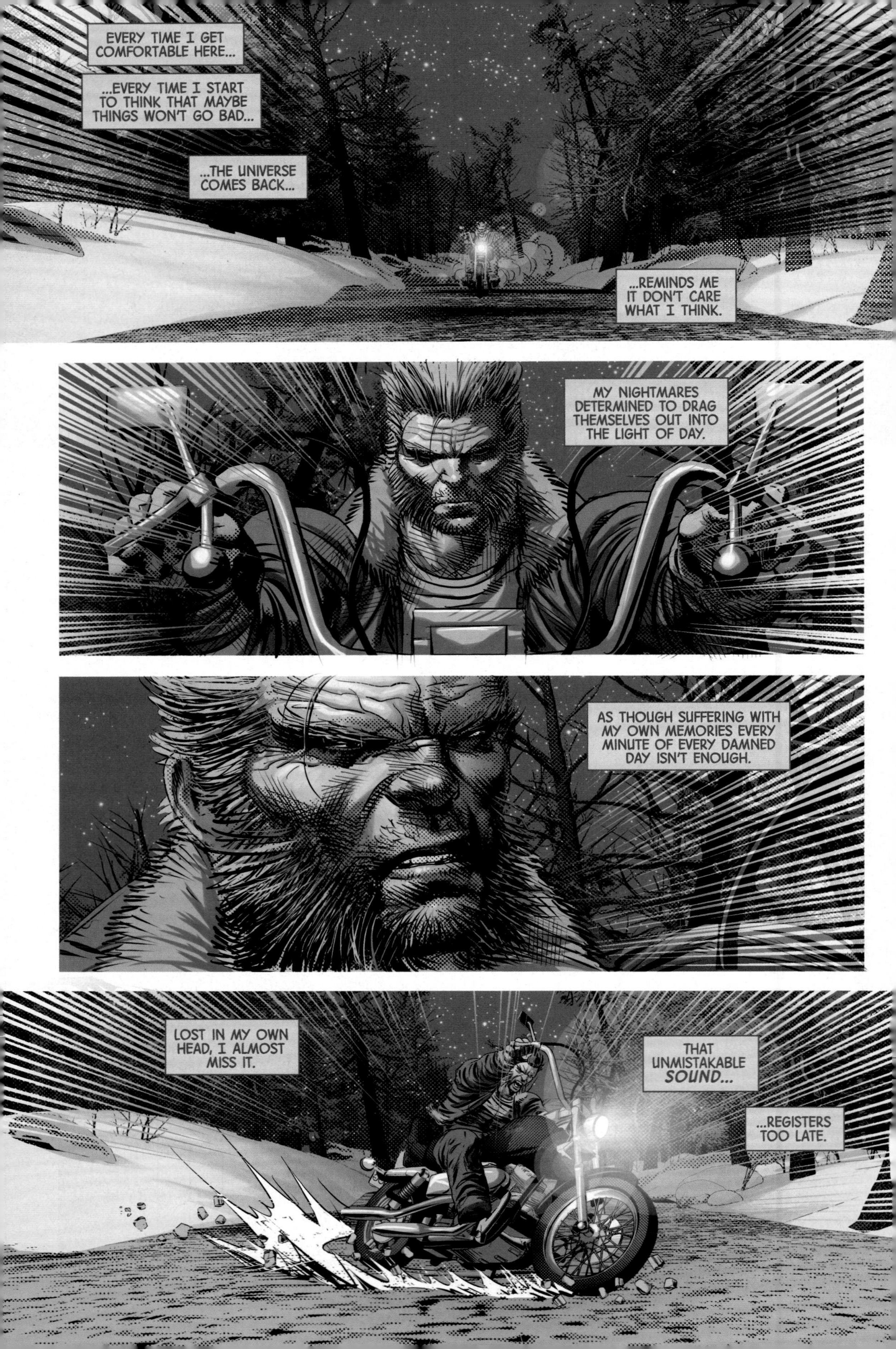
EVERY TIME I GET COMFORTABLE HERE...
...EVERY TIME I START TO THINK THAT MAYBE THINGS WON'T GO BAD...
...THE UNIVERSE COMES BACK...
...REMINDS ME IT DON'T CARE WHAT I THINK.
MY NIGHTMARES DETERMINED TO DRAG THEMSELVES OUT INTO THE LIGHT OF DAY.
AS THOUGH SUFFERING WITH MY OWN MEMORIES EVERY MINUTE OF EVERY DAMNED DAY ISN'T ENOUGH.
LOST IN MY OWN HEAD, I ALMOST MISS IT.
THAT UNMISTAKABLE SOUND...
...REGISTERS TOO LATE.

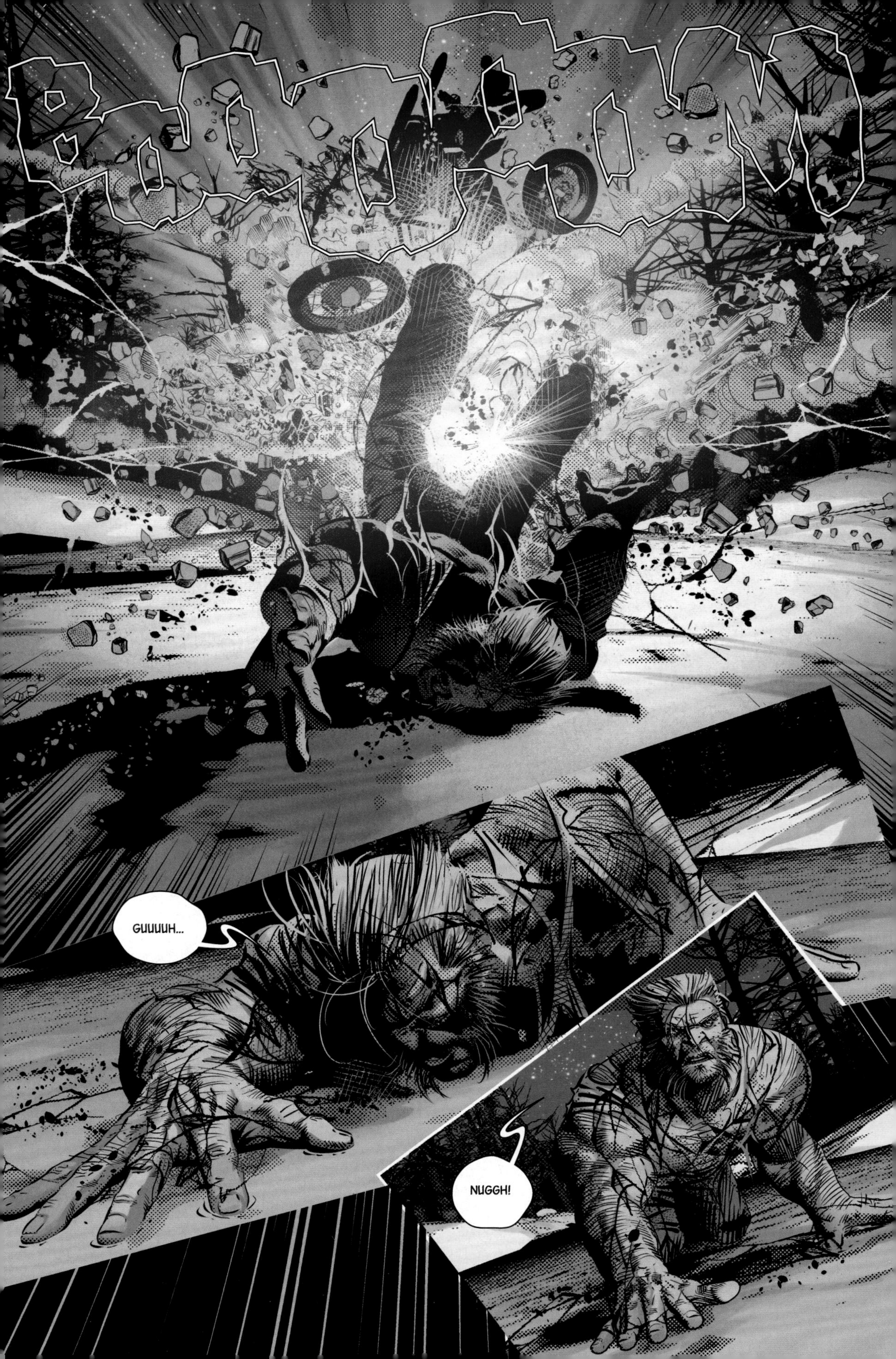
BADOOOM
GUUUUH...
NUGGH!

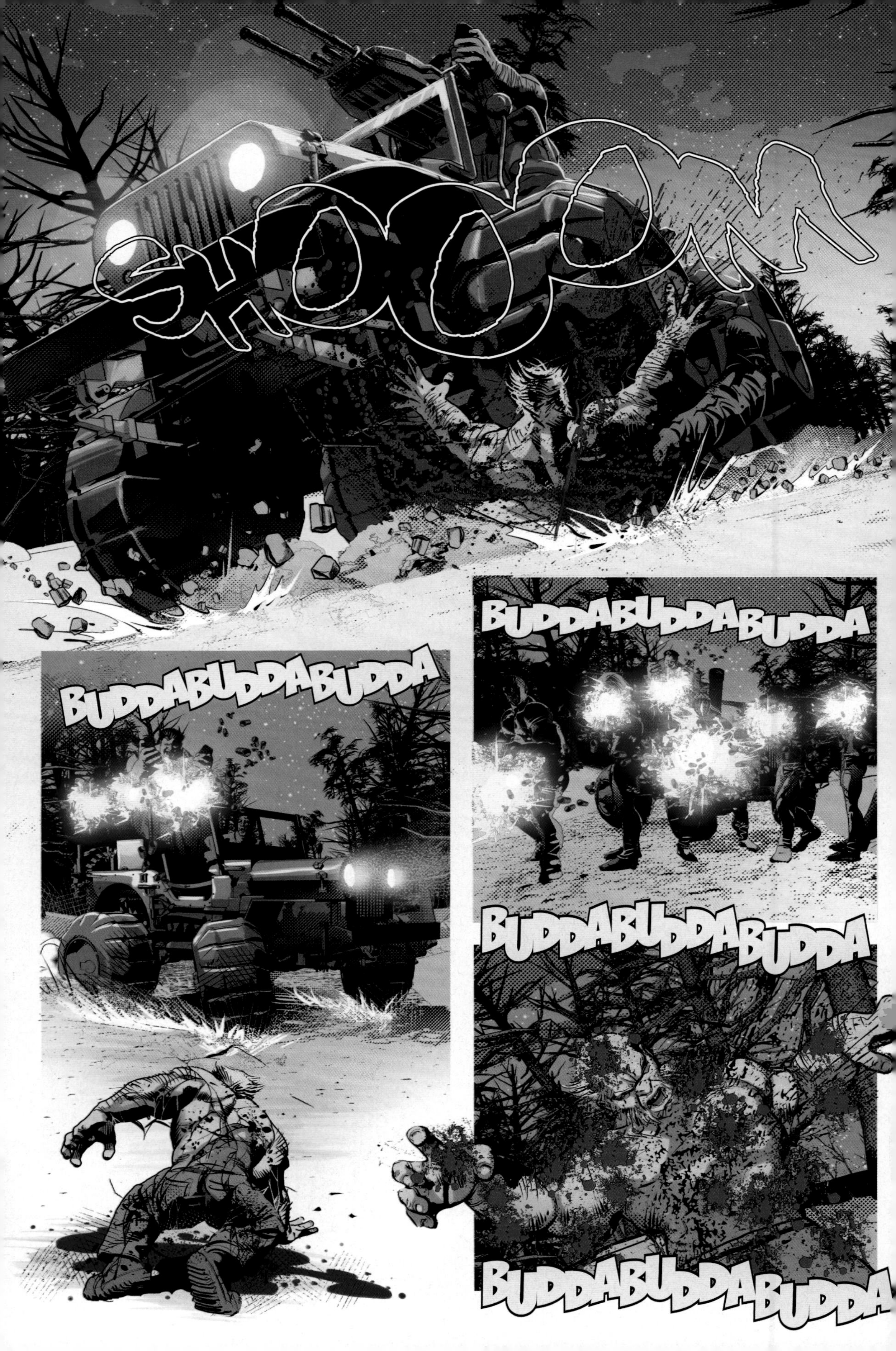
SHOOOM
BUDDABUDDABUDDA
BUDDABUDDABUDDA
BUDDABUDDABUDDA
BUDDABUDDABUDDA

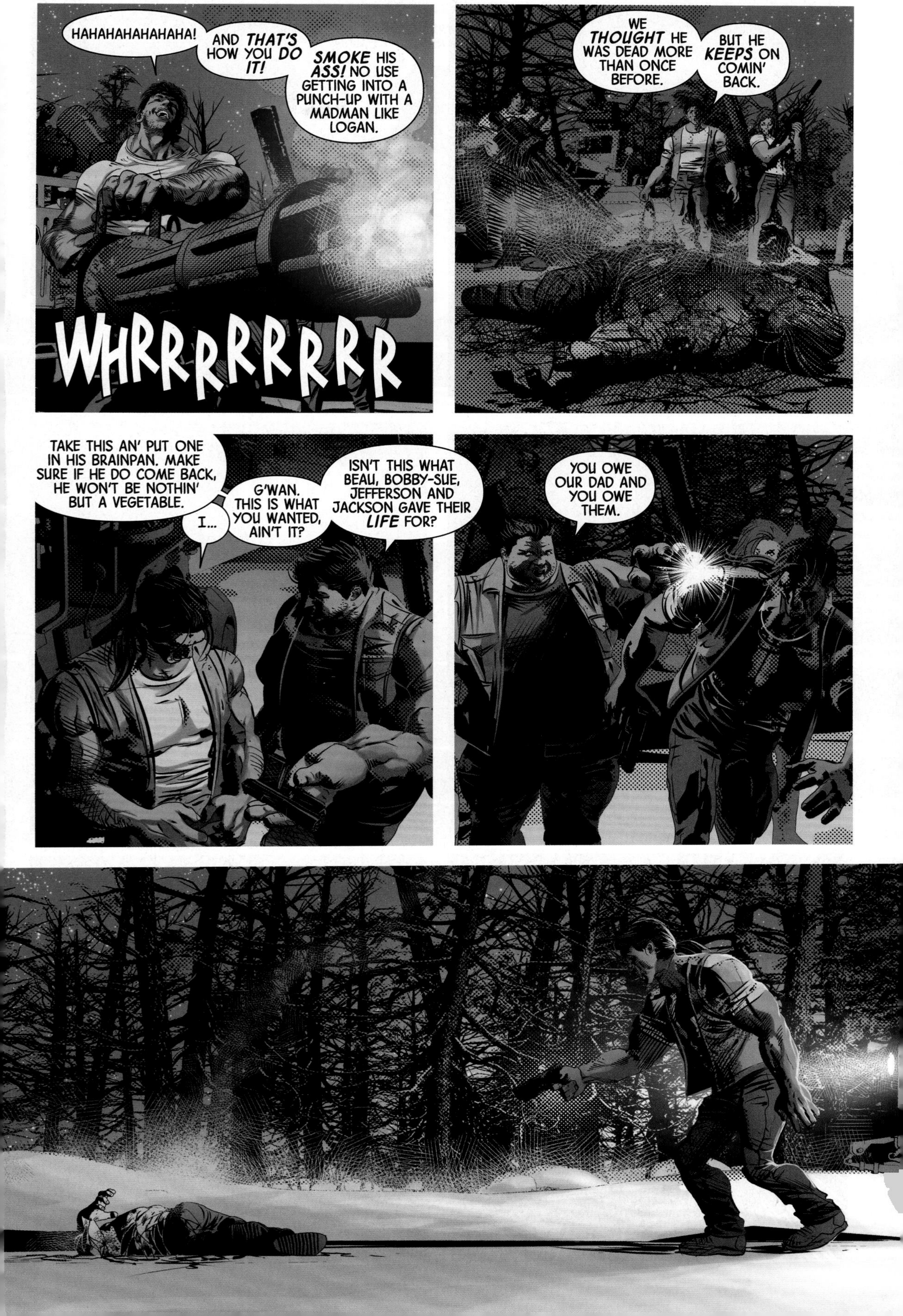
HAHAHAHAHAHAHA!
AND THAT'S HOW YOU DO IT!
SMOKE HIS ASS! NO USE GETTING INTO A PUNCH-UP WITH A MADMAN LIKE LOGAN.
WHRRRRRRRR
WE THOUGHT HE WAS DEAD MORE THAN ONCE BEFORE.
BUT HE KEEPS ON COMIN' BACK.
TAKE THIS AN' PUT ONE IN HIS BRAINPAN. MAKE SURE IF HE DO COME BACK, HE WON'T BE NOTHIN' BUT A VEGETABLE.
I...
G'WAN. THIS IS WHAT YOU WANTED, AIN'T IT?
ISN'T THIS WHAT BEAU, BOBBY-SUE, JEFFERSON AND JACKSON GAVE THEIR LIFE FOR?
YOU OWE OUR DAD AND YOU OWE THEM.

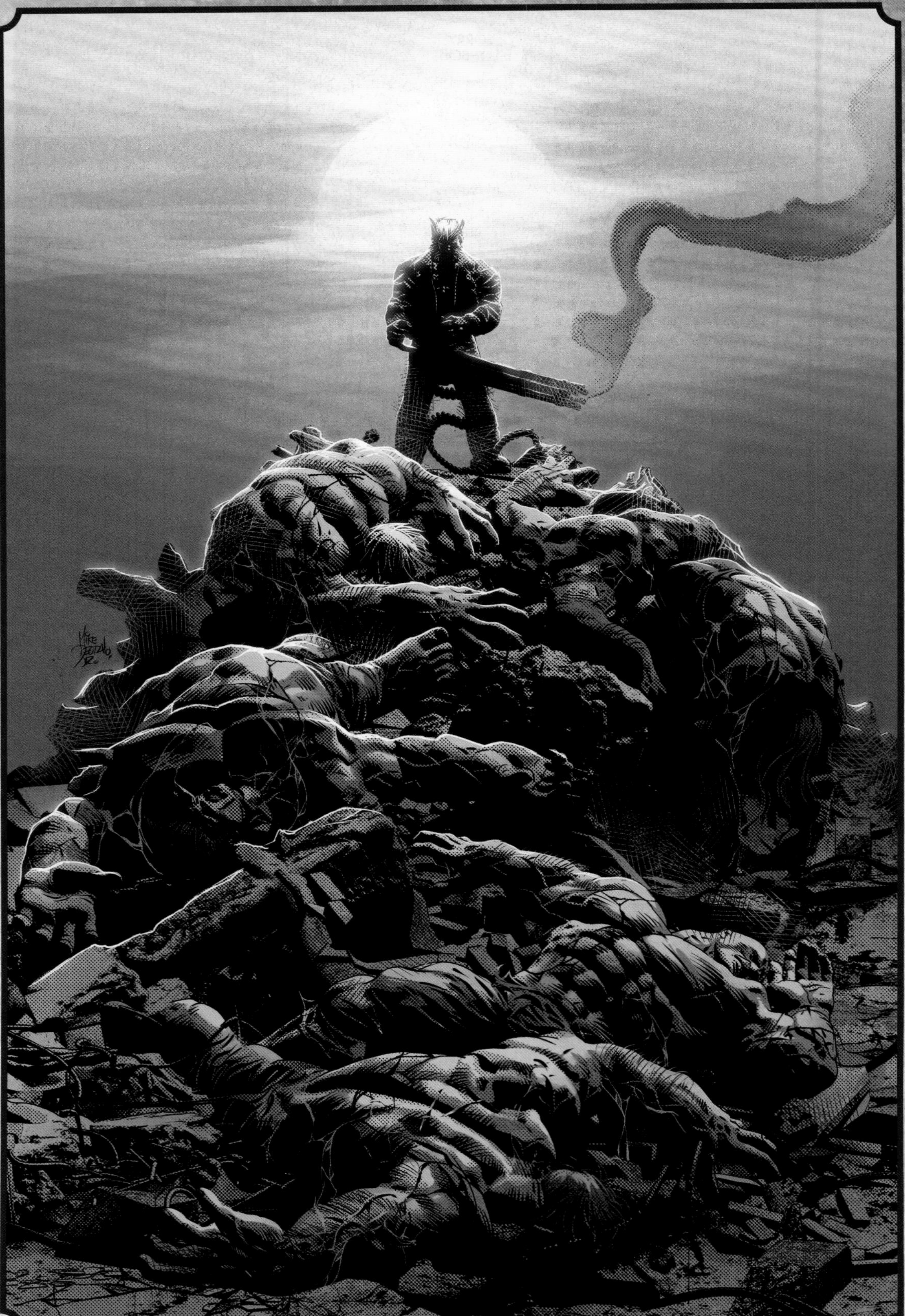

27

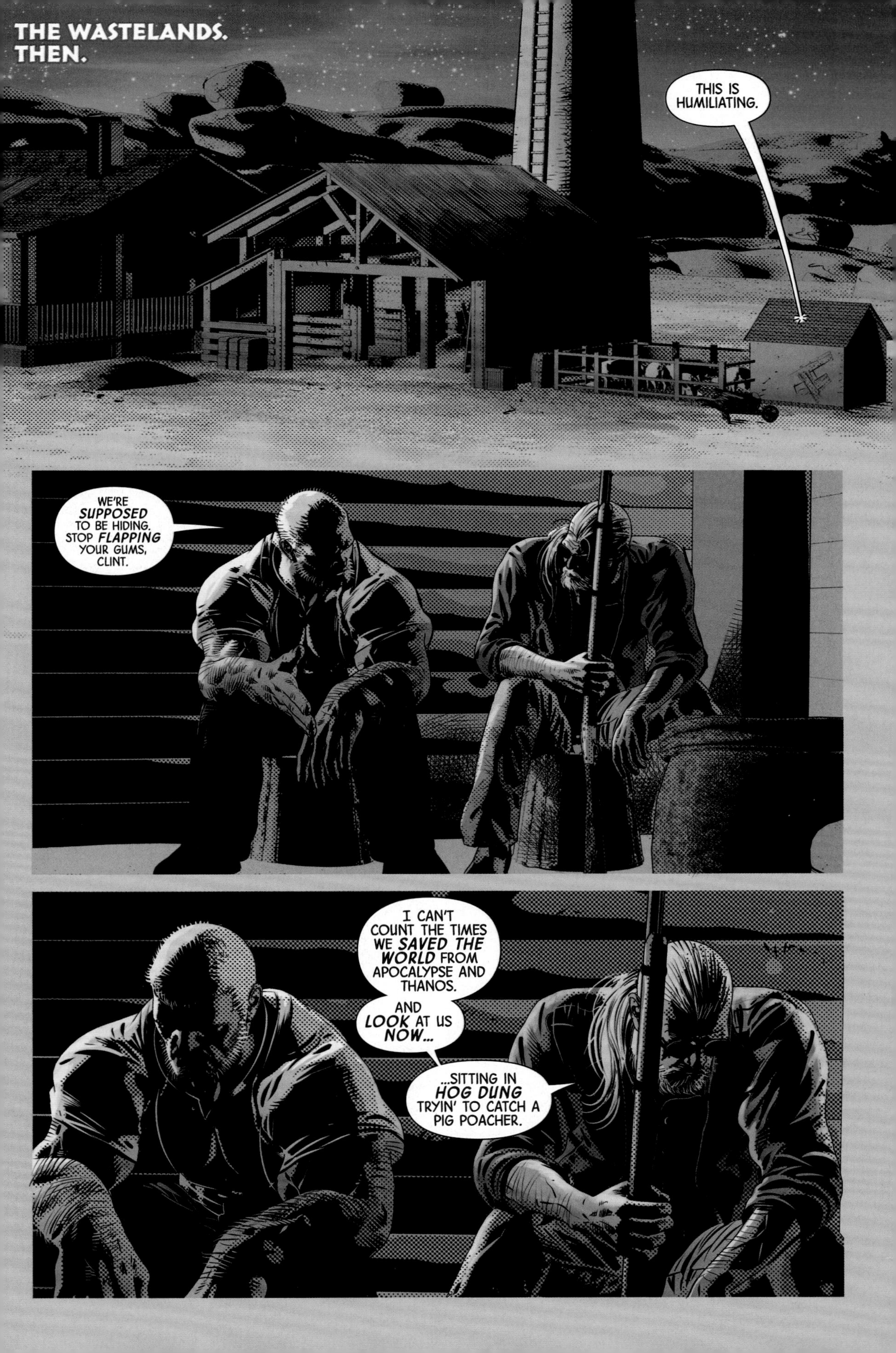
THE WASTELANDS. THEN.
THIS IS HUMILIATING.
WE'RE SUPPOSED TO BE HIDING. STOP FLAPPING YOUR GUMS, CLINT.
I CAN'T COUNT THE TIMES WE SAVED THE WORLD FROM APOCALYPSE AND THANOS.
AND LOOK AT US NOW...
...SITTING IN HOG DUNG TRYIN' TO CATCH A PIG POACHER.

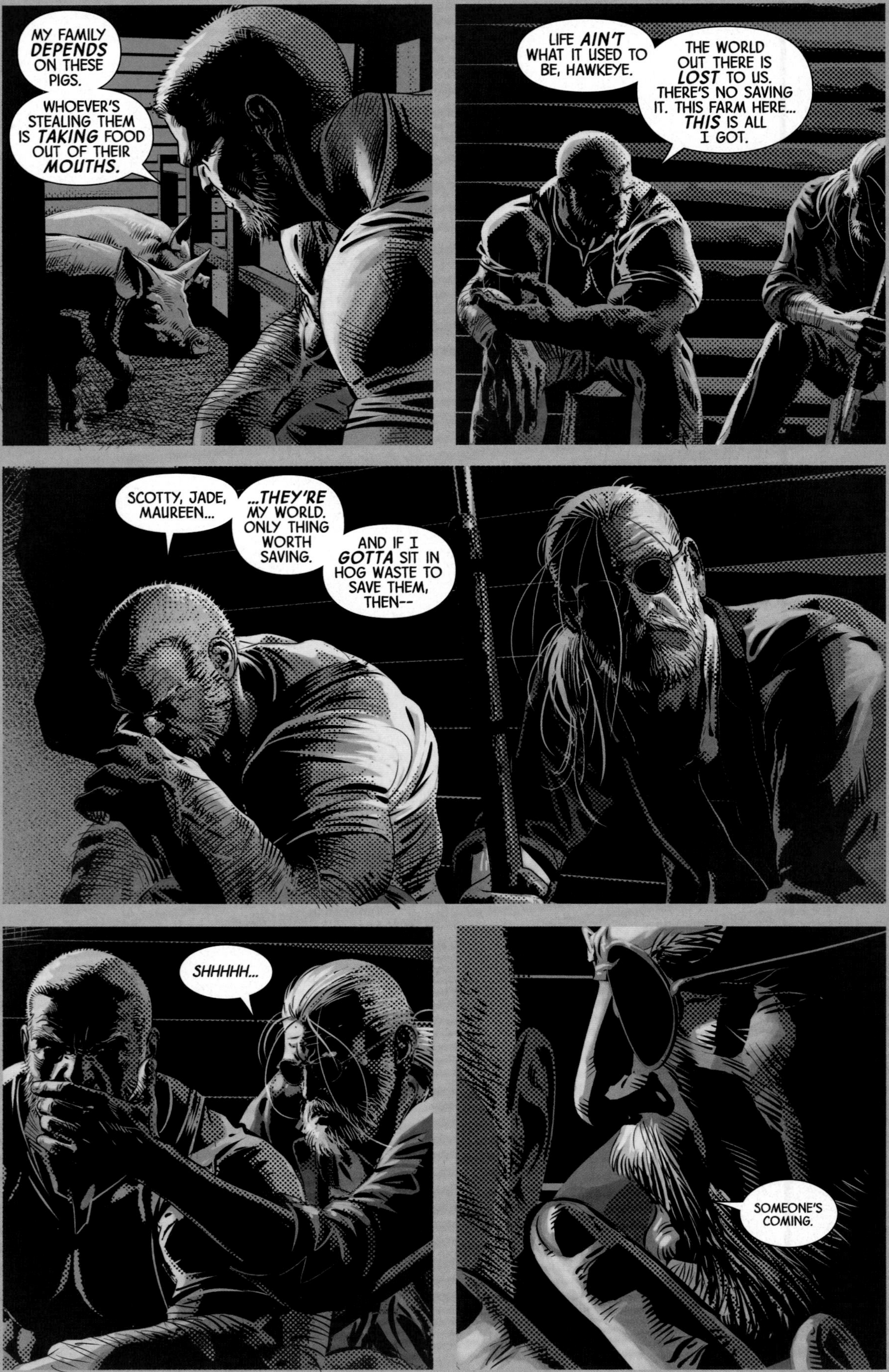

MY FAMILY DEPENDS ON THESE PIGS.
WHOEVER'S STEALING THEM IS TAKING FOOD OUT OF THEIR MOUTHS.
LIFE AIN'T WHAT IT USED TO BE, HAWKEYE.
THE WORLD OUT THERE IS LOST TO US. THERE'S NO SAVING IT. THIS FARM HERE... THIS IS ALL I GOT.
SCOTTY, JADE, MAUREEN...
...THEY'RE MY WORLD. ONLY THING WORTH SAVING.
AND IF I GOTTA SIT IN HOG WASTE TO SAVE THEM, THEN--
SHHHHH...
SOMEONE'S COMING.

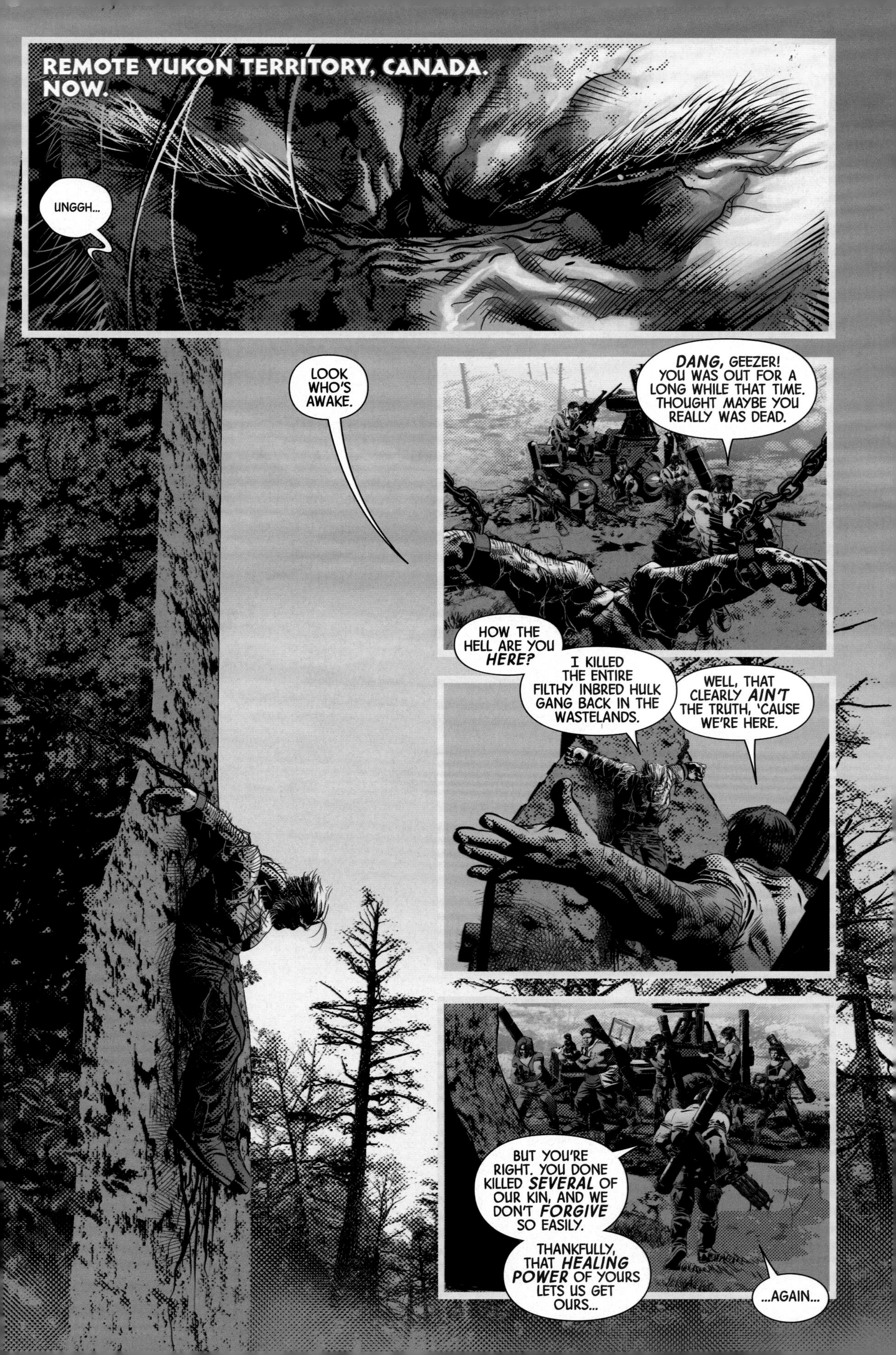
REMOTE YUKON TERRITORY, CANADA. NOW.
UNGGH...
LOOK WHO'S AWAKE.
DANG, GEEZER! YOU WAS OUT FOR A LONG WHILE THAT TIME. THOUGHT MAYBE YOU REALLY WAS DEAD.
HOW THE HELL ARE YOU HERE?
I KILLED THE ENTIRE FILTHY INBRED HULK GANG BACK IN THE WASTELANDS.
WELL, THAT CLEARLY AIN'T THE TRUTH, 'CAUSE WE'RE HERE.
BUT YOU'RE RIGHT. YOU DONE KILLED SEVERAL OF OUR KIN, AND WE DON'T FORGIVE SO EASILY.
THANKFULLY, THAT HEALING POWER OF YOURS LETS US GET OURS...
...AGAIN...

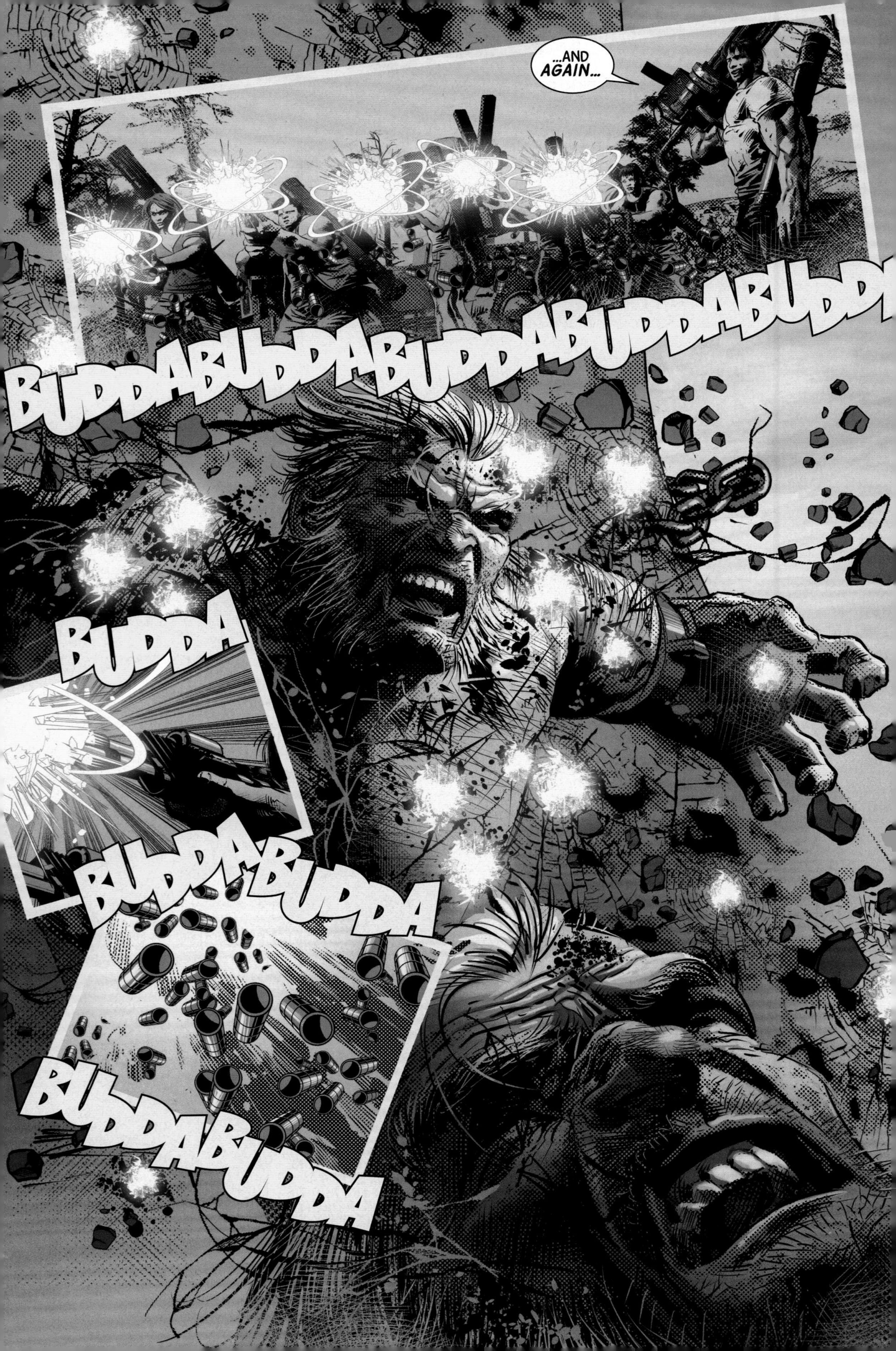
...AND AGAIN...
BUDDABUDDABUDDABUDDABUDDABUDD
BUDDA
BUDDABUDDA
BUDDABUDDA

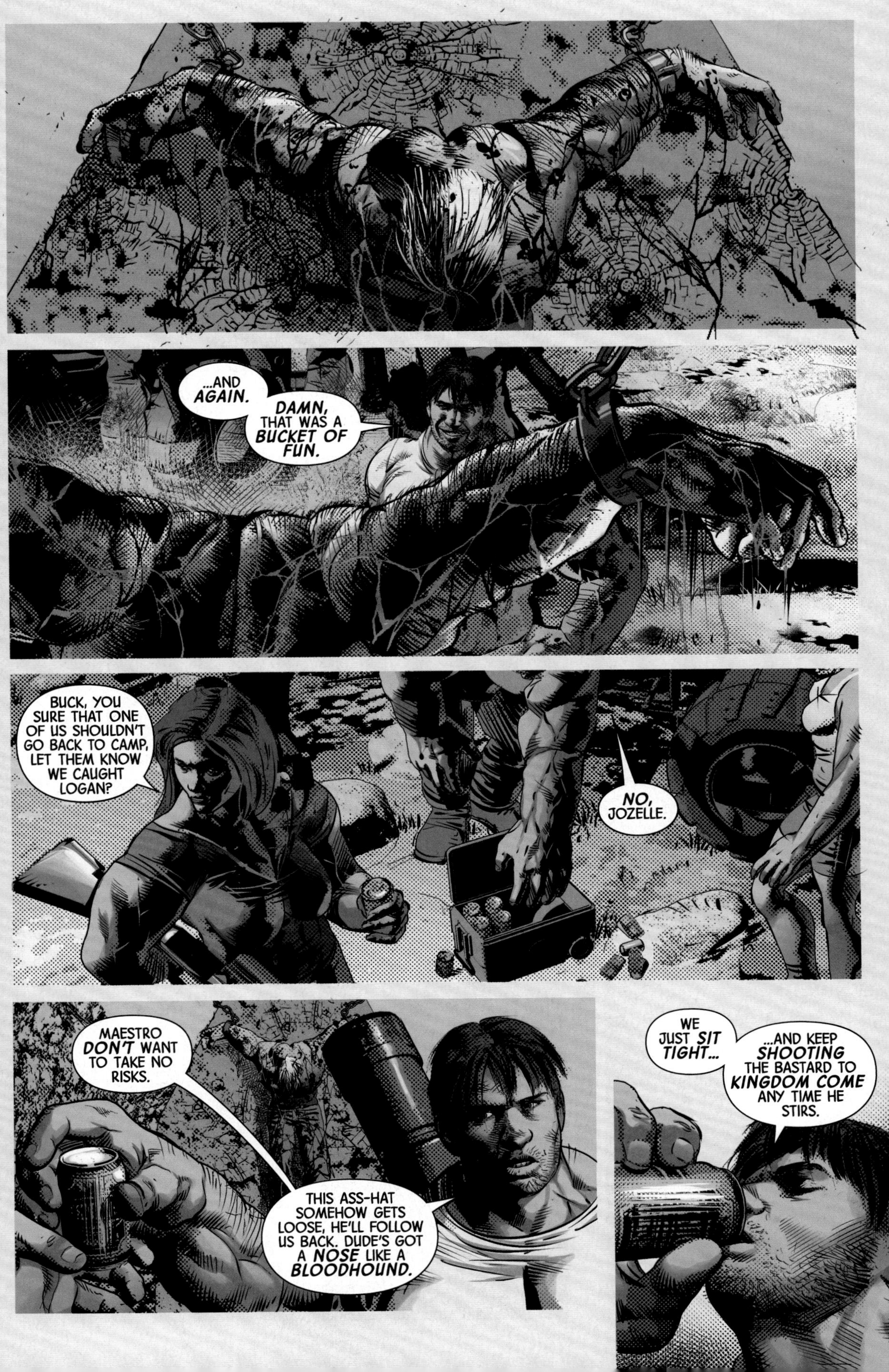

...AND AGAIN.
DAMN, THAT WAS A BUCKET OF FUN.
BUCK, YOU SURE THAT ONE OF US SHOULDN'T GO BACK TO CAMP, LET THEM KNOW WE CAUGHT LOGAN?
NO, JOZELLE.
MAESTRO DON'T WANT TO TAKE NO RISKS.
THIS ASS-HAT SOMEHOW GETS LOOSE, HE'LL FOLLOW US BACK. DUDE'S GOT A NOSE LIKE A BLOODHOUND.
WE JUST SIT TIGHT...
...AND KEEP SHOOTING THE BASTARD TO KINGDOM COME ANY TIME HE STIRS.

MAESTRO'S COMPOUND.
SOMEWHERE IN THE YUKON.

IT'S STILL ALARMING TO SEE YOU IN HUMAN FORM, MAESTRO.

I'LL ADMIT, I DON'T USUALLY ENJOY BEING IN THIS FORM.

BUT THERE'S SOMETHING TO BE SAID FOR THE *NIMBLE* FINGERS OF HUMANS.

COMES IN HANDY WHEN WORKING WITH SUCH *ARCHAIC WEAPONRY* THAT, WITH ONE WRONG MOVE, COULD BLOW US BACK TO THE STONE AGE.

NOT THAT WE AREN'T ALREADY THERE.

NOW, CAMBRIA, IS THERE SOMETHING I CAN HELP YOU WITH?

I'M *BUSY* WITH MY WORK.

I... WE'RE *REALLY* GOING TO DO THIS?

IT'S SO STRANGE TO THINK THAT SOMETHING SO SMALL COULD CAUSE SO MUCH DESTRUCTION.

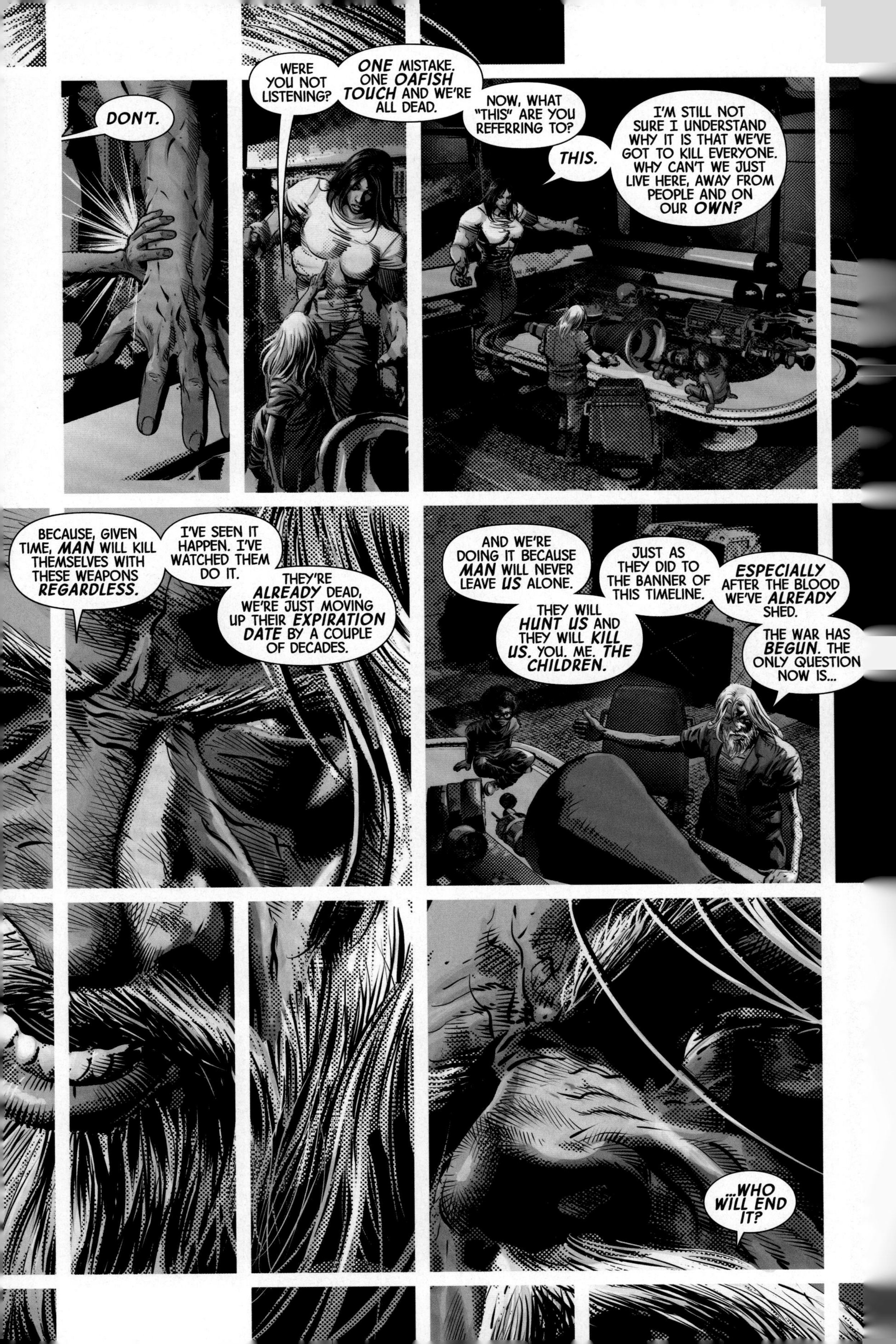
DON'T.
WERE YOU NOT LISTENING?
ONE MISTAKE. ONE OAFISH TOUCH AND WE'RE ALL DEAD.
NOW, WHAT "THIS" ARE YOU REFERRING TO?
THIS.
I'M STILL NOT SURE I UNDERSTAND WHY IT IS THAT WE'VE GOT TO KILL EVERYONE. WHY CAN'T WE JUST LIVE HERE, AWAY FROM PEOPLE AND ON OUR OWN?
BECAUSE, GIVEN TIME, MAN WILL KILL THEMSELVES WITH THESE WEAPONS REGARDLESS.
I'VE SEEN IT HAPPEN. I'VE WATCHED THEM DO IT.
THEY'RE ALREADY DEAD, WE'RE JUST MOVING UP THEIR EXPIRATION DATE BY A COUPLE OF DECADES.
AND WE'RE DOING IT BECAUSE MAN WILL NEVER LEAVE US ALONE.
THEY WILL HUNT US AND THEY WILL KILL US. YOU. ME. THE CHILDREN.
JUST AS THEY DID TO THE BANNER OF THIS TIMELINE.
ESPECIALLY AFTER THE BLOOD WE'VE ALREADY SHED.
THE WAR HAS BEGUN. THE ONLY QUESTION NOW IS...
...WHO WILL END IT?

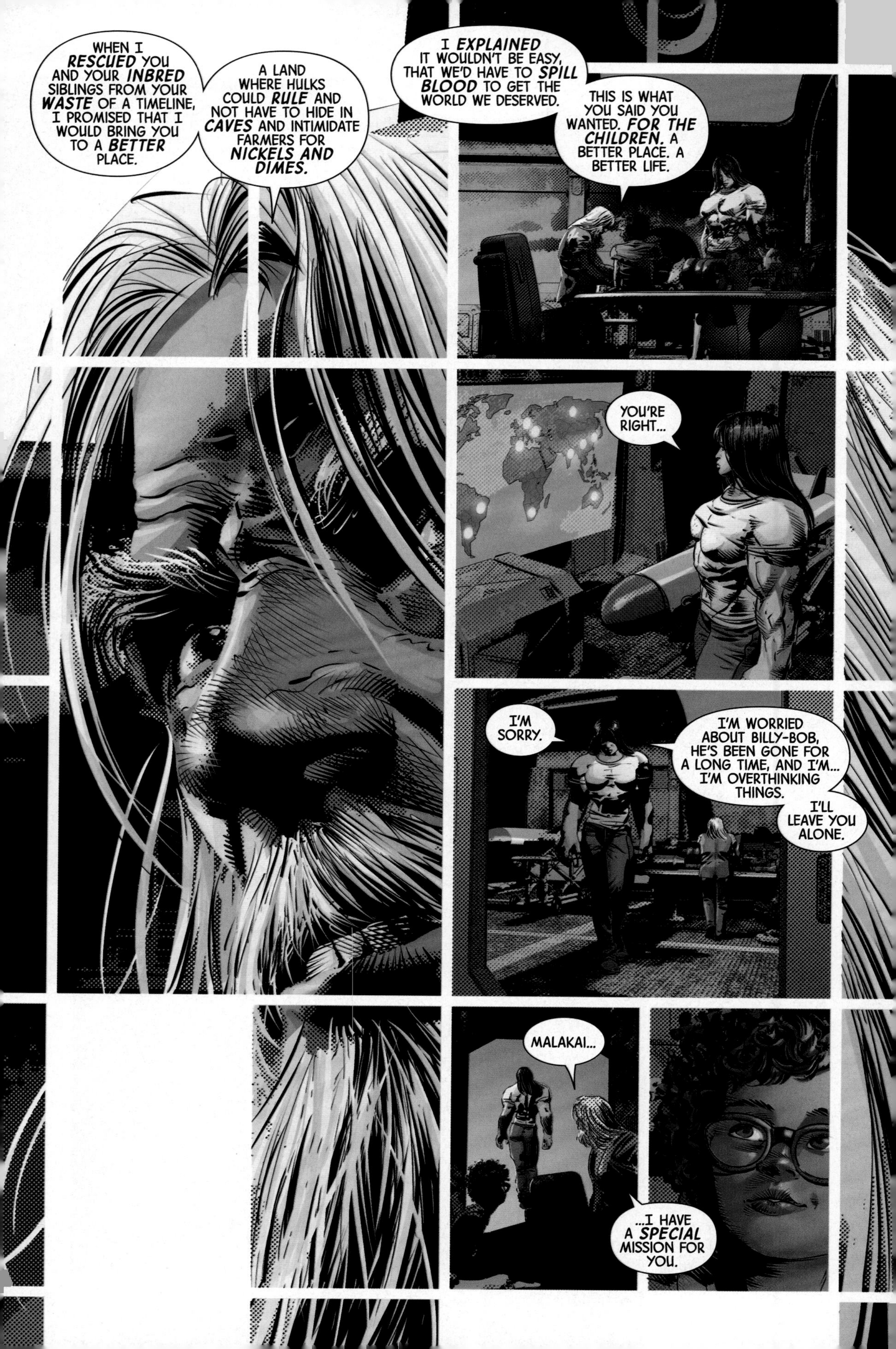
WHEN I *RESCUED* YOU AND YOUR *INBRED* SIBLINGS FROM YOUR *WASTE* OF A TIMELINE, I PROMISED THAT I WOULD BRING YOU TO A *BETTER* PLACE.
A LAND WHERE HULKS COULD *RULE* AND NOT HAVE TO HIDE IN *CAVES* AND INTIMIDATE FARMERS FOR *NICKELS AND DIMES.*
I *EXPLAINED* IT WOULDN'T BE EASY, THAT WE'D HAVE TO *SPILL BLOOD* TO GET THE WORLD WE DESERVED.
THIS IS WHAT YOU SAID YOU WANTED. *FOR THE CHILDREN.* A BETTER PLACE. A BETTER LIFE.
YOU'RE RIGHT...
I'M SORRY.
I'M WORRIED ABOUT BILLY-BOB, HE'S BEEN GONE FOR A LONG TIME, AND I'M... I'M OVERTHINKING THINGS.
I'LL LEAVE YOU ALONE.
MALAKAI...
...I HAVE A *SPECIAL* MISSION FOR YOU.

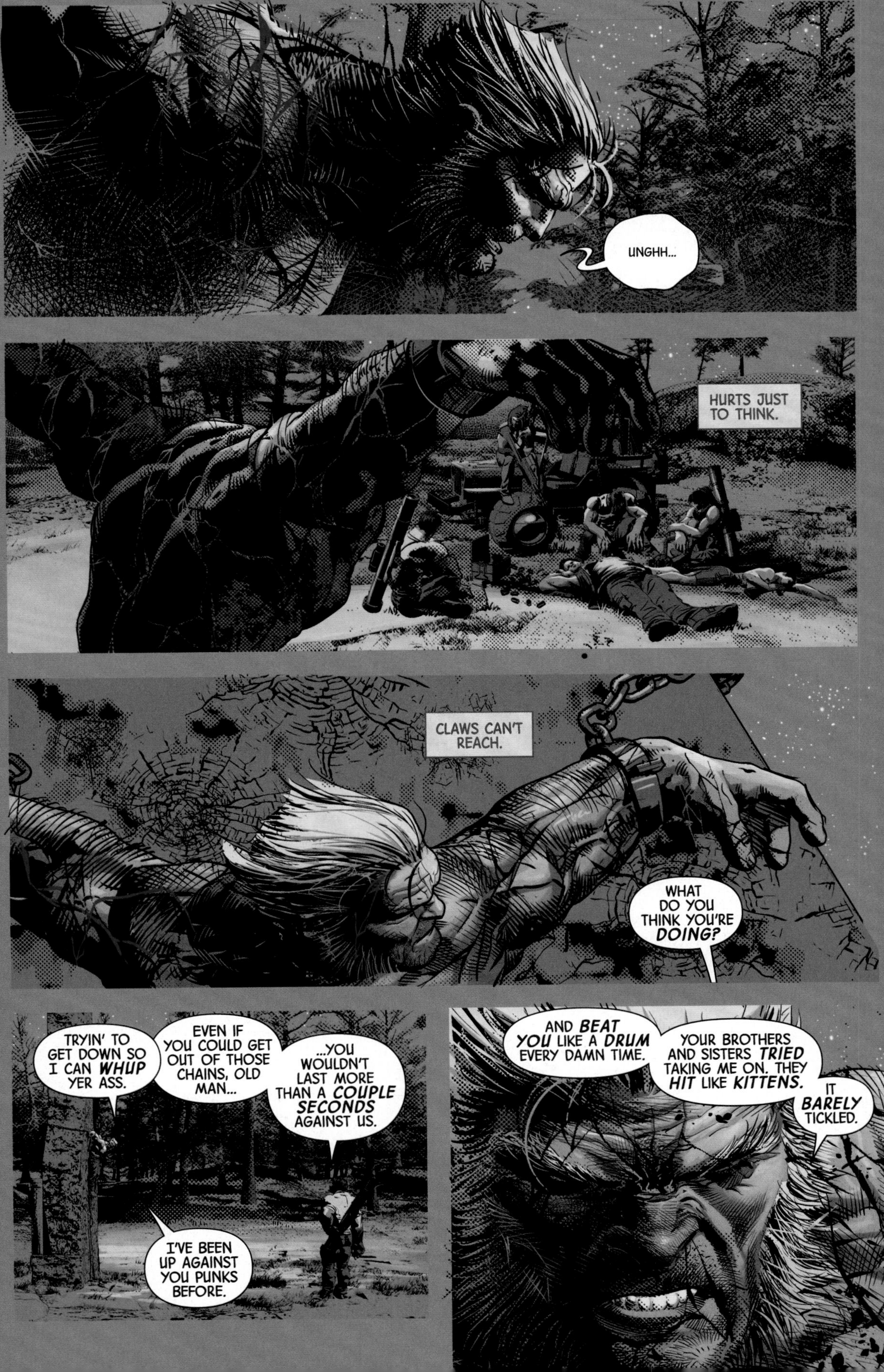
UNGHH...
HURTS JUST TO THINK.
CLAWS CAN'T REACH.
WHAT DO YOU THINK YOU'RE DOING?
TRYIN' TO GET DOWN SO I CAN WHUP YER ASS.
EVEN IF YOU COULD GET OUT OF THOSE CHAINS, OLD MAN...
...YOU WOULDN'T LAST MORE THAN A COUPLE SECONDS AGAINST US.
I'VE BEEN UP AGAINST YOU PUNKS BEFORE.
AND BEAT YOU LIKE A DRUM EVERY DAMN TIME.
YOUR BROTHERS AND SISTERS TRIED TAKING ME ON. THEY HIT LIKE KITTENS.
IT BARELY TICKLED.

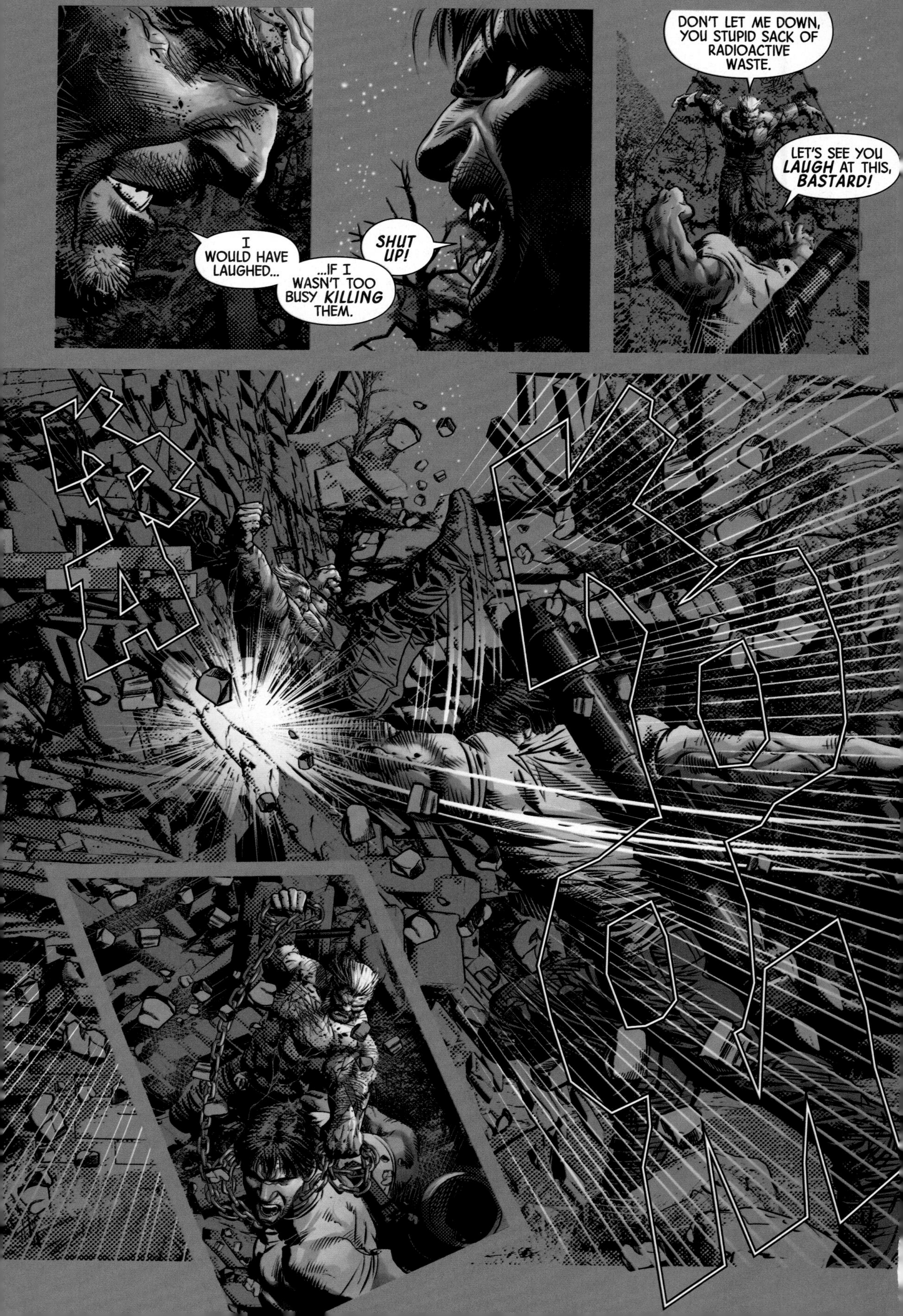
I WOULD HAVE LAUGHED...
...IF I WASN'T TOO BUSY KILLING THEM.
SHUT UP!
DON'T LET ME DOWN, YOU STUPID SACK OF RADIOACTIVE WASTE.
LET'S SEE YOU LAUGH AT THIS, BASTARD!

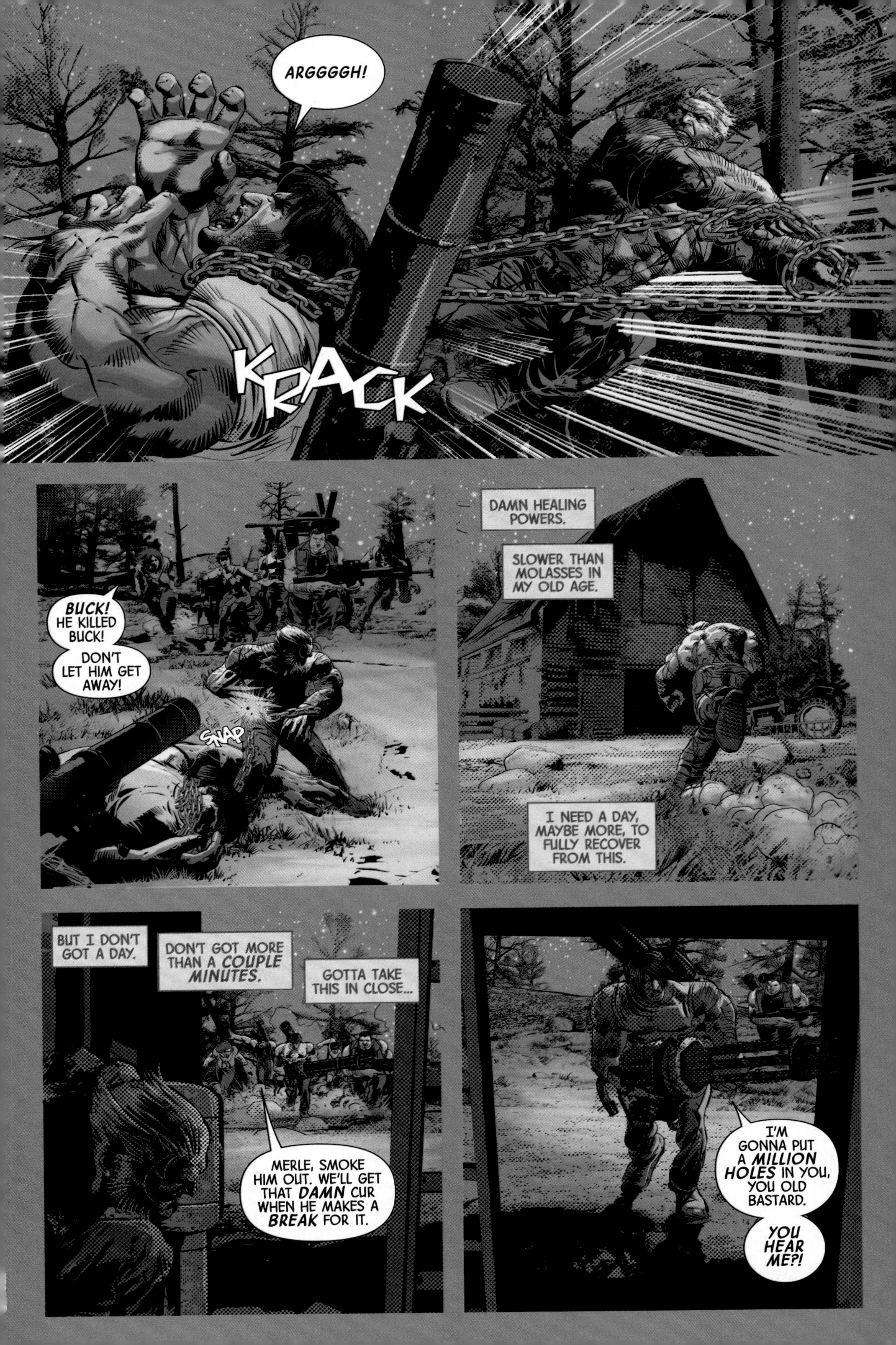
ARGGGGH!
KRACK
BUCK! HE KILLED BUCK!
DON'T LET HIM GET AWAY!
SNAP
DAMN HEALING POWERS.
SLOWER THAN MOLASSES IN MY OLD AGE.
I NEED A DAY, MAYBE MORE, TO FULLY RECOVER FROM THIS.
BUT I DON'T GOT A DAY.
DON'T GOT MORE THAN A COUPLE MINUTES.
GOTTA TAKE THIS IN CLOSE...
MERLE, SMOKE HIM OUT. WE'LL GET THAT DAMN CUR WHEN HE MAKES A BREAK FOR IT.
I'M GONNA PUT A MILLION HOLES IN YOU, YOU OLD BASTARD.
YOU HEAR ME?!

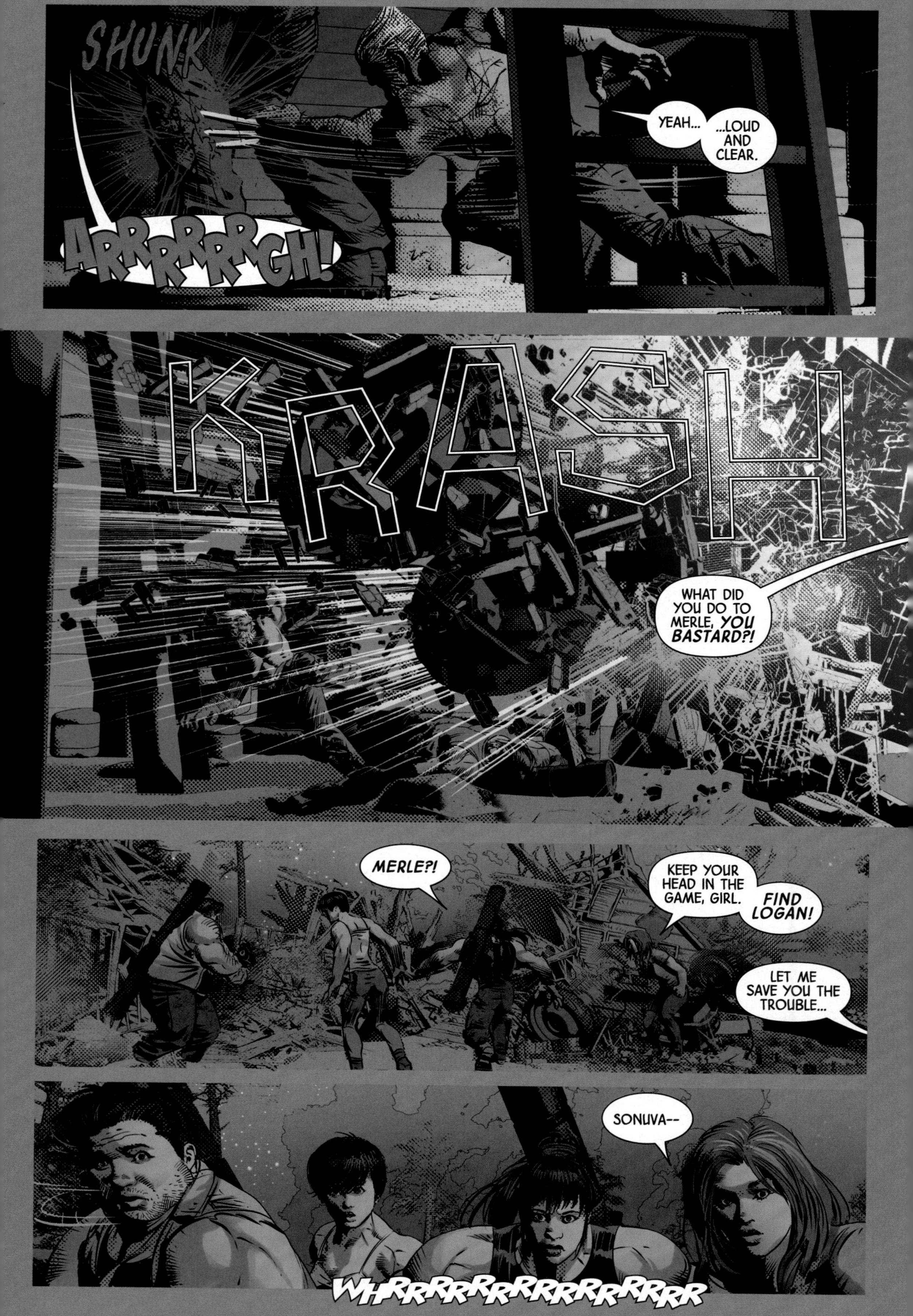
SHUNK
ARRRRRRGH!
YEAH...
...LOUD AND CLEAR.
KRASH
WHAT DID YOU DO TO MERLE, *YOU BASTARD?!*
*MERLE?!*
KEEP YOUR HEAD IN THE GAME, GIRL.
*FIND LOGAN!*
LET ME SAVE YOU THE TROUBLE...
SONUVA--
WHRRRRRRRRRRRRRRR

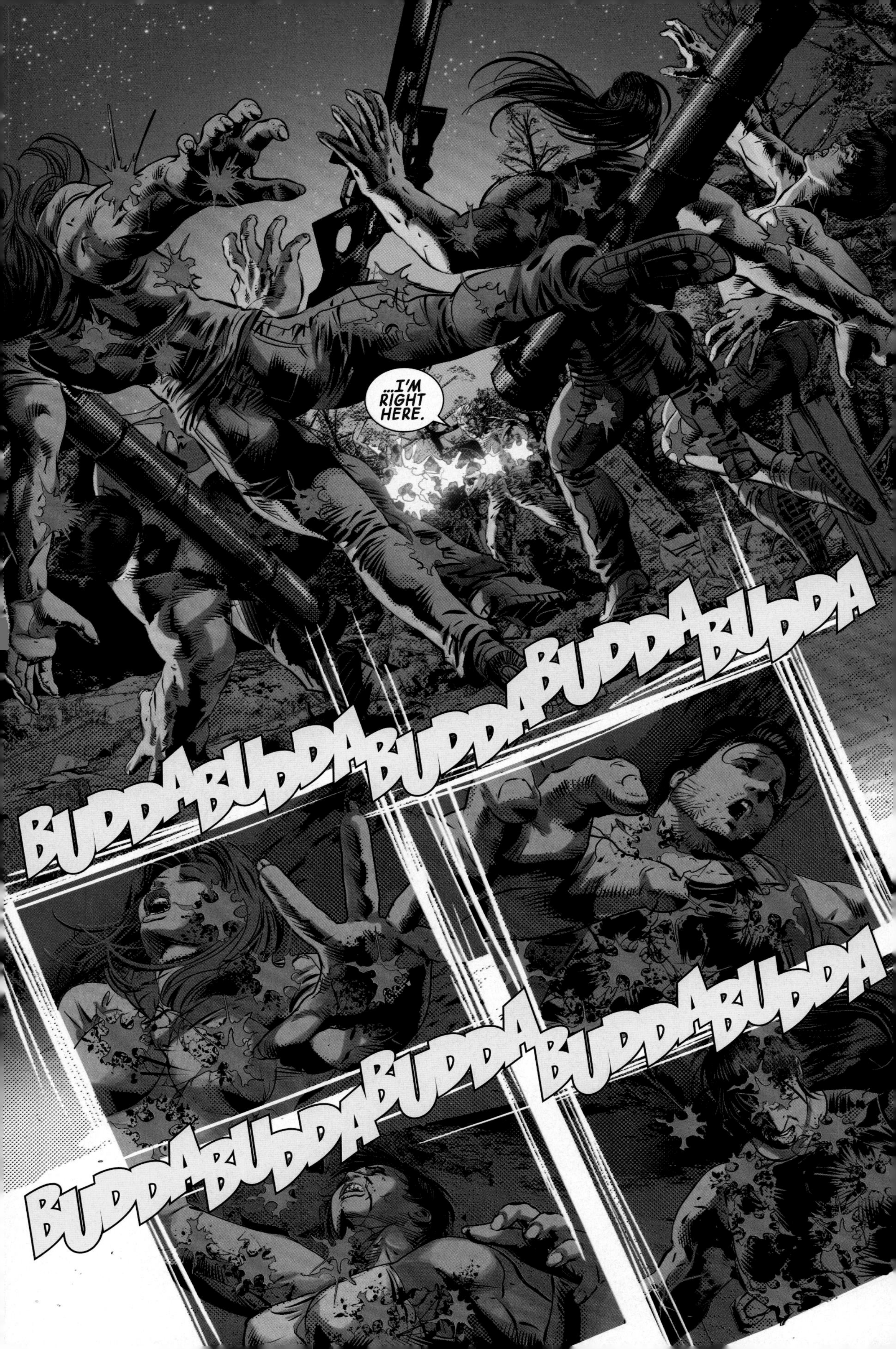
...I'M RIGHT HERE.
BUDDABUDDA
BUDDABUDDABUDDA
BUDDABUDDABUDDA
BUDDABUDDA

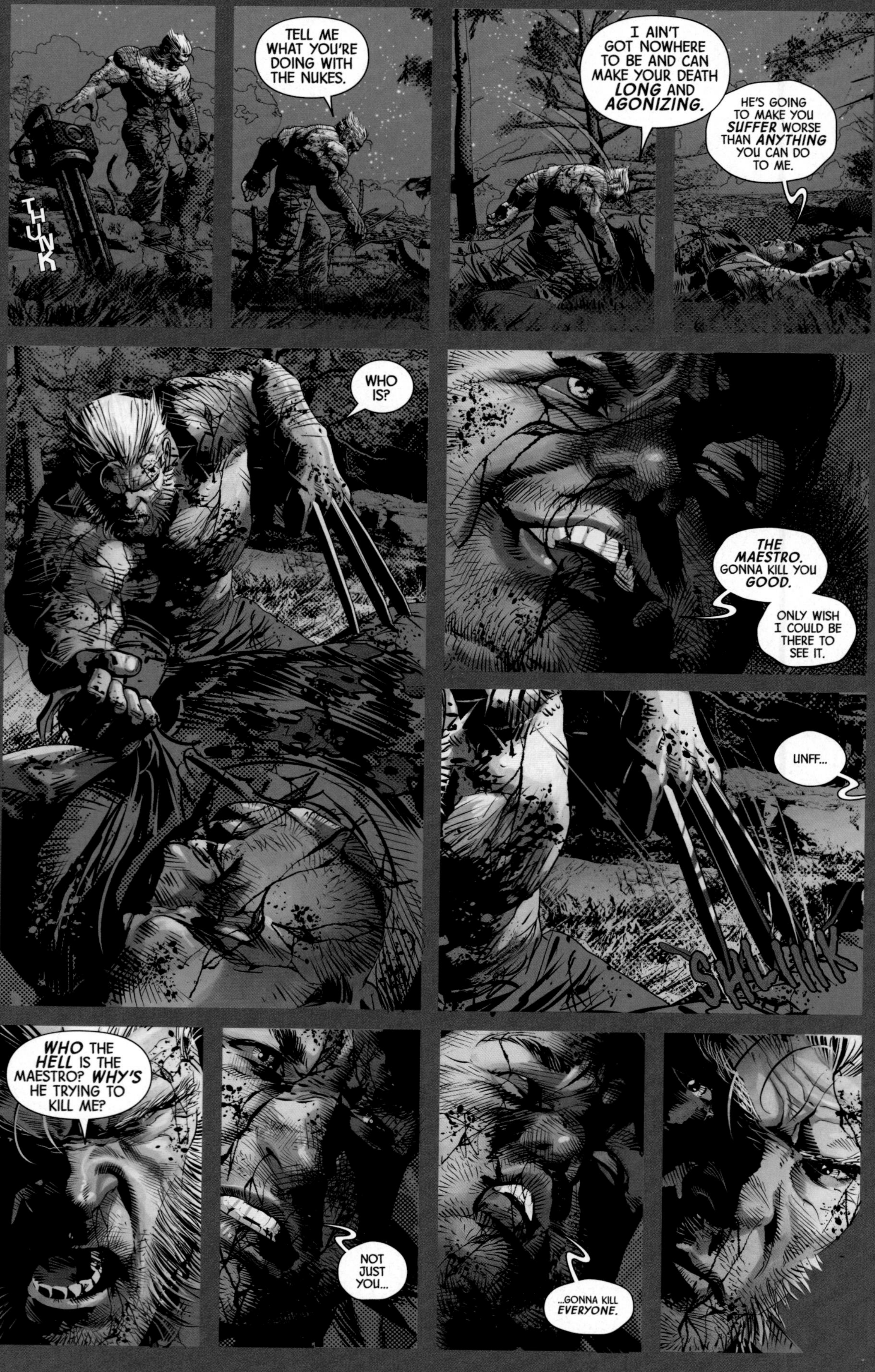

THUNK
TELL ME WHAT YOU'RE DOING WITH THE NUKES.
I AIN'T GOT NOWHERE TO BE AND CAN MAKE YOUR DEATH *LONG* AND *AGONIZING.*
HE'S GOING TO MAKE YOU *SUFFER* WORSE THAN *ANYTHING* YOU CAN DO TO ME.
WHO IS?
*THE MAESTRO.* GONNA KILL YOU *GOOD.*
ONLY WISH I COULD BE THERE TO SEE IT.
UNFF...
*WHO* THE *HELL* IS THE MAESTRO? *WHY'S* HE TRYING TO KILL ME?
NOT JUST YOU...
...GONNA KILL *EVERYONE.*

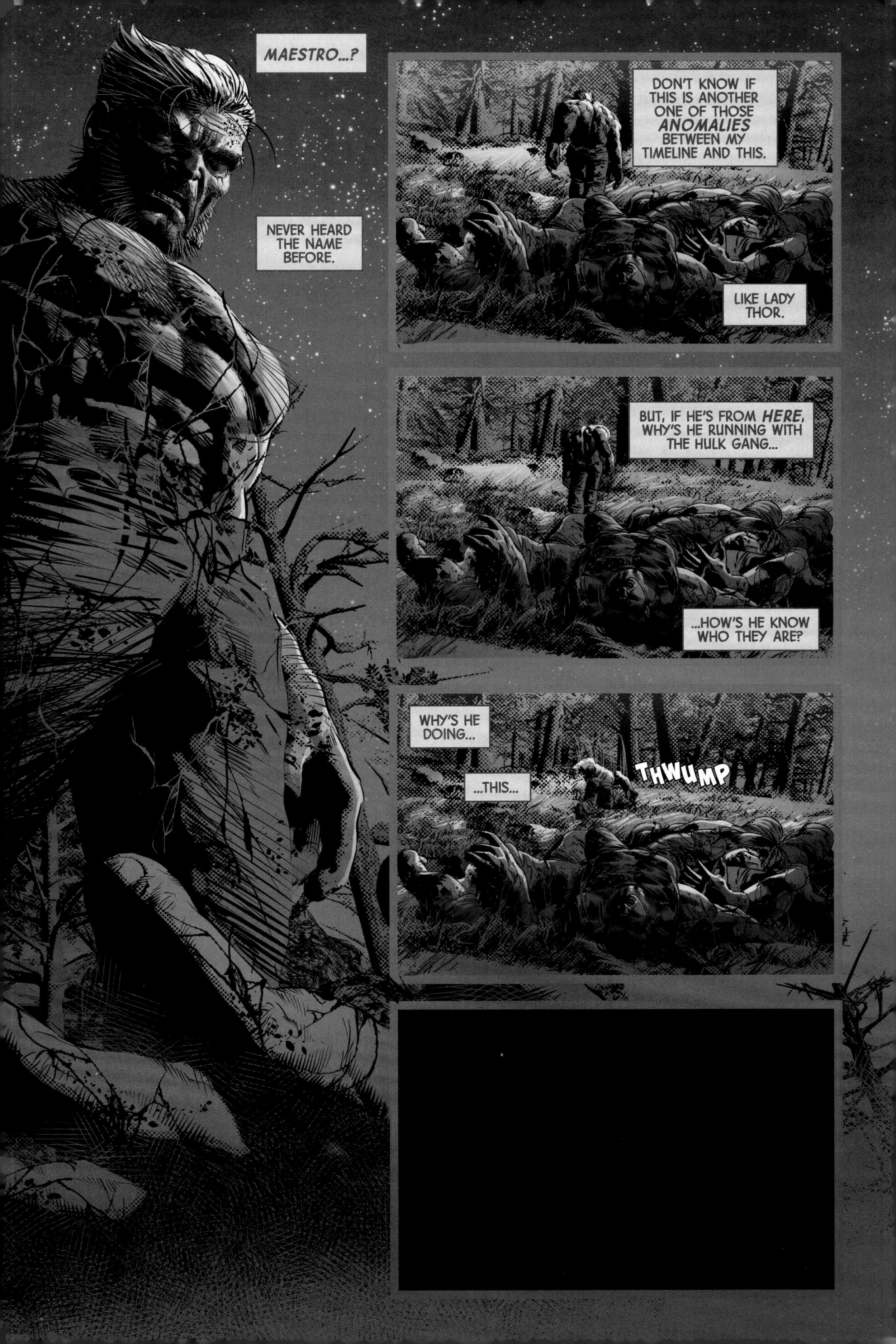

MAESTRO...?
NEVER HEARD THE NAME BEFORE.
DON'T KNOW IF THIS IS ANOTHER ONE OF THOSE *ANOMALIES* BETWEEN MY TIMELINE AND THIS.
LIKE LADY THOR.
BUT, IF HE'S FROM *HERE*, WHY'S HE RUNNING WITH THE HULK GANG...
...HOW'S HE KNOW WHO THEY ARE?
WHY'S HE DOING...
...THIS...
THWUMP

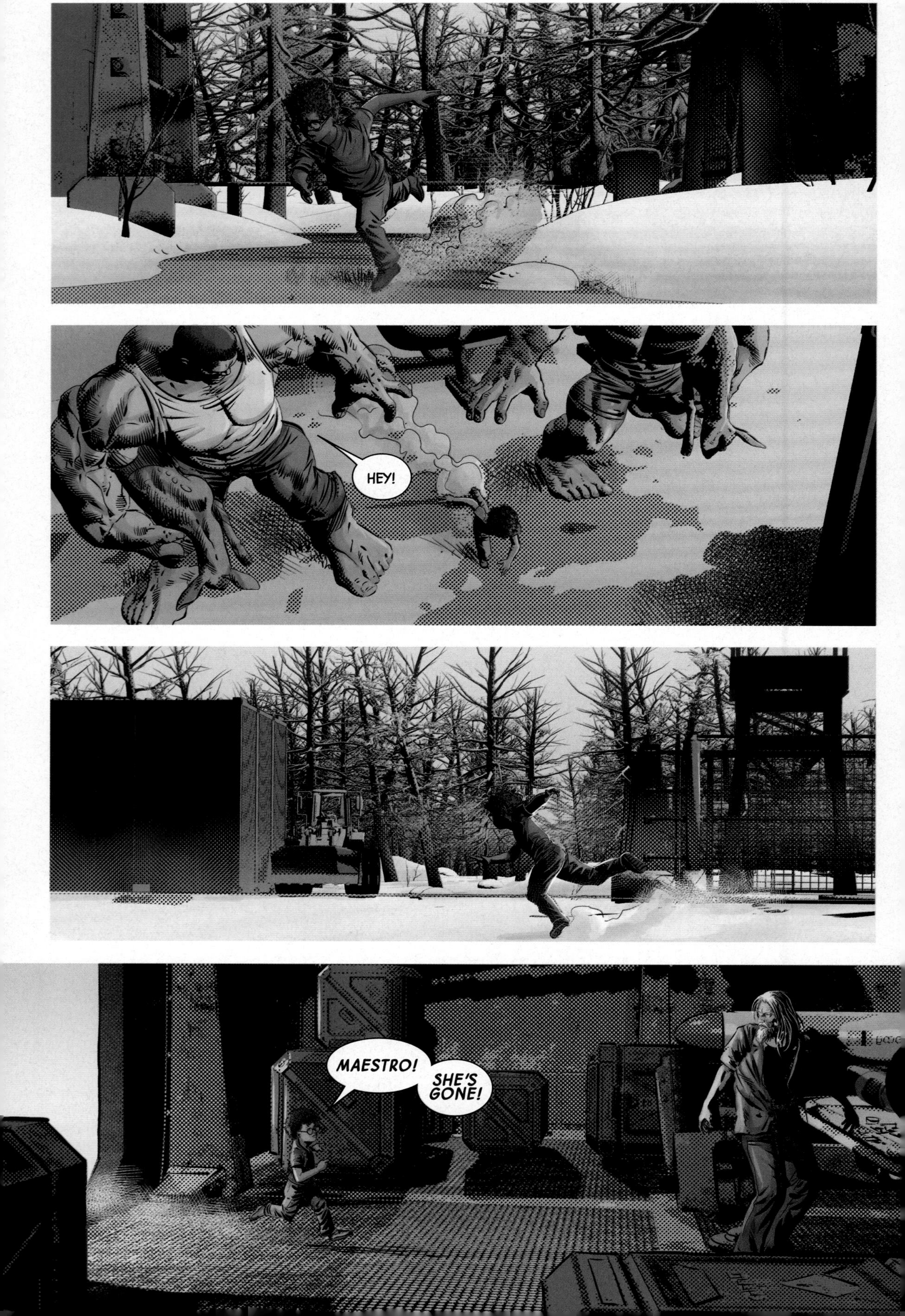
HEY!
MAESTRO!
SHE'S GONE!

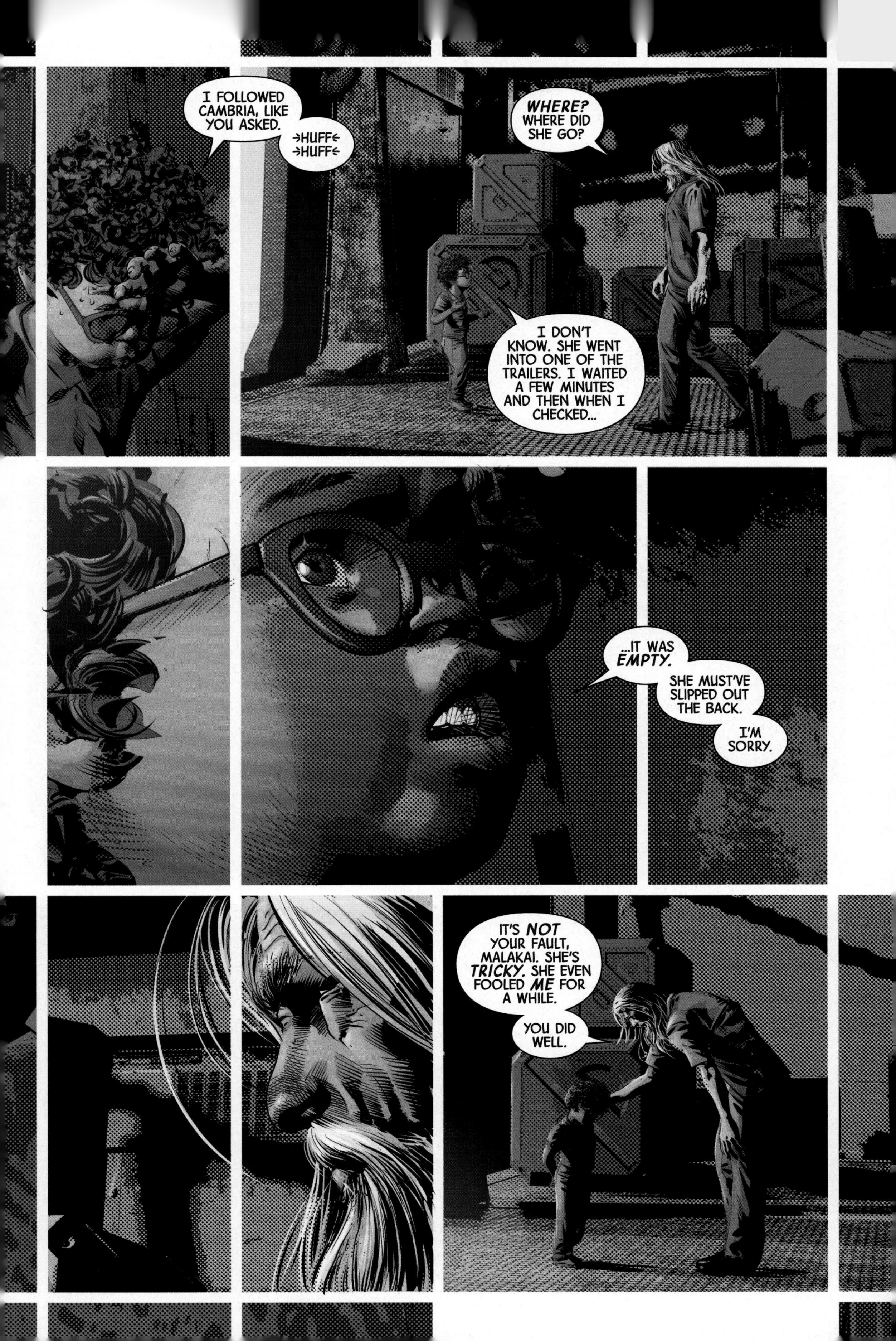

I FOLLOWED CAMBRIA, LIKE YOU ASKED.
HUFF
HUFF
WHERE? WHERE DID SHE GO?
I DON'T KNOW. SHE WENT INTO ONE OF THE TRAILERS. I WAITED A FEW MINUTES AND THEN WHEN I CHECKED...
...IT WAS EMPTY.
SHE MUST'VE SLIPPED OUT THE BACK.
I'M SORRY.
IT'S NOT YOUR FAULT, MALAKAI. SHE'S TRICKY. SHE EVEN FOOLED ME FOR A WHILE.
YOU DID WELL.

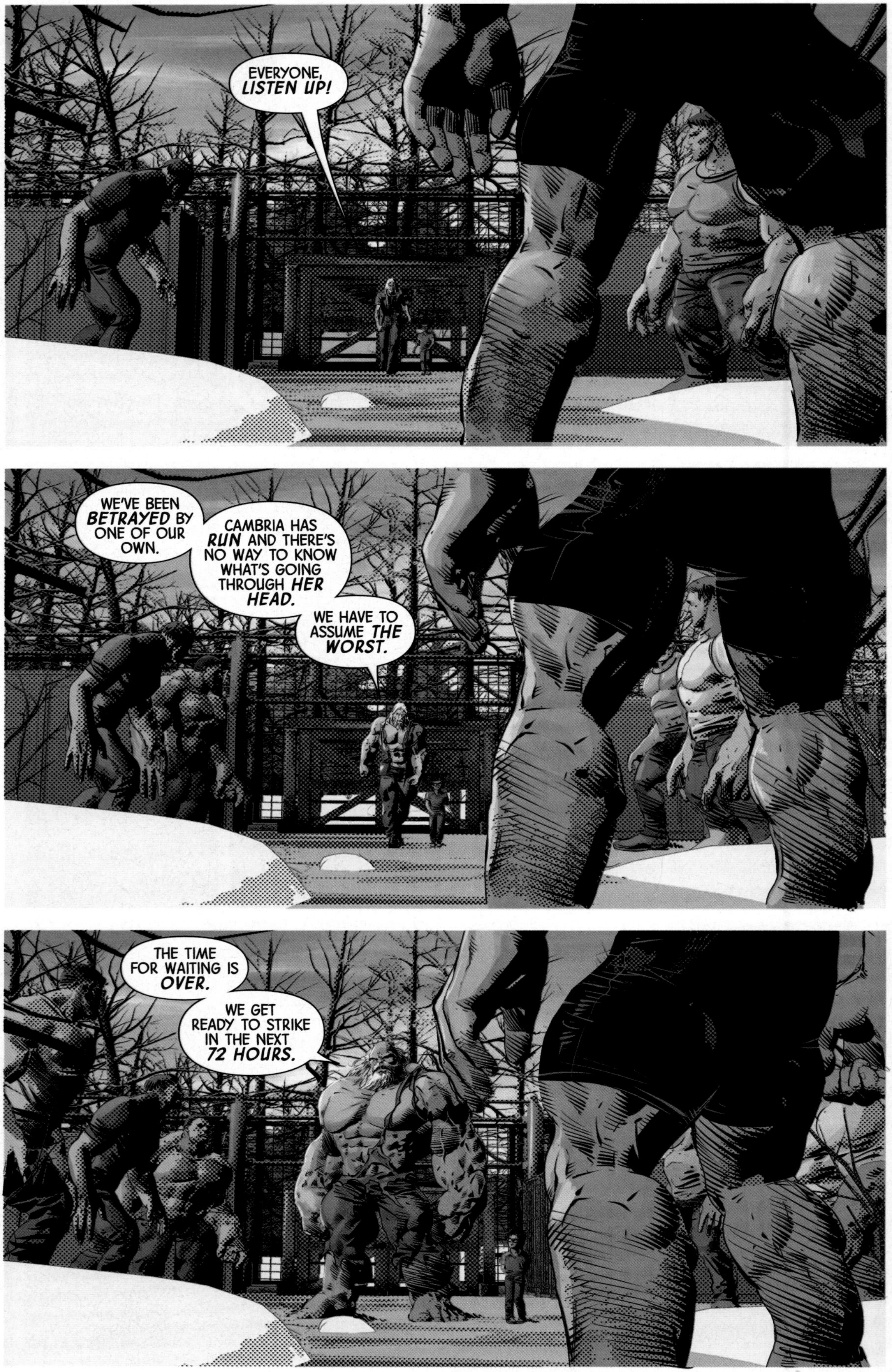
EVERYONE, LISTEN UP!
WE'VE BEEN BETRAYED BY ONE OF OUR OWN.
CAMBRIA HAS RUN AND THERE'S NO WAY TO KNOW WHAT'S GOING THROUGH HER HEAD.
WE HAVE TO ASSUME THE WORST.
THE TIME FOR WAITING IS OVER.
WE GET READY TO STRIKE IN THE NEXT 72 HOURS.

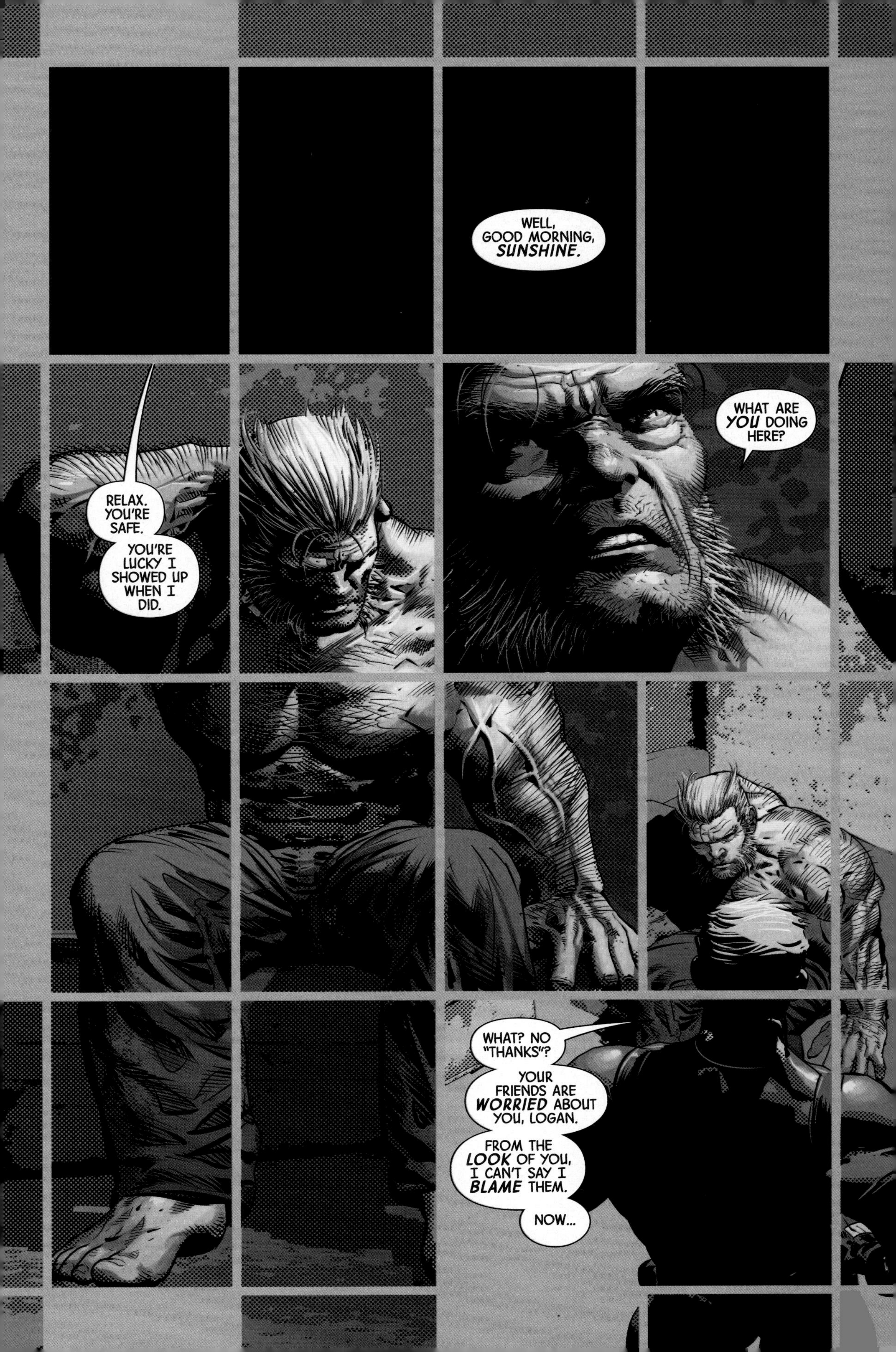
WELL, GOOD MORNING, SUNSHINE.
RELAX. YOU'RE SAFE.
YOU'RE LUCKY I SHOWED UP WHEN I DID.
WHAT ARE YOU DOING HERE?
WHAT? NO "THANKS"?
YOUR FRIENDS ARE WORRIED ABOUT YOU, LOGAN.
FROM THE LOOK OF YOU, I CAN'T SAY I BLAME THEM.
NOW...

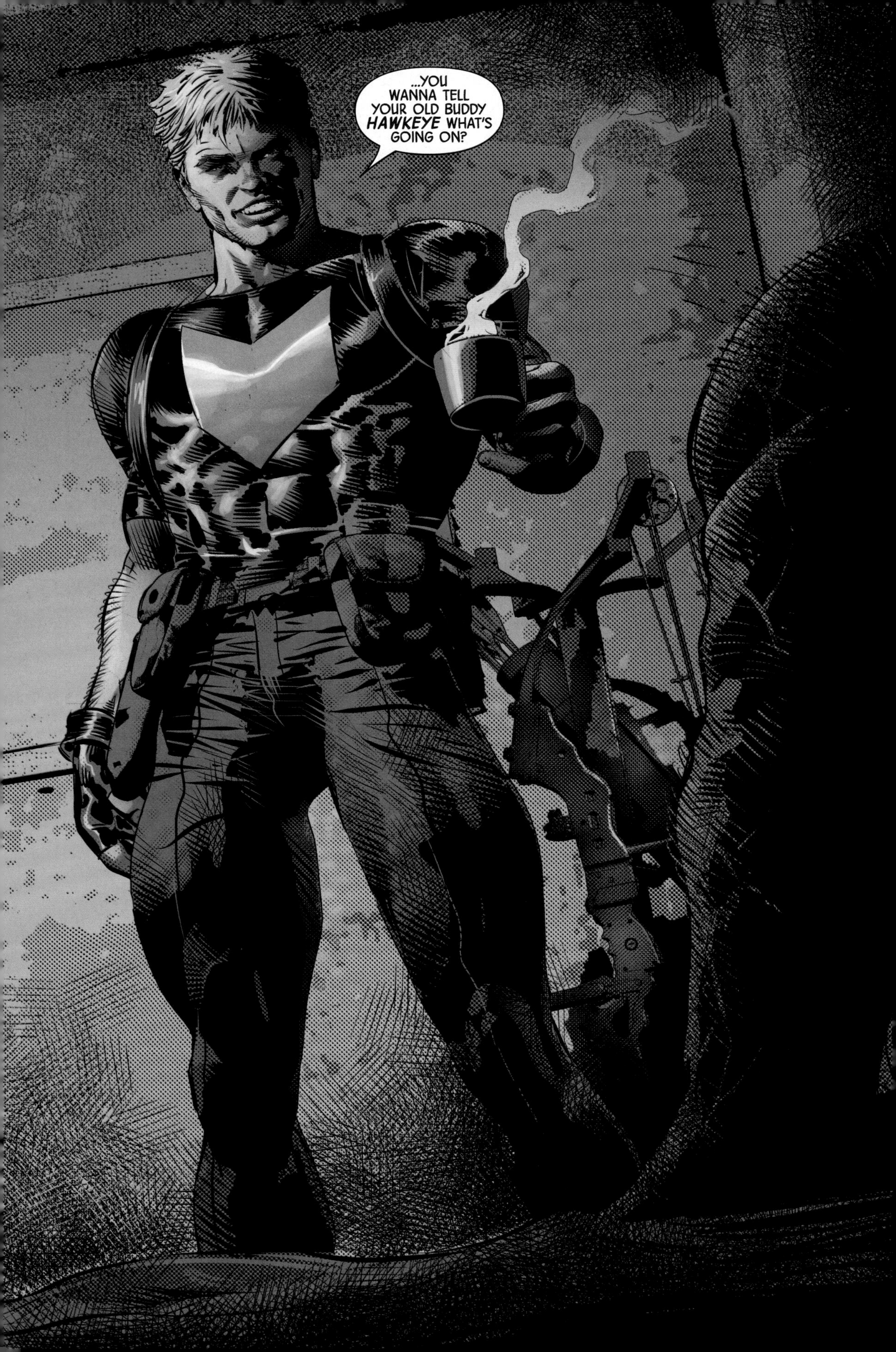
...YOU WANNA TELL YOUR OLD BUDDY HAWKEYE WHAT'S GOING ON?

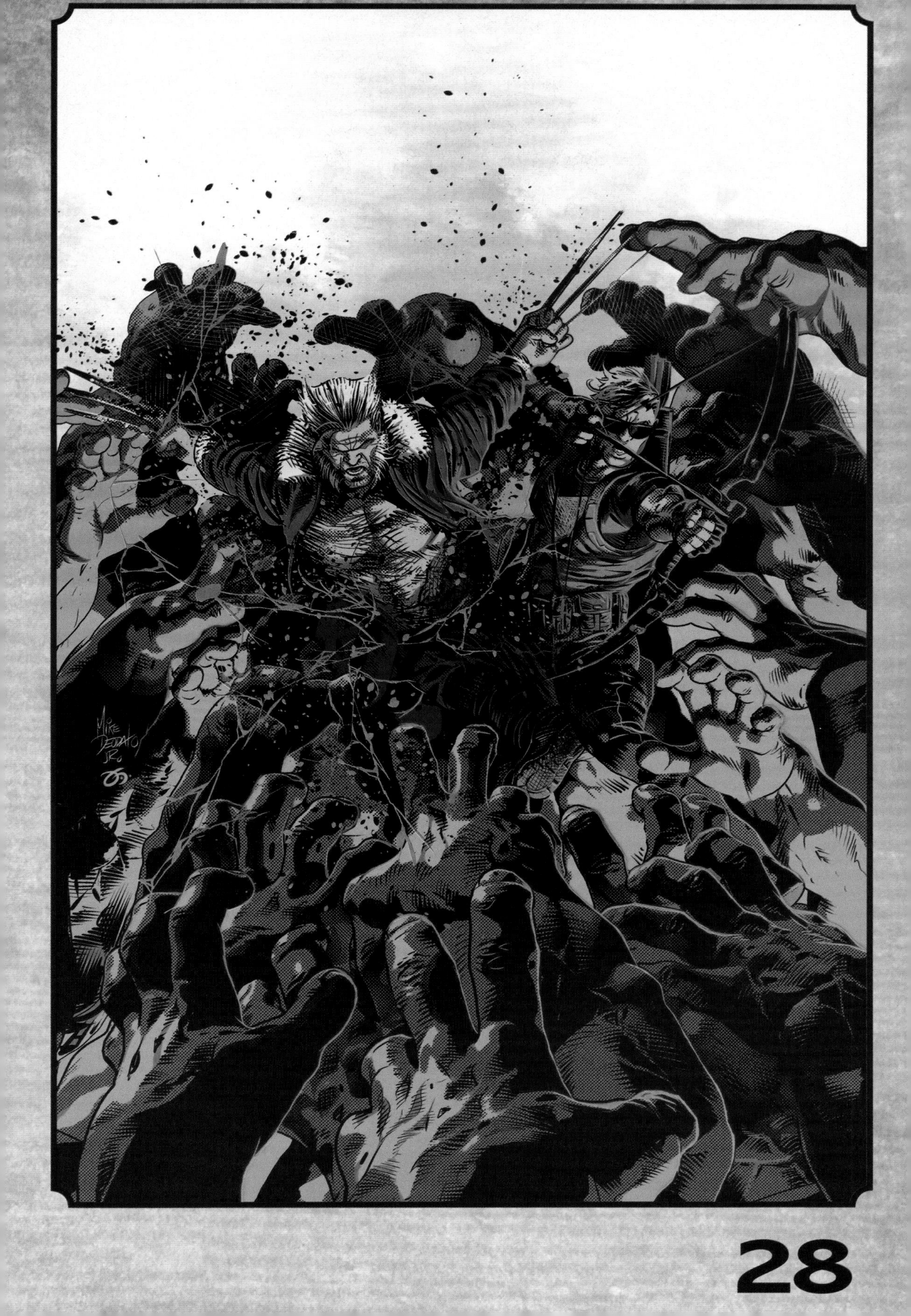
MIKE DEODATO JR.

28

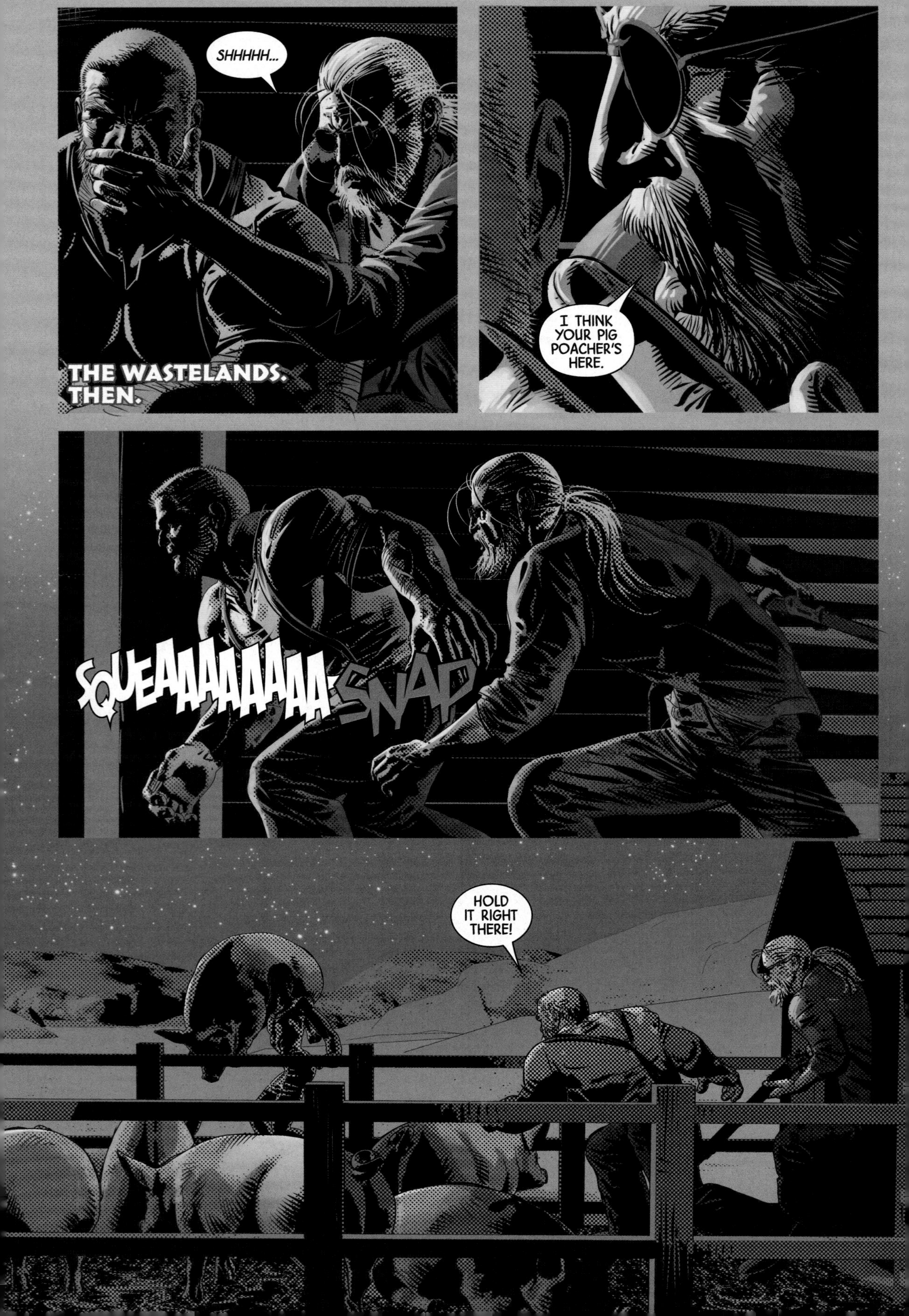
SHHHHH...
THE WASTELANDS. THEN.
I THINK YOUR PIG POACHER'S HERE.
SQUEAAAAAAAA-SNAP
HOLD IT RIGHT THERE!

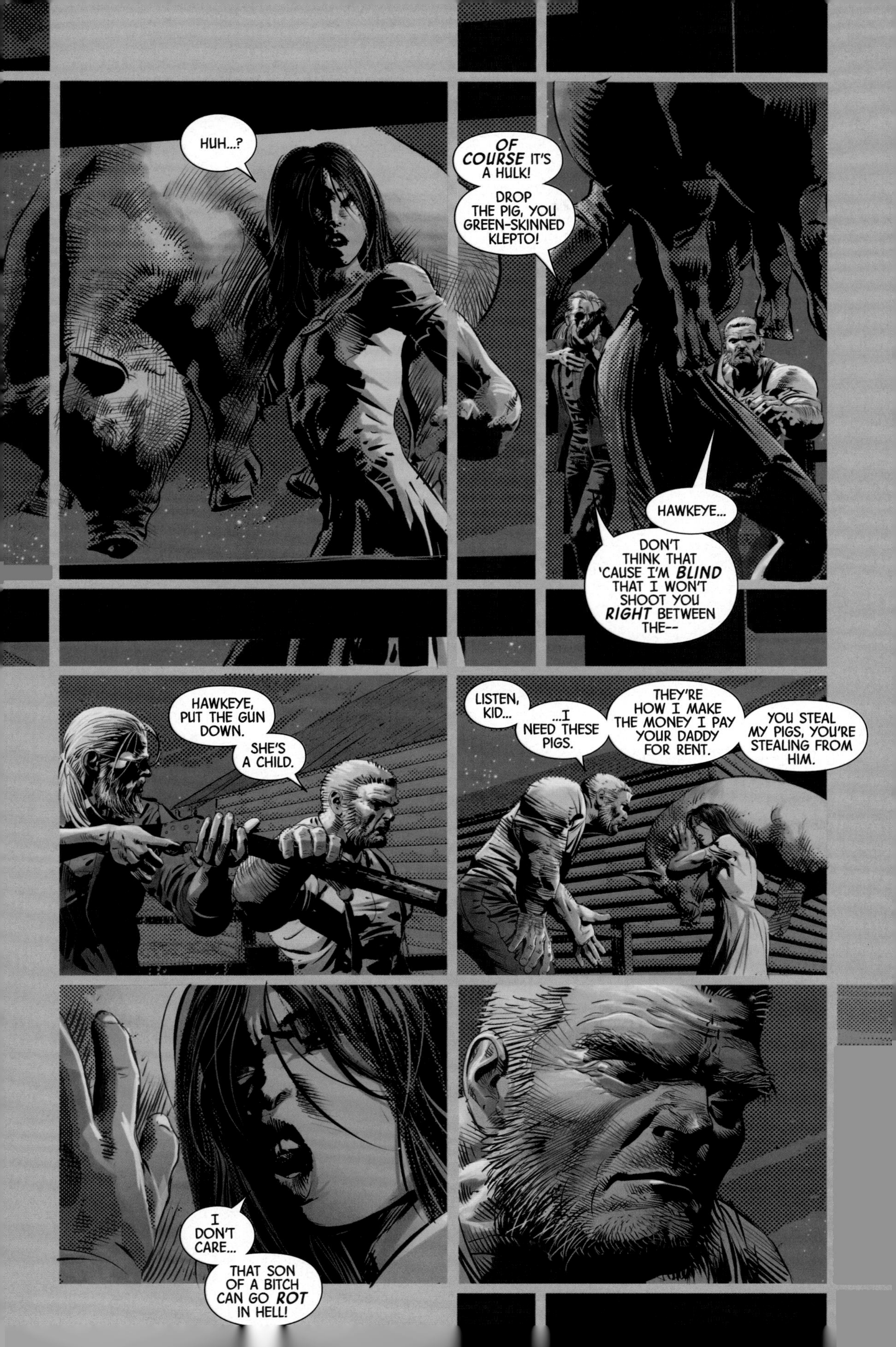

HUH...?
OF COURSE IT'S A HULK!
DROP THE PIG, YOU GREEN-SKINNED KLEPTO!
HAWKEYE...
DON'T THINK THAT 'CAUSE I'M BLIND THAT I WON'T SHOOT YOU RIGHT BETWEEN THE--
HAWKEYE, PUT THE GUN DOWN.
SHE'S A CHILD.
LISTEN, KID...
...I NEED THESE PIGS.
THEY'RE HOW I MAKE THE MONEY I PAY YOUR DADDY FOR RENT.
YOU STEAL MY PIGS, YOU'RE STEALING FROM HIM.
I DON'T CARE...
THAT SON OF A BITCH CAN GO ROT IN HELL!

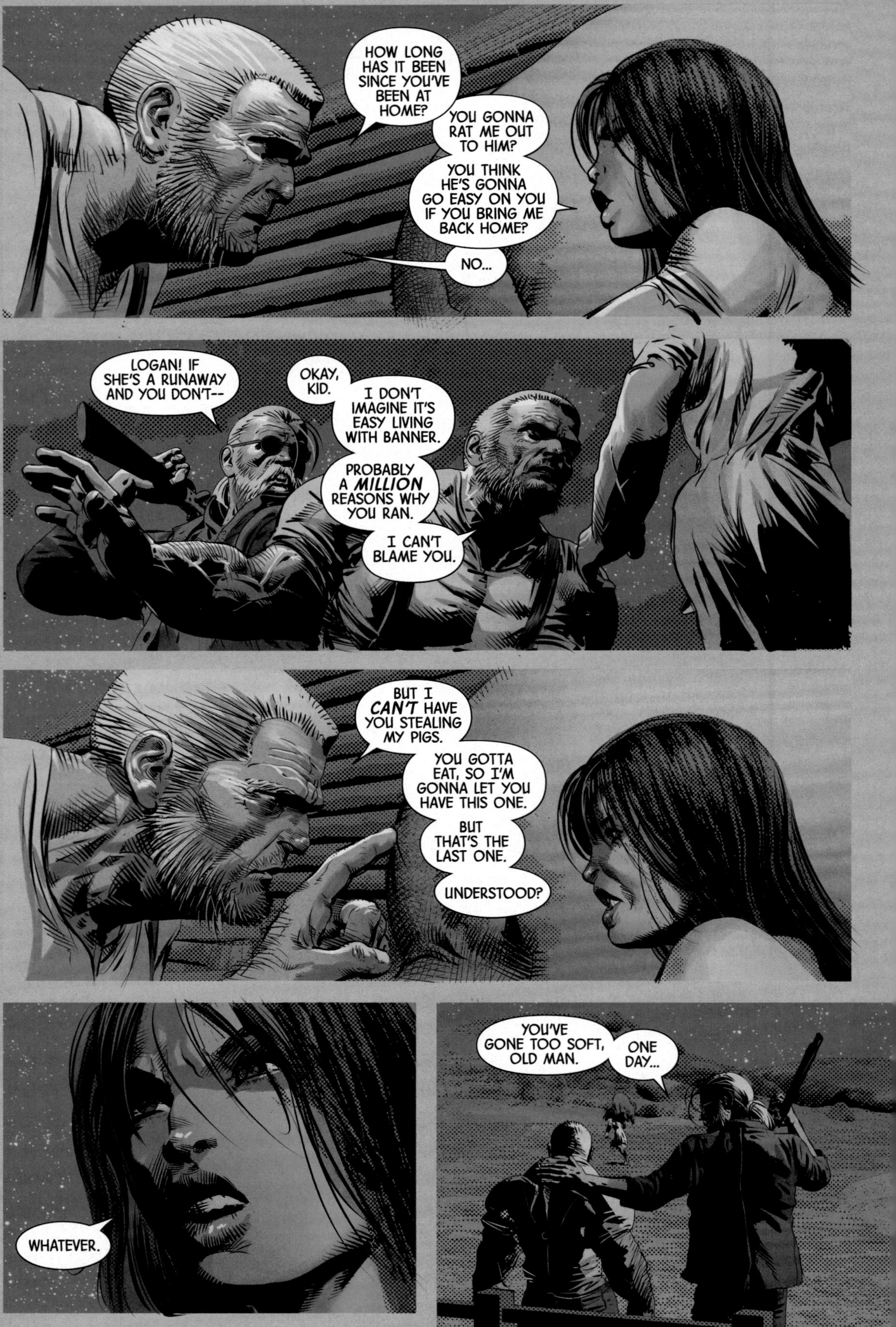
HOW LONG HAS IT BEEN SINCE YOU'VE BEEN AT HOME?
YOU GONNA RAT ME OUT TO HIM?
YOU THINK HE'S GONNA GO EASY ON YOU IF YOU BRING ME BACK HOME?
NO...
LOGAN! IF SHE'S A RUNAWAY AND YOU DON'T--
OKAY, KID.
I DON'T IMAGINE IT'S EASY LIVING WITH BANNER.
PROBABLY A *MILLION* REASONS WHY YOU RAN.
I CAN'T BLAME YOU.
BUT I *CAN'T* HAVE YOU STEALING MY PIGS.
YOU GOTTA EAT, SO I'M GONNA LET YOU HAVE THIS ONE.
BUT THAT'S THE LAST ONE.
UNDERSTOOD?
WHATEVER.
YOU'VE GONE TOO SOFT, OLD MAN.
ONE DAY...

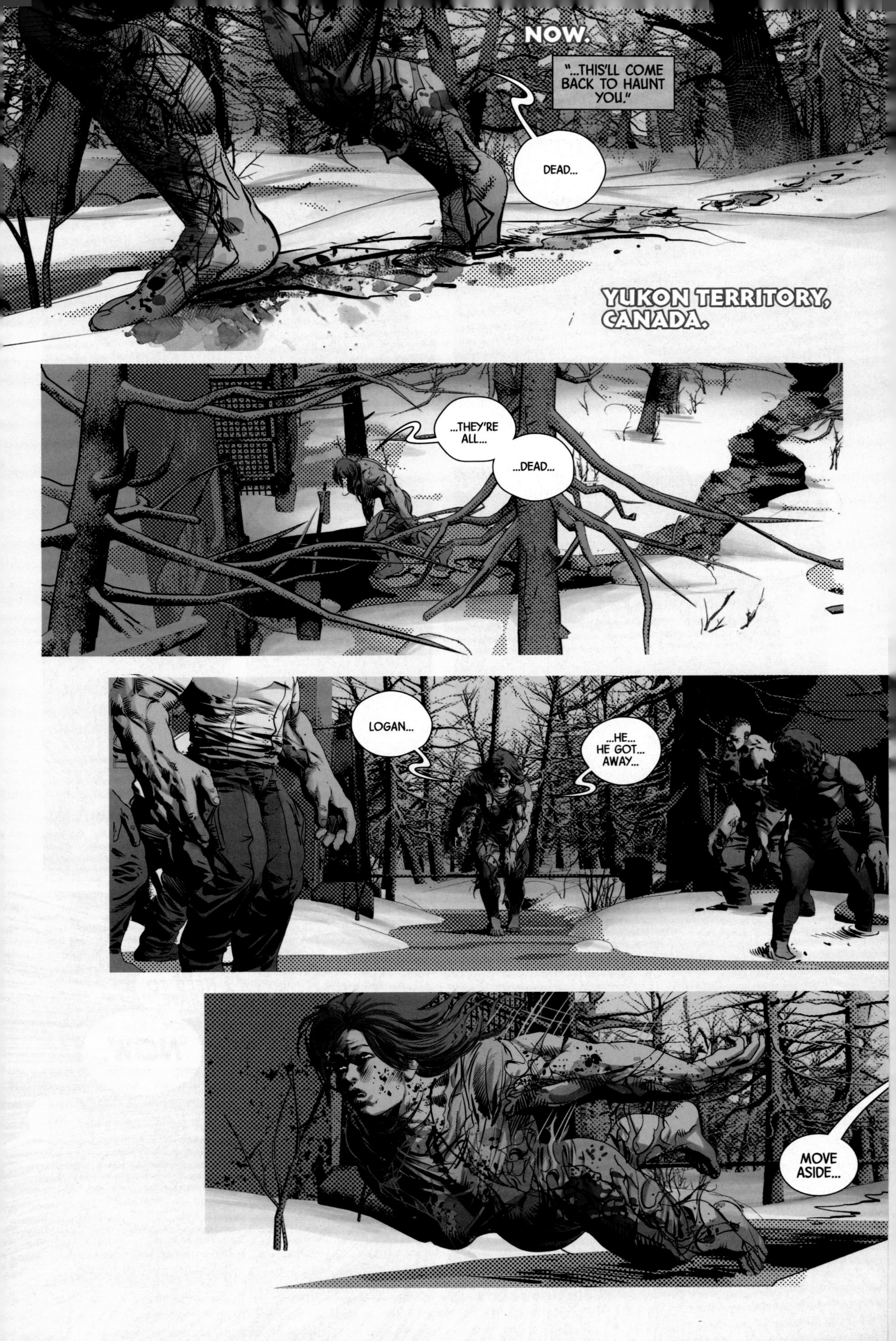
NOW.
"...THIS'LL COME BACK TO HAUNT YOU."
DEAD...
YUKON TERRITORY, CANADA.
...THEY'RE ALL...
...DEAD...
LOGAN...
...HE... HE GOT... AWAY...
MOVE ASIDE...

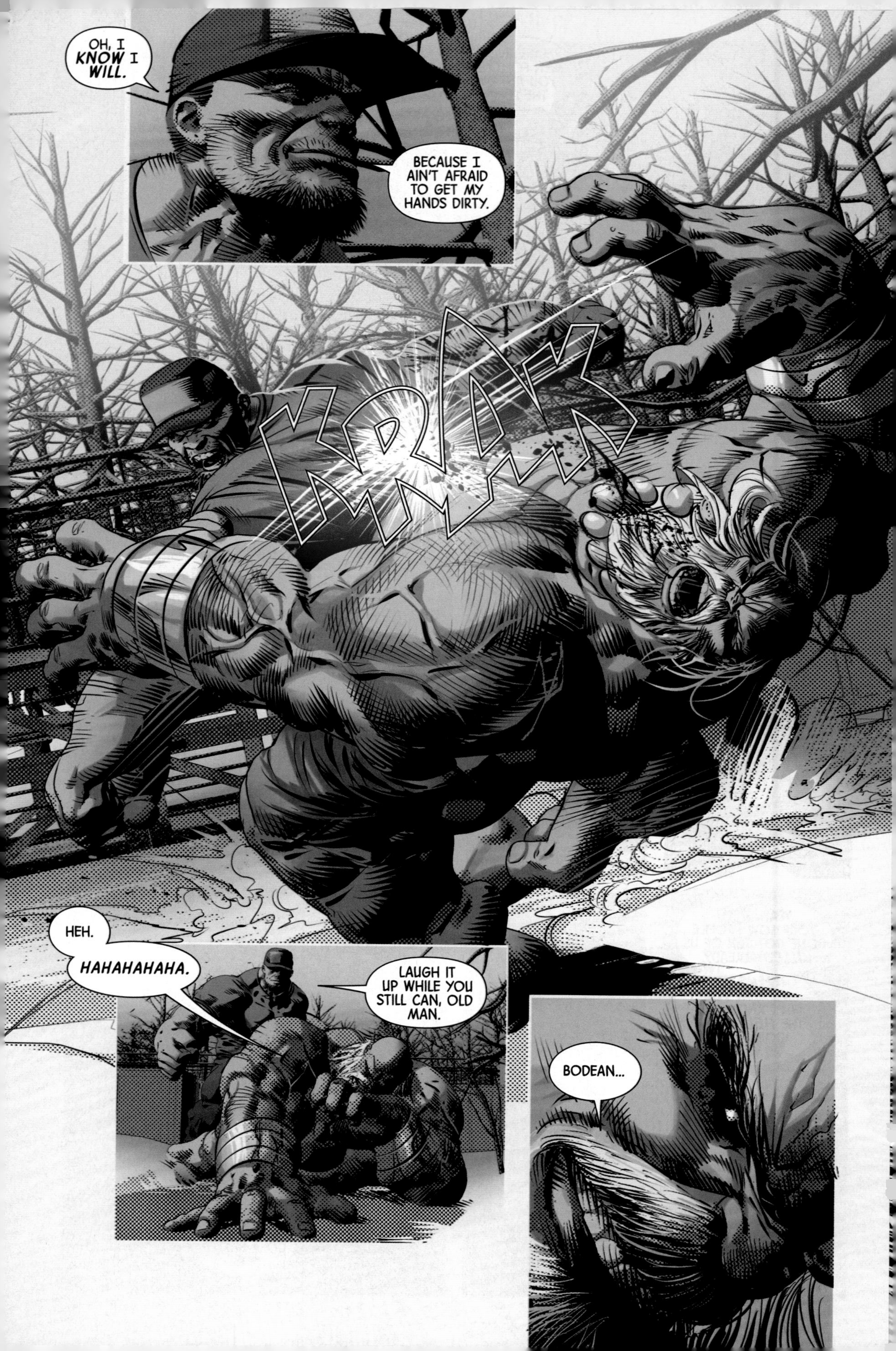
OH, I KNOW I WILL.
BECAUSE I AIN'T AFRAID TO GET MY HANDS DIRTY.
KRAK
HEH.
HAHAHAHAHA.
LAUGH IT UP WHILE YOU STILL CAN, OLD MAN.
BODEAN...

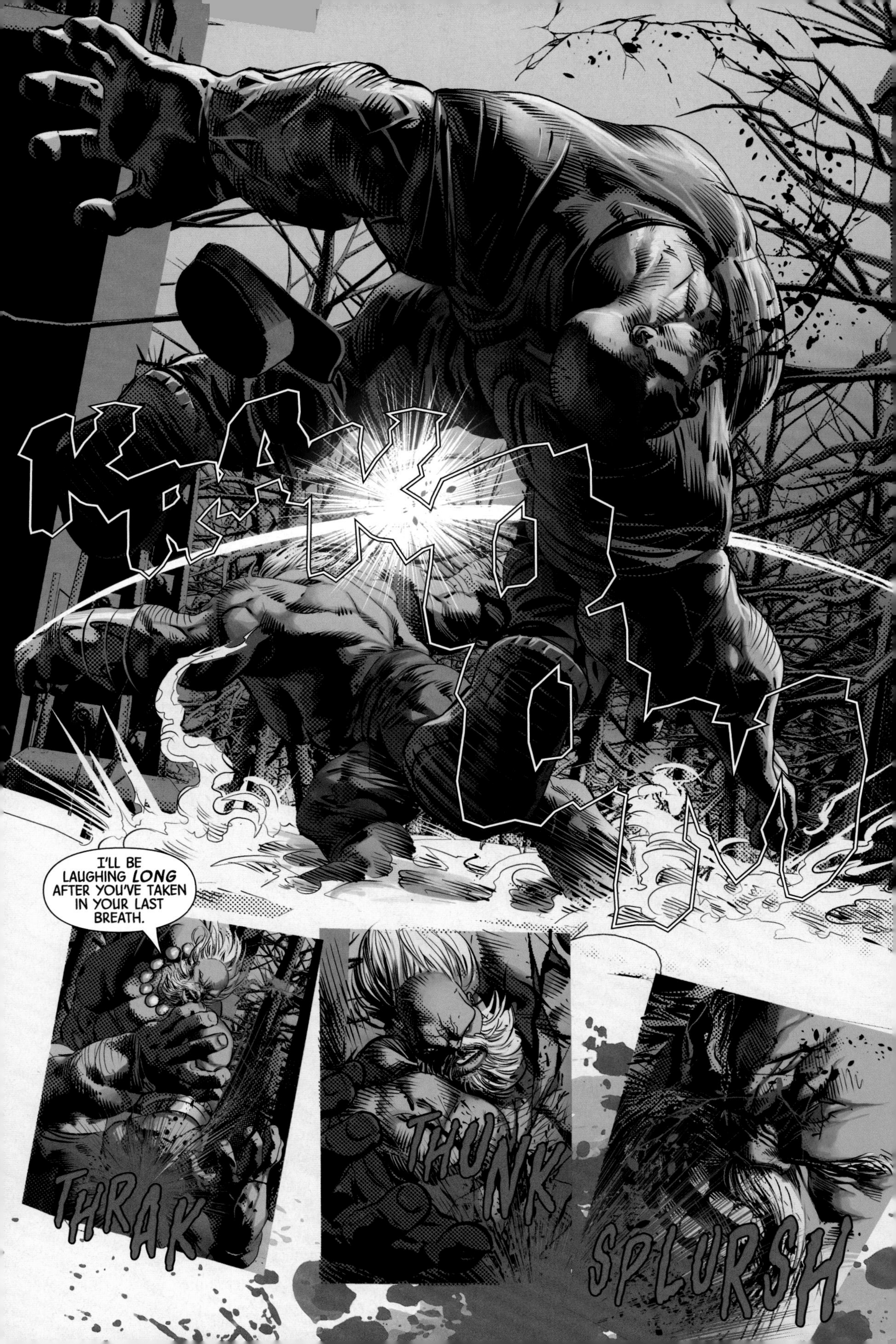
KRAKOOM
I'LL BE LAUGHING LONG AFTER YOU'VE TAKEN IN YOUR LAST BREATH.
THRAK
THUNK
SPLURSH

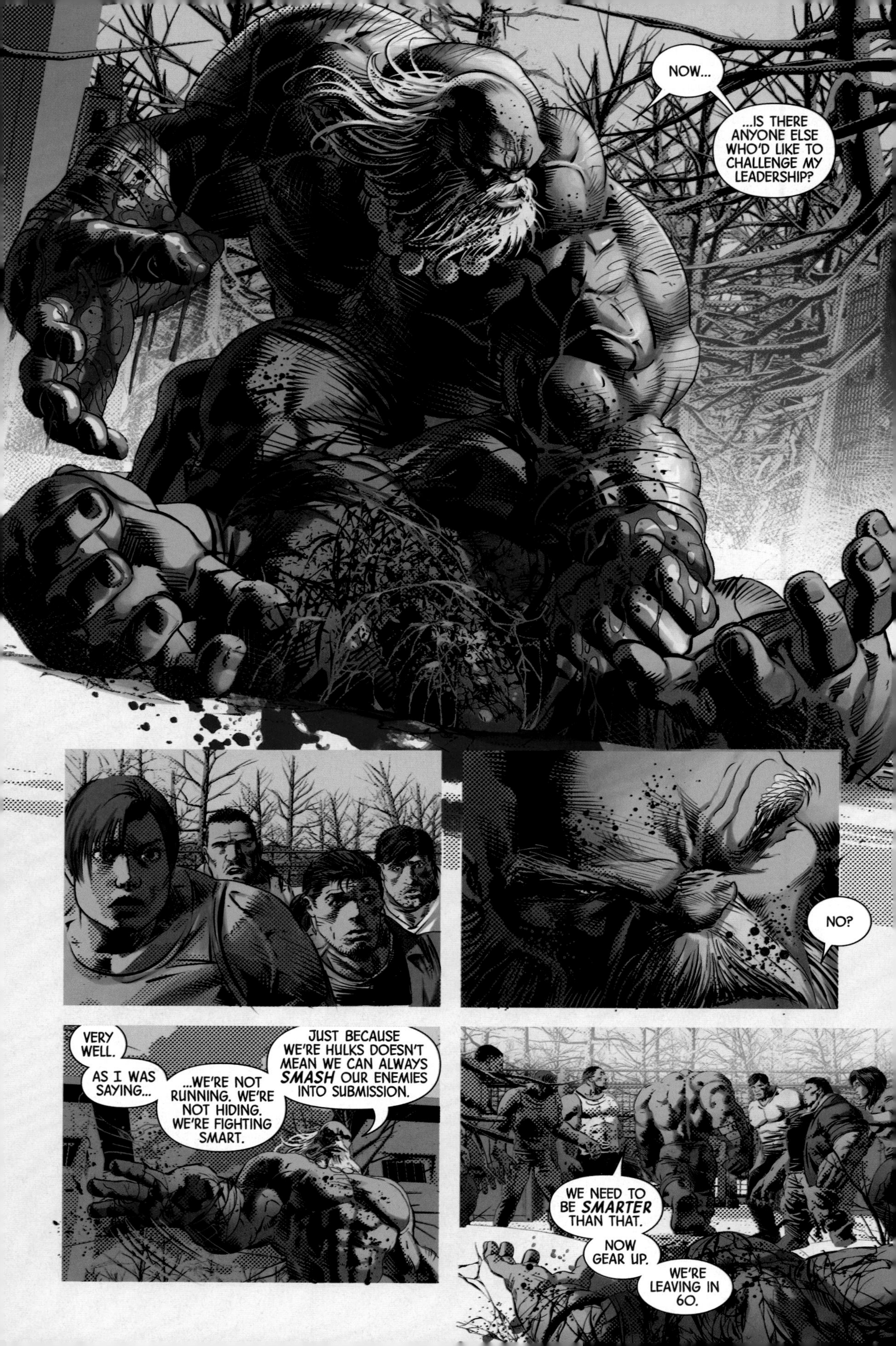
NOW...
...IS THERE ANYONE ELSE WHO'D LIKE TO CHALLENGE MY LEADERSHIP?
NO?
VERY WELL.
AS I WAS SAYING...
...WE'RE NOT RUNNING. WE'RE NOT HIDING. WE'RE FIGHTING SMART.
JUST BECAUSE WE'RE HULKS DOESN'T MEAN WE CAN ALWAYS SMASH OUR ENEMIES INTO SUBMISSION.
WE NEED TO BE SMARTER THAN THAT.
NOW GEAR UP.
WE'RE LEAVING IN 60.

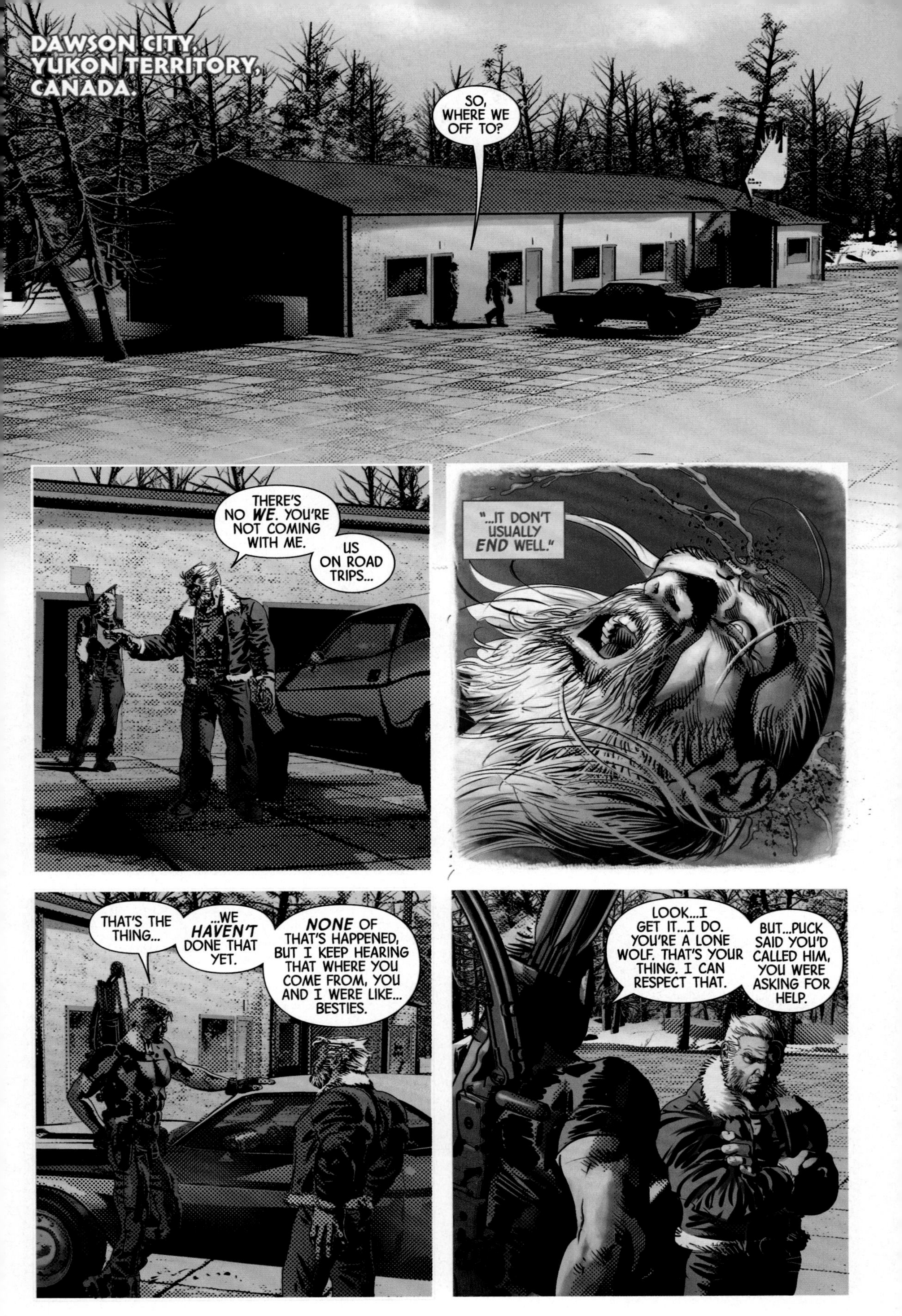
DAWSON CITY, YUKON TERRITORY, CANADA.
SO, WHERE WE OFF TO?
THERE'S NO WE. YOU'RE NOT COMING WITH ME.
US ON ROAD TRIPS...
"...IT DON'T USUALLY END WELL."
THAT'S THE THING...
...WE HAVEN'T DONE THAT YET.
NONE OF THAT'S HAPPENED, BUT I KEEP HEARING THAT WHERE YOU COME FROM, YOU AND I WERE LIKE... BESTIES.
LOOK...I GET IT...I DO. YOU'RE A LONE WOLF. THAT'S YOUR THING. I CAN RESPECT THAT.
BUT...PUCK SAID YOU'D CALLED HIM, YOU WERE ASKING FOR HELP.

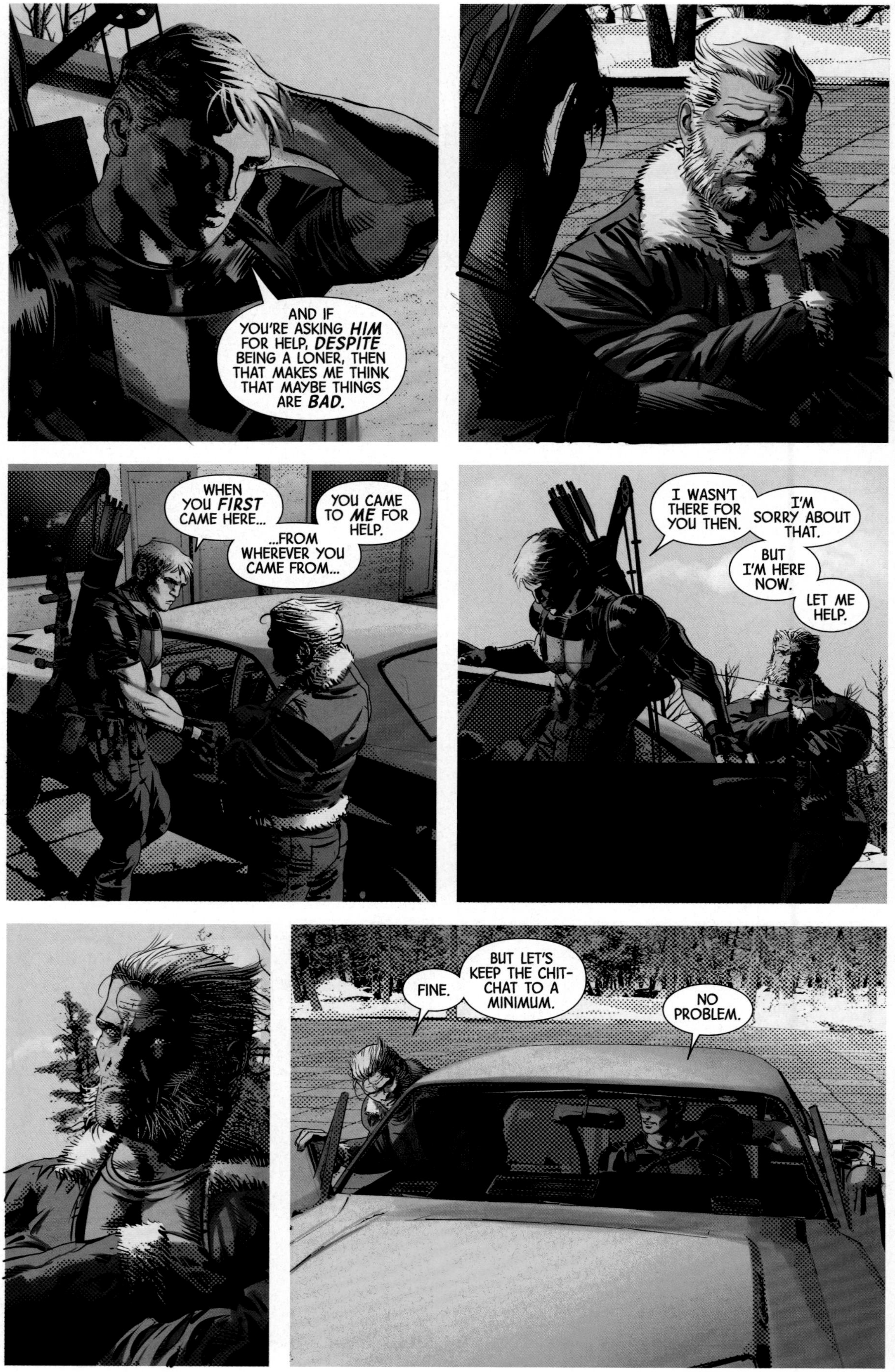
AND IF YOU'RE ASKING *HIM* FOR HELP, *DESPITE* BEING A LONER, THEN THAT MAKES ME THINK THAT MAYBE THINGS ARE *BAD.*
WHEN YOU *FIRST* CAME HERE...
...FROM WHEREVER YOU CAME FROM...
YOU CAME TO *ME* FOR HELP.
I WASN'T THERE FOR YOU THEN.
I'M SORRY ABOUT THAT.
BUT I'M HERE NOW.
LET ME HELP.
FINE.
BUT LET'S KEEP THE CHIT-CHAT TO A MINIMUM.
NO PROBLEM.

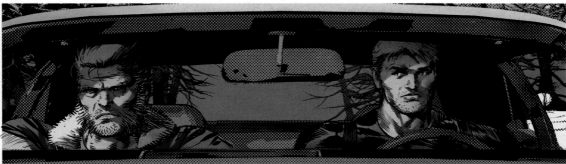

SORRY. I KNOW I'M SUPPOSED TO KEEP IT ZIPPED. BUT I GOTTA ASK...

...WHAT'S FUTURE, INTERDIMENSIONAL ME LIKE?

AM I A REAL BADASS?

NO. YOU MARRY SPIDER-MAN'S DAUGHTER, HAVE A KID. SHE LEAVES YOU FOR AN ULTRON.

YOU GET CATARACTS, GO *BLIND*, RUN DRUGS FOR A LIVING AND NEVER FIGURE OUT HOW TO KEEP YOUR YAP SHUT FOR MORE THAN FIVE MINUTES.

OH.

WAIT. BACK UP...

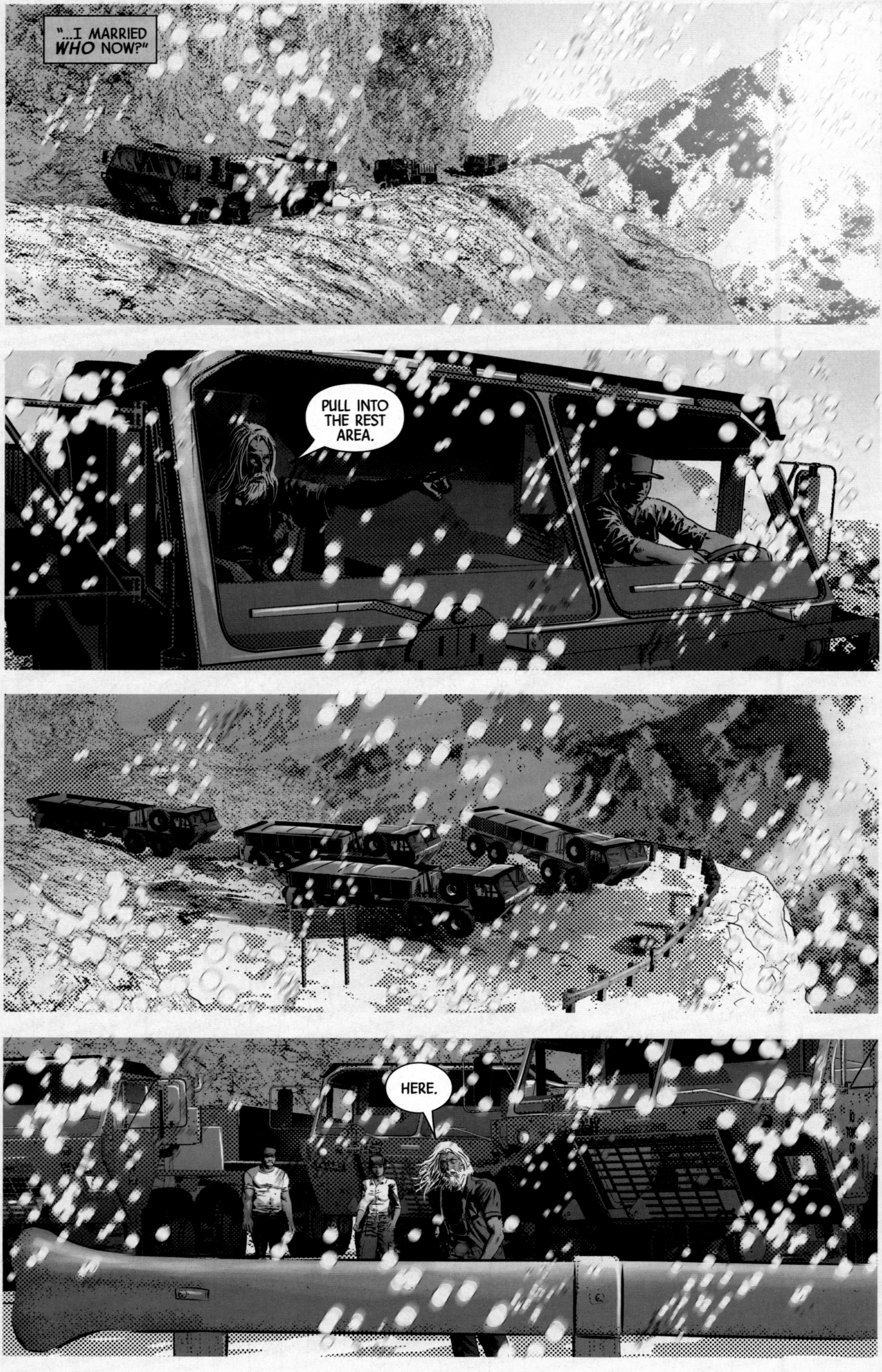
"...I MARRIED WHO NOW?"
PULL INTO THE REST AREA.
HERE.

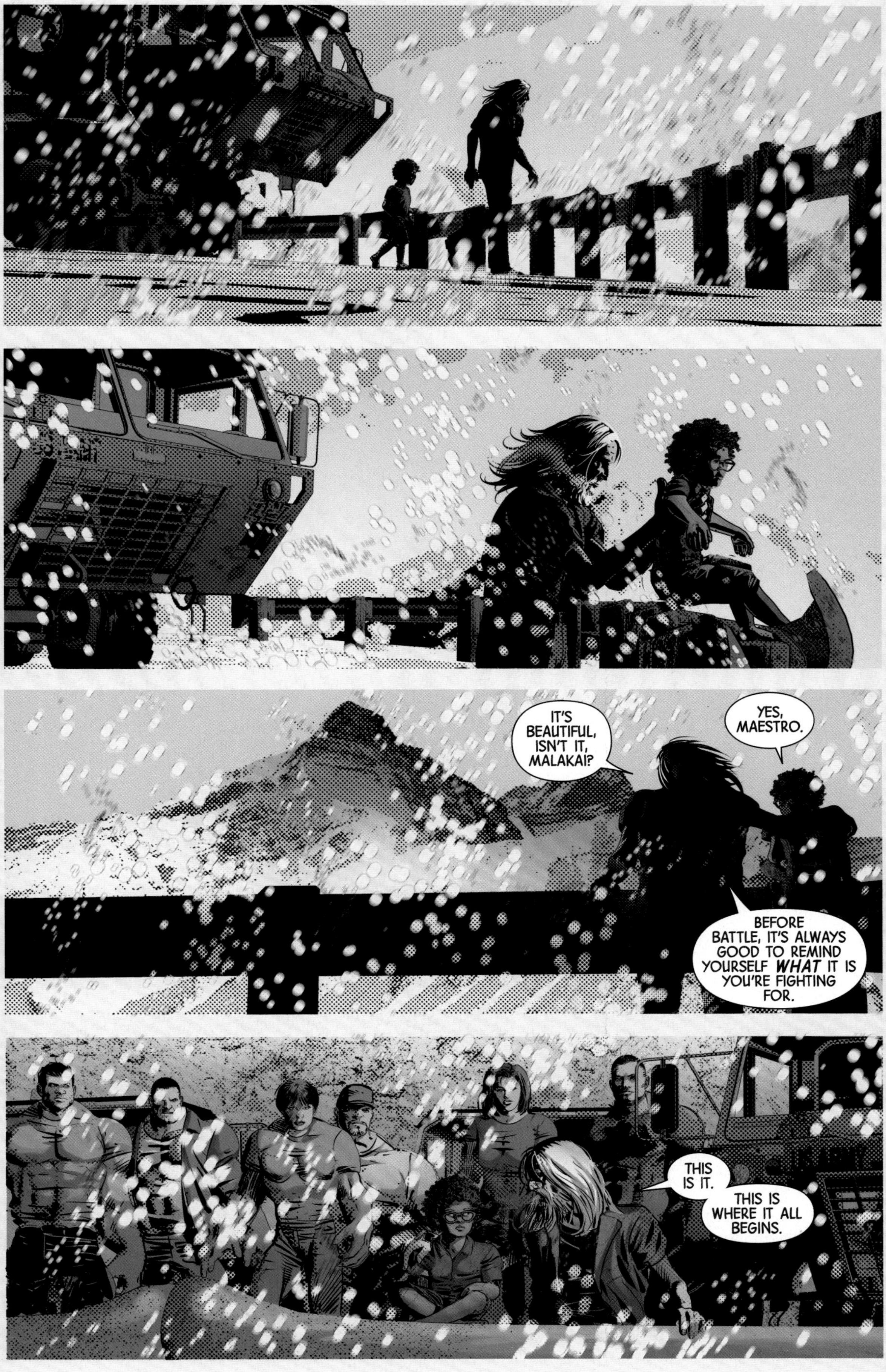
IT'S BEAUTIFUL, ISN'T IT, MALAKAI?
YES, MAESTRO.
BEFORE BATTLE, IT'S ALWAYS GOOD TO REMIND YOURSELF *WHAT* IT IS YOU'RE FIGHTING FOR.
THIS IS IT.
THIS IS WHERE IT ALL BEGINS.

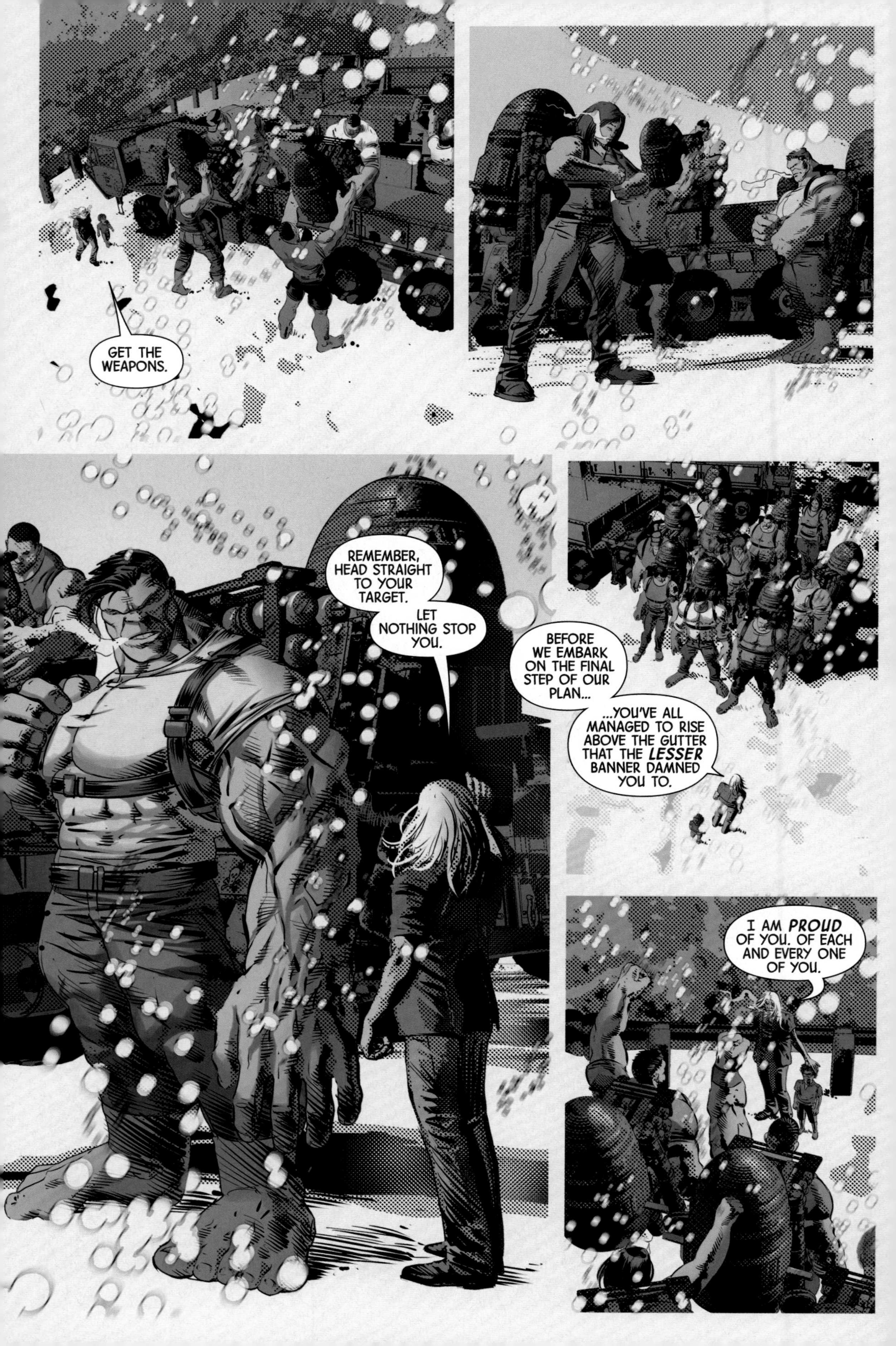
GET THE WEAPONS.
REMEMBER, HEAD STRAIGHT TO YOUR TARGET.
LET NOTHING STOP YOU.
BEFORE WE EMBARK ON THE FINAL STEP OF OUR PLAN...
...YOU'VE ALL MANAGED TO RISE ABOVE THE GUTTER THAT THE LESSER BANNER DAMNED YOU TO.
I AM PROUD OF YOU. OF EACH AND EVERY ONE OF YOU.

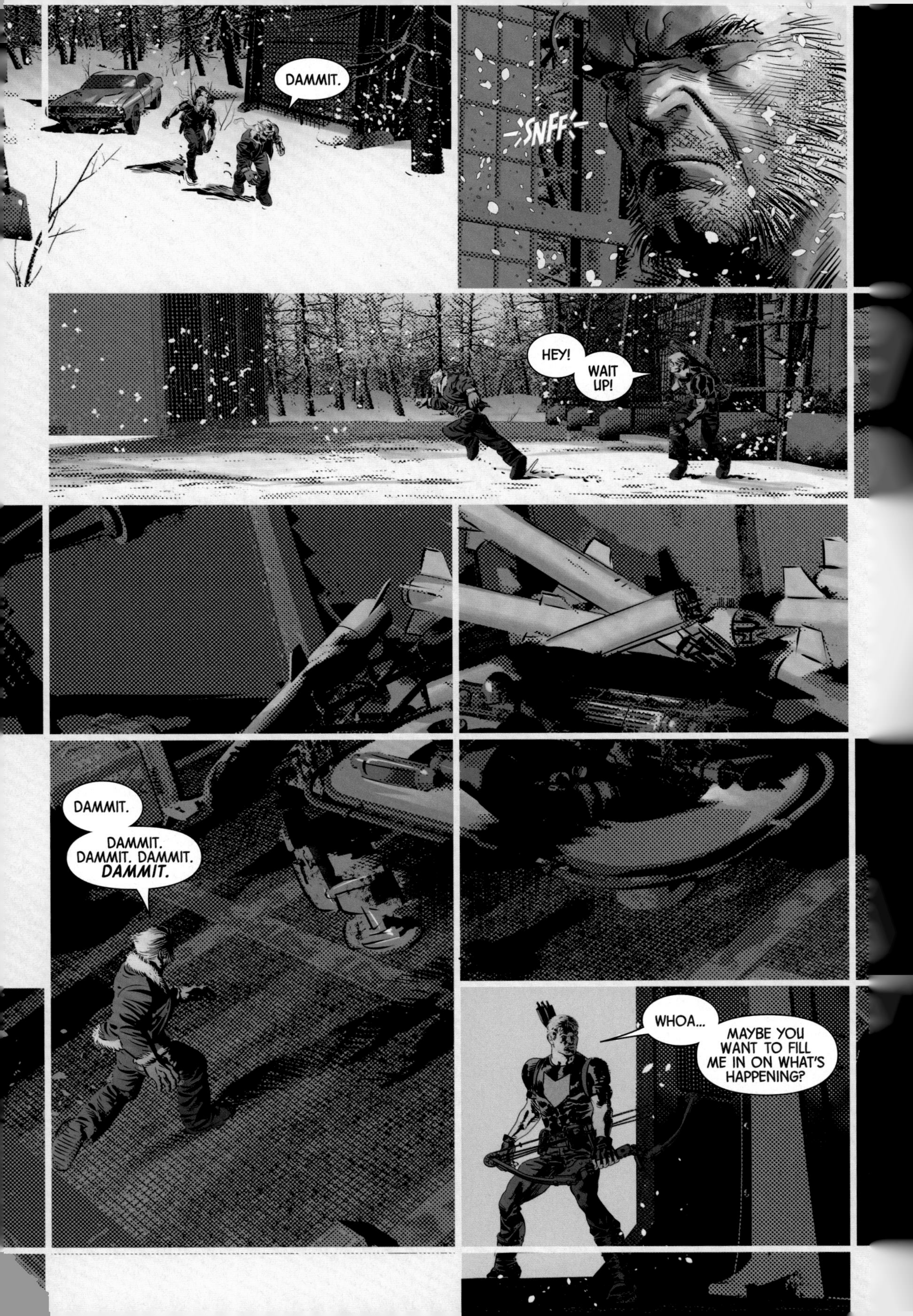
DAMMIT.
SNFF
HEY!
WAIT UP!
DAMMIT.
DAMMIT. DAMMIT. DAMMIT. *DAMMIT.*
WHOA...
MAYBE YOU WANT TO FILL ME IN ON WHAT'S HAPPENING?

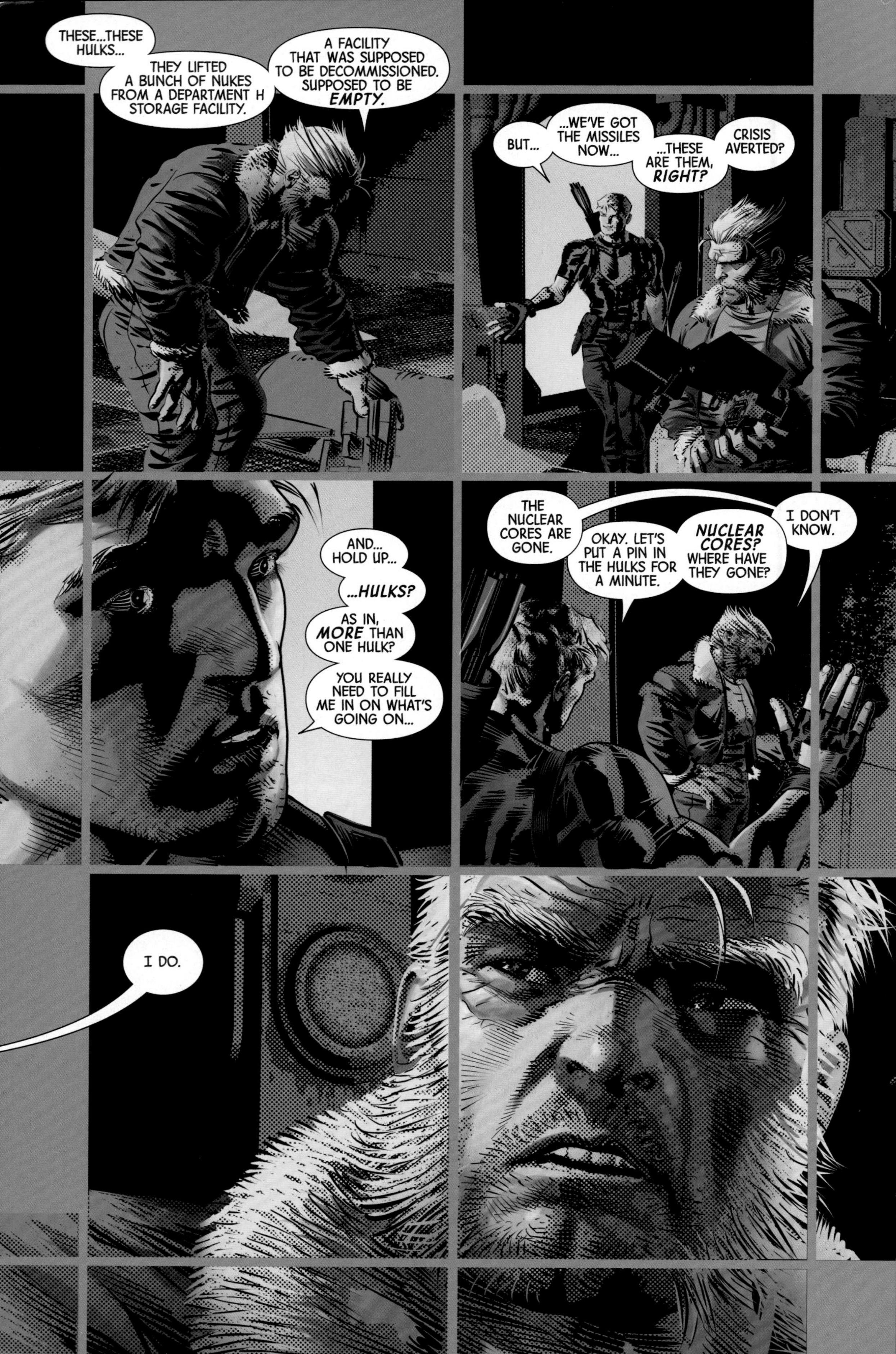

THESE...THESE HULKS...
THEY LIFTED A BUNCH OF NUKES FROM A DEPARTMENT H STORAGE FACILITY.
A FACILITY THAT WAS SUPPOSED TO BE DECOMMISSIONED. SUPPOSED TO BE EMPTY.
BUT...
...WE'VE GOT THE MISSILES NOW...
...THESE ARE THEM, RIGHT?
CRISIS AVERTED?
AND... HOLD UP...
...HULKS?
AS IN, MORE THAN ONE HULK?
YOU REALLY NEED TO FILL ME IN ON WHAT'S GOING ON...
OKAY. LET'S PUT A PIN IN THE HULKS FOR A MINUTE.
NUCLEAR CORES? WHERE HAVE THEY GONE?
THE NUCLEAR CORES ARE GONE.
I DON'T KNOW.
I DO.

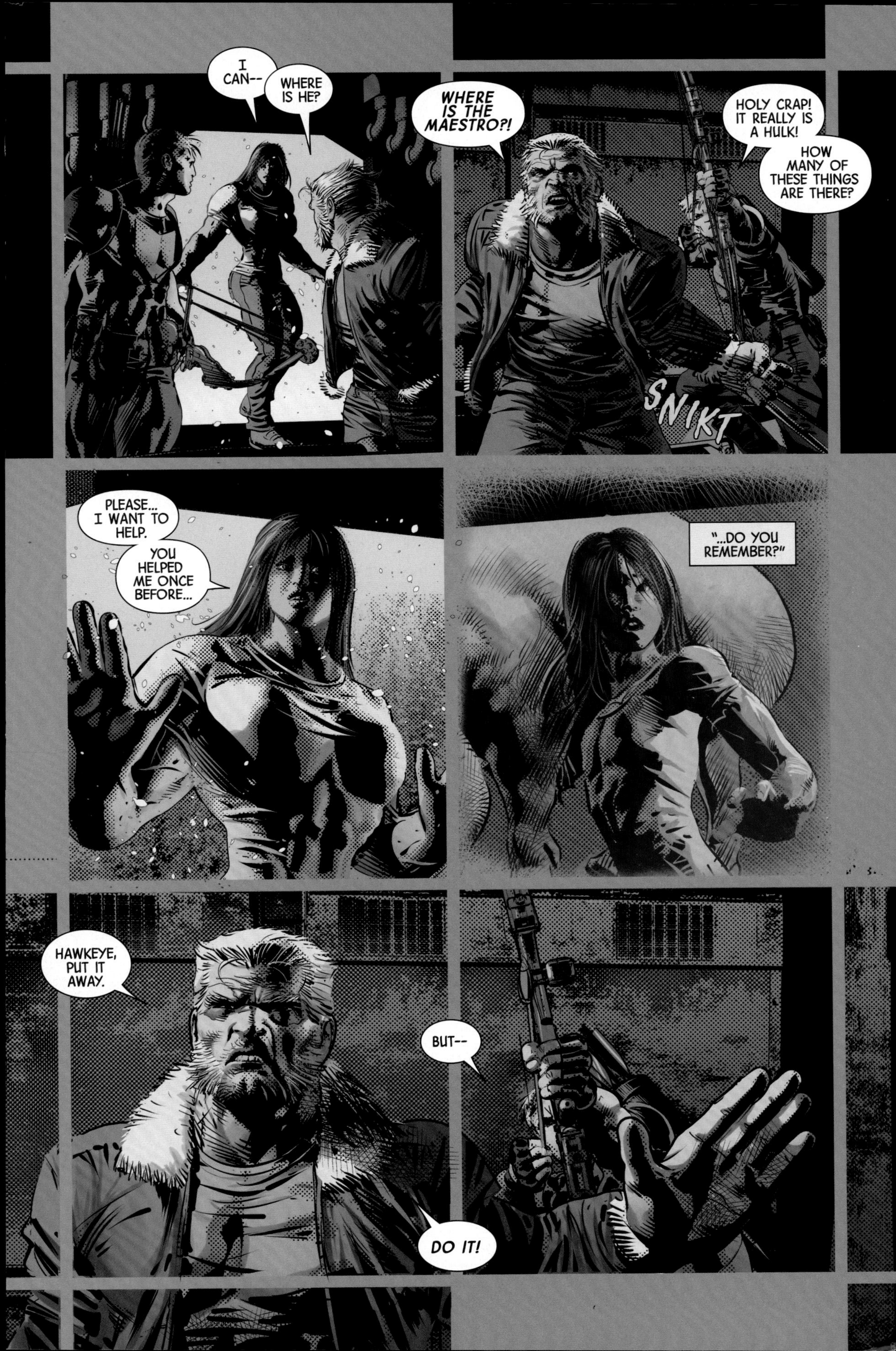
I CAN--
WHERE IS HE?
WHERE IS THE MAESTRO?!
HOLY CRAP! IT REALLY IS A HULK!
HOW MANY OF THESE THINGS ARE THERE?
SNIKT
PLEASE... I WANT TO HELP.
YOU HELPED ME ONCE BEFORE...
"...DO YOU REMEMBER?"
HAWKEYE, PUT IT AWAY.
BUT--
DO IT!

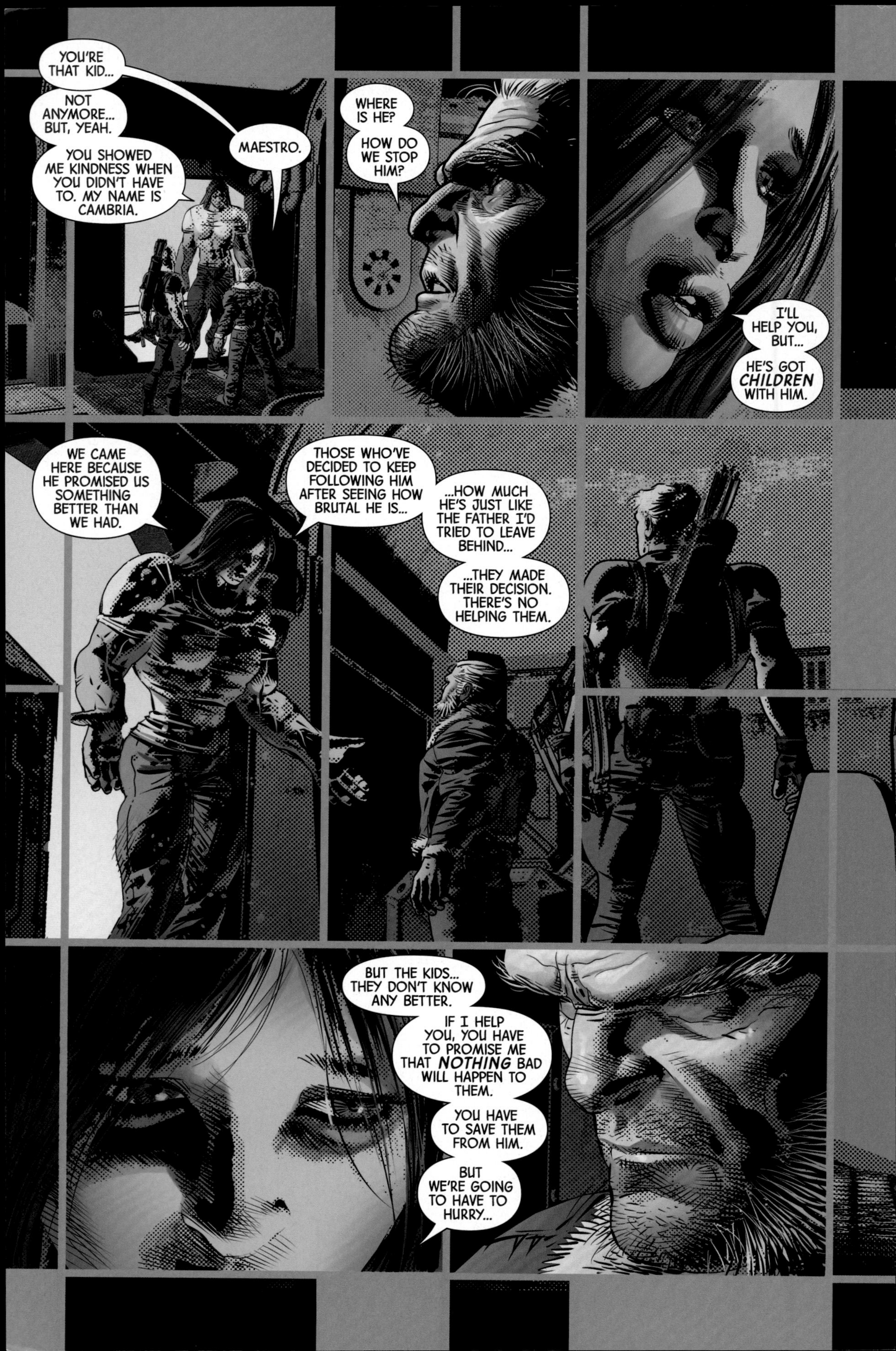
YOU'RE THAT KID...
NOT ANYMORE... BUT, YEAH.
YOU SHOWED ME KINDNESS WHEN YOU DIDN'T HAVE TO. MY NAME IS CAMBRIA.
MAESTRO.
WHERE IS HE?
HOW DO WE STOP HIM?
I'LL HELP YOU, BUT...
HE'S GOT *CHILDREN* WITH HIM.
WE CAME HERE BECAUSE HE PROMISED US SOMETHING BETTER THAN WE HAD.
THOSE WHO'VE DECIDED TO KEEP FOLLOWING HIM AFTER SEEING HOW BRUTAL HE IS...
...HOW MUCH HE'S JUST LIKE THE FATHER I'D TRIED TO LEAVE BEHIND...
...THEY MADE THEIR DECISION. THERE'S NO HELPING THEM.
BUT THE KIDS... THEY DON'T KNOW ANY BETTER.
IF I HELP YOU, YOU HAVE TO PROMISE ME THAT *NOTHING* BAD WILL HAPPEN TO THEM.
YOU HAVE TO SAVE THEM FROM HIM.
BUT WE'RE GOING TO HAVE TO HURRY...

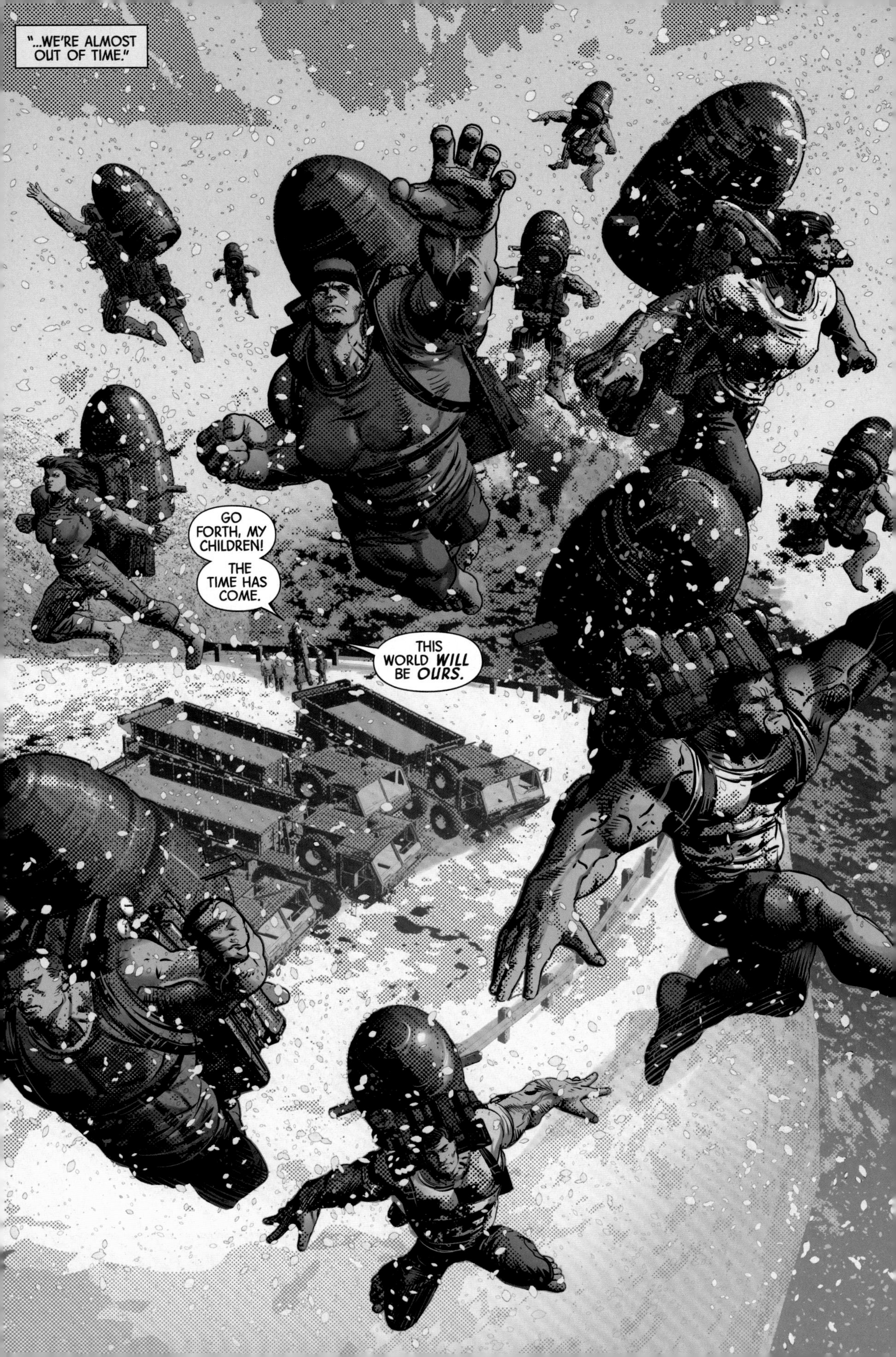
"...WE'RE ALMOST OUT OF TIME."
GO FORTH, MY CHILDREN!
THE TIME HAS COME.
THIS WORLD *WILL* BE *OURS*.

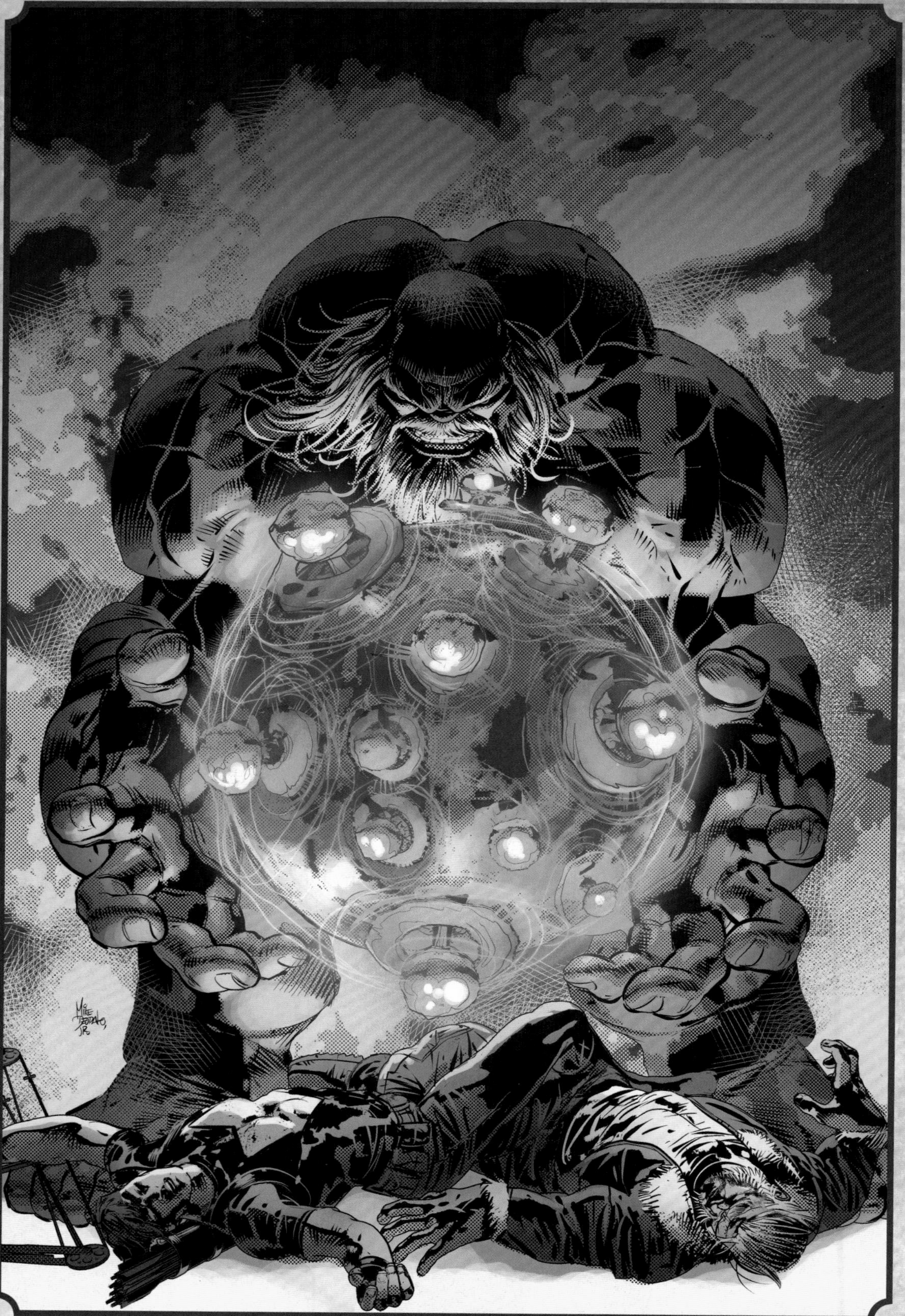

29

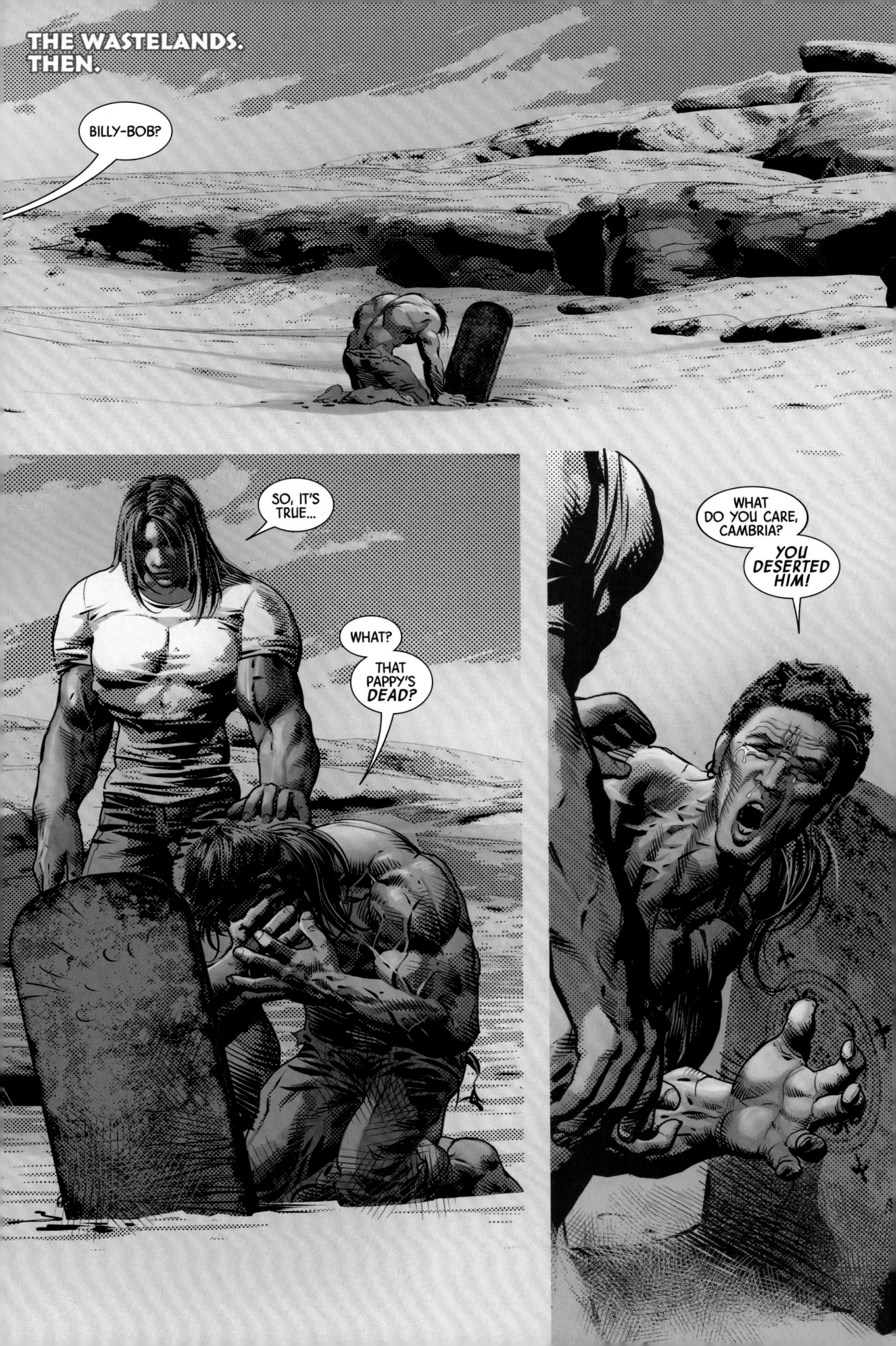
THE WASTELANDS.
THEN.
BILLY-BOB?
SO, IT'S TRUE...
WHAT?
THAT PAPPY'S DEAD?
WHAT DO YOU CARE, CAMBRIA?
YOU DESERTED HIM!

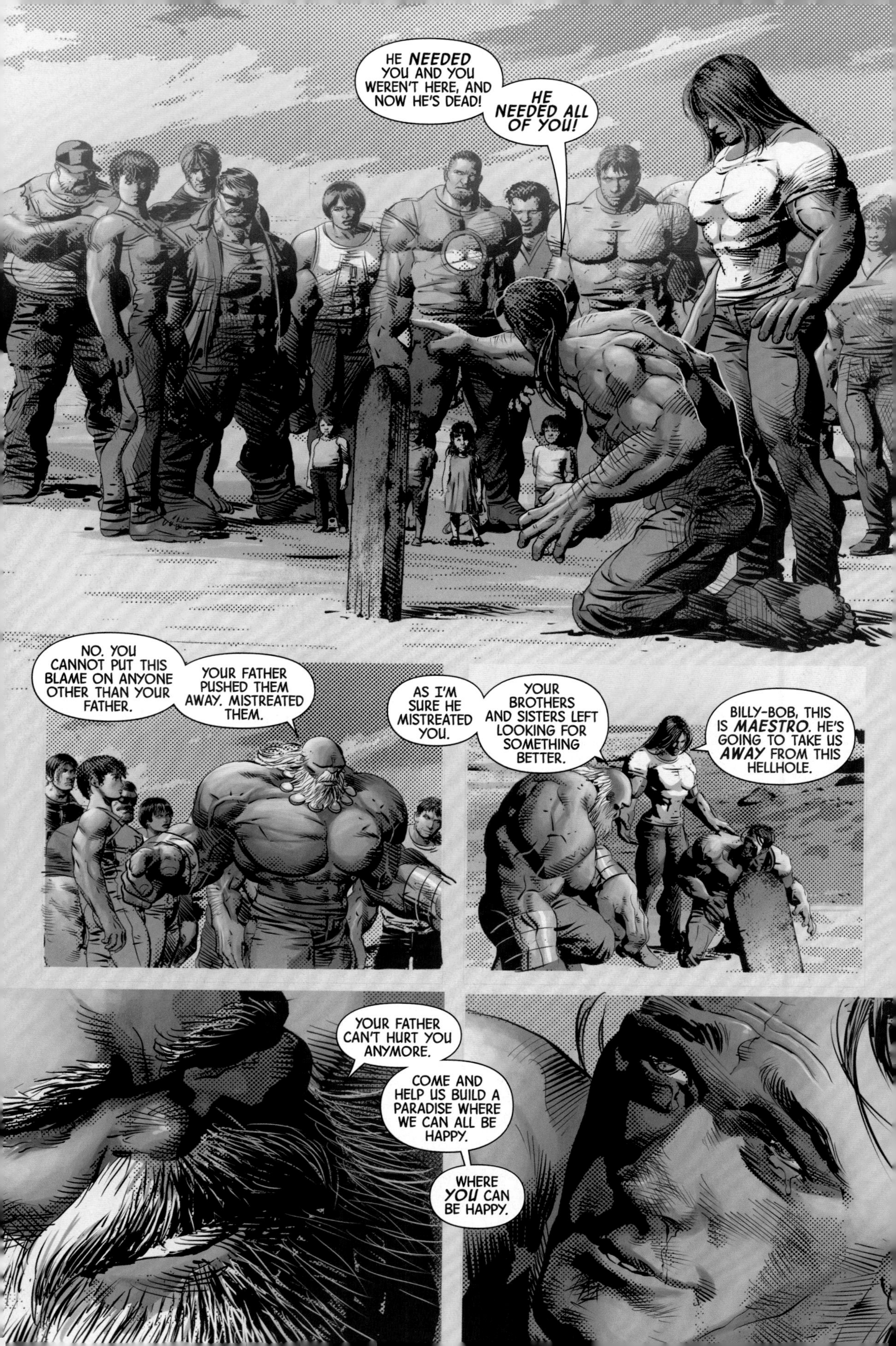
HE NEEDED YOU AND YOU WEREN'T HERE, AND NOW HE'S DEAD!
HE NEEDED ALL OF YOU!
NO. YOU CANNOT PUT THIS BLAME ON ANYONE OTHER THAN YOUR FATHER.
YOUR FATHER PUSHED THEM AWAY. MISTREATED THEM.
AS I'M SURE HE MISTREATED YOU.
YOUR BROTHERS AND SISTERS LEFT LOOKING FOR SOMETHING BETTER.
BILLY-BOB, THIS IS MAESTRO. HE'S GOING TO TAKE US AWAY FROM THIS HELLHOLE.
YOUR FATHER CAN'T HURT YOU ANYMORE.
COME AND HELP US BUILD A PARADISE WHERE WE CAN ALL BE HAPPY.
WHERE YOU CAN BE HAPPY.

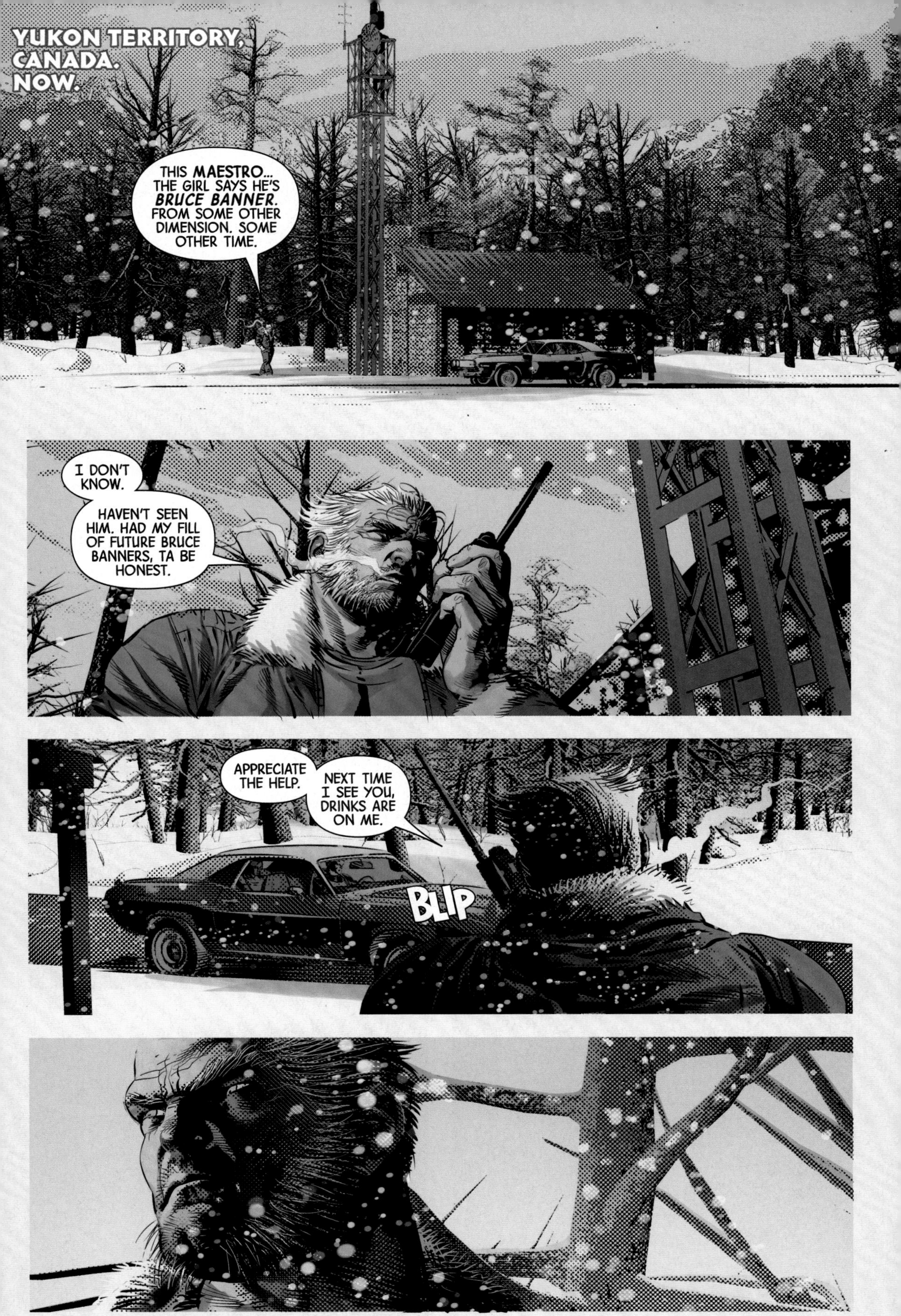
YUKON TERRITORY, CANADA. NOW.
THIS MAESTRO... THE GIRL SAYS HE'S BRUCE BANNER. FROM SOME OTHER DIMENSION. SOME OTHER TIME.
I DON'T KNOW.
HAVEN'T SEEN HIM. HAD MY FILL OF FUTURE BRUCE BANNERS, TA BE HONEST.
APPRECIATE THE HELP.
NEXT TIME I SEE YOU, DRINKS ARE ON ME.
BLIP

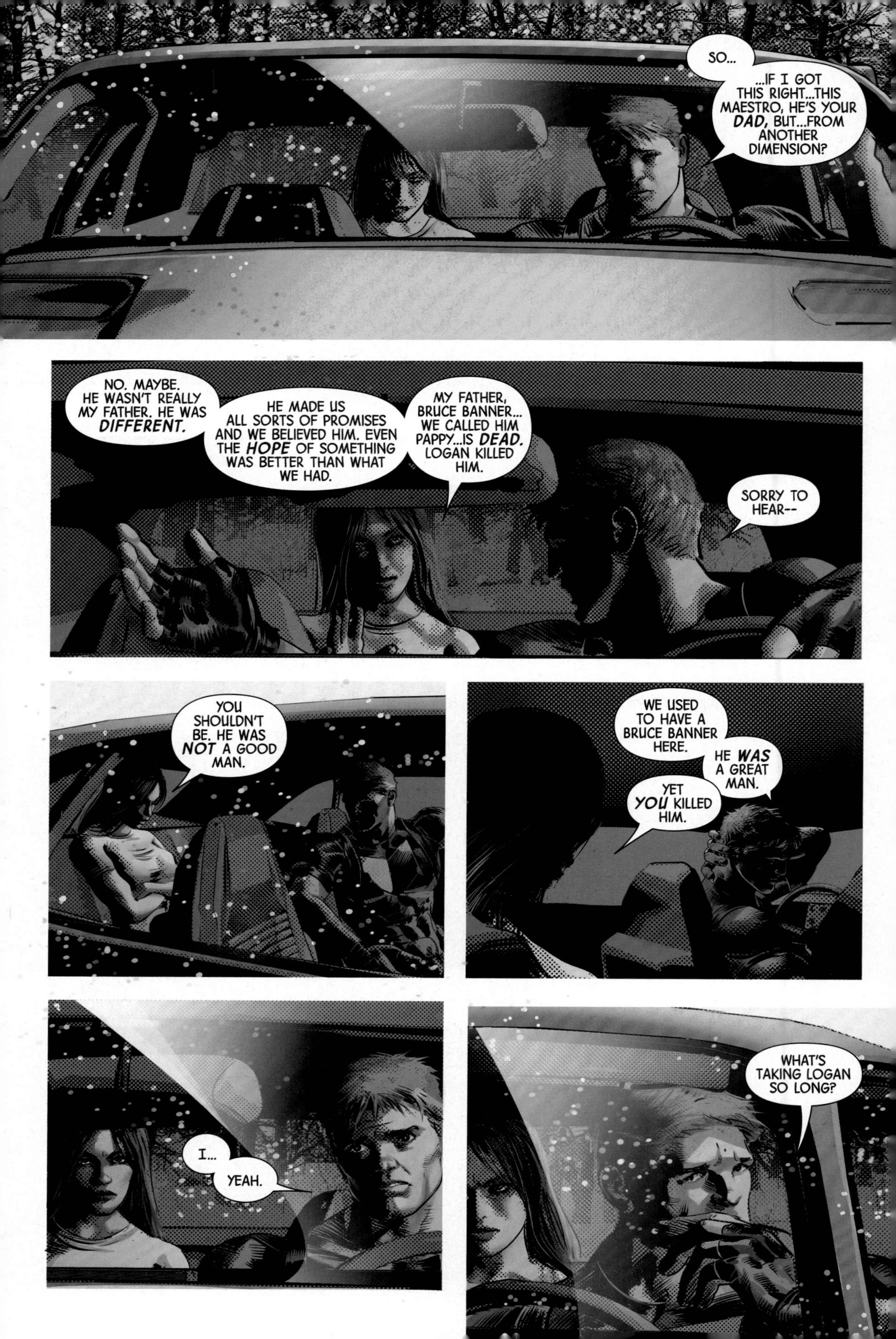
SO...
...IF I GOT THIS RIGHT...THIS MAESTRO, HE'S YOUR DAD, BUT...FROM ANOTHER DIMENSION?
NO. MAYBE. HE WASN'T REALLY MY FATHER. HE WAS DIFFERENT.
HE MADE US ALL SORTS OF PROMISES AND WE BELIEVED HIM. EVEN THE HOPE OF SOMETHING WAS BETTER THAN WHAT WE HAD.
MY FATHER, BRUCE BANNER... WE CALLED HIM PAPPY...IS DEAD. LOGAN KILLED HIM.
SORRY TO HEAR--
YOU SHOULDN'T BE. HE WAS NOT A GOOD MAN.
WE USED TO HAVE A BRUCE BANNER HERE.
HE WAS A GREAT MAN.
YET YOU KILLED HIM.
I...
YEAH.
WHAT'S TAKING LOGAN SO LONG?

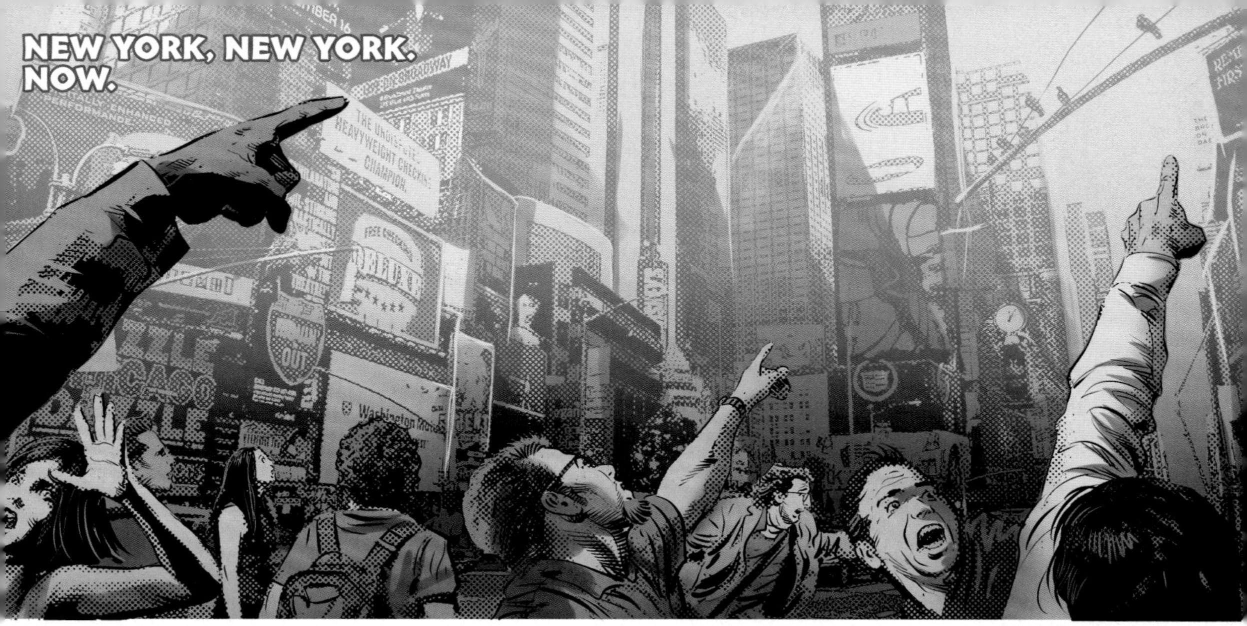
NEW YORK, NEW YORK.
NOW.

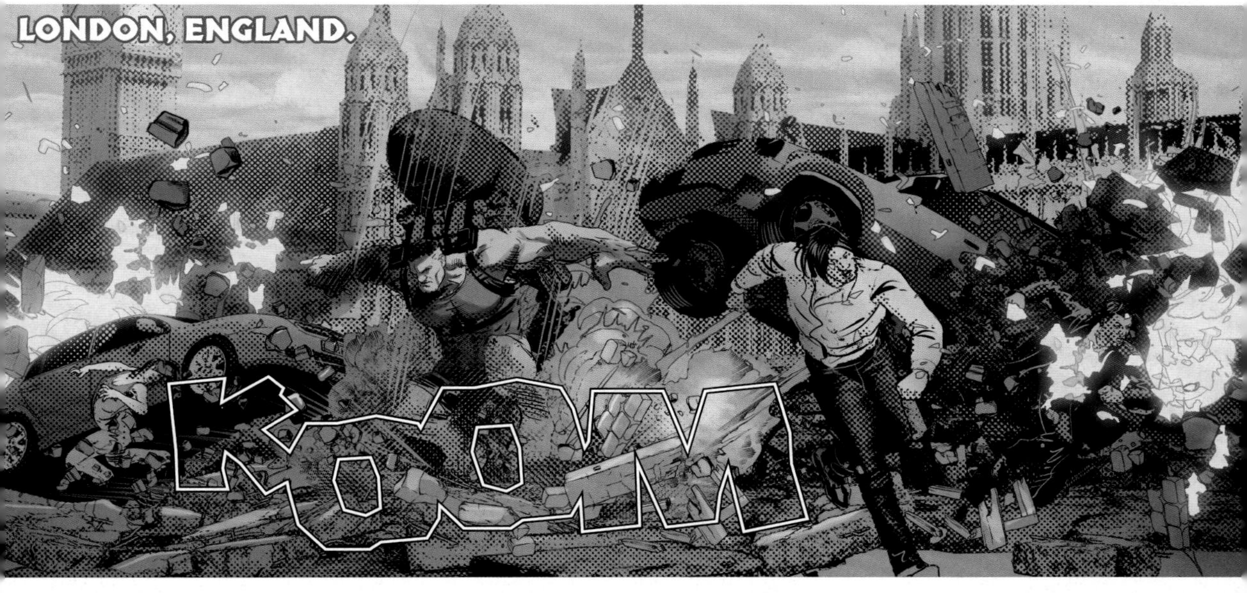
LONDON, ENGLAND.
KOOM

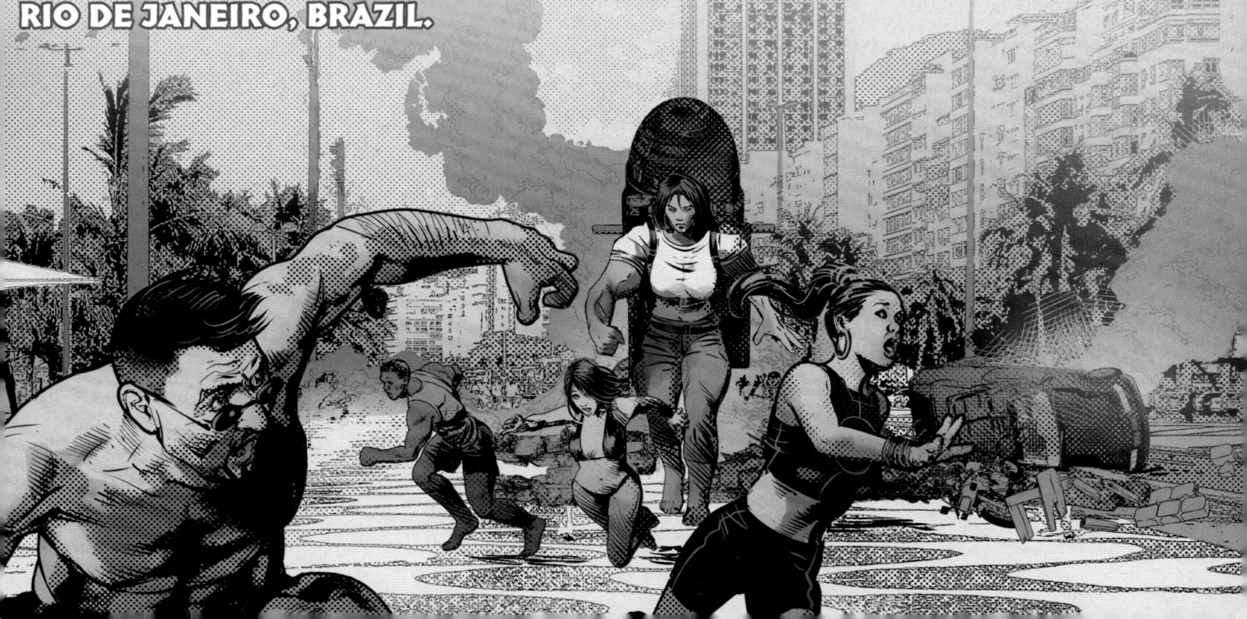
RIO DE JANEIRO, BRAZIL.

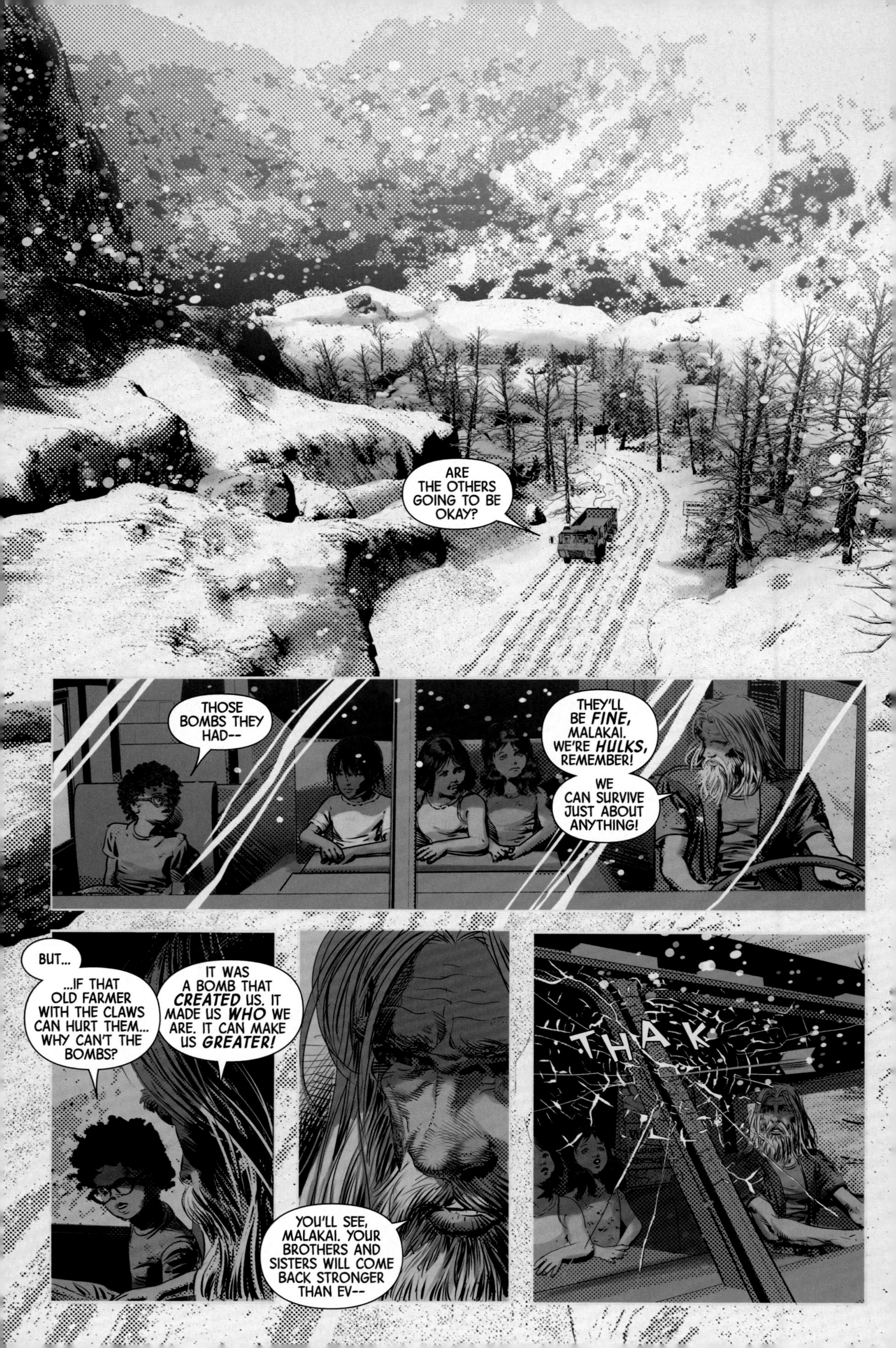
ARE THE OTHERS GOING TO BE OKAY?
THOSE BOMBS THEY HAD--
THEY'LL BE FINE, MALAKAI. WE'RE HULKS, REMEMBER!
WE CAN SURVIVE JUST ABOUT ANYTHING!
BUT...
...IF THAT OLD FARMER WITH THE CLAWS CAN HURT THEM... WHY CAN'T THE BOMBS?
IT WAS A BOMB THAT CREATED US. IT MADE US WHO WE ARE. IT CAN MAKE US GREATER!
YOU'LL SEE, MALAKAI. YOUR BROTHERS AND SISTERS WILL COME BACK STRONGER THAN EV--
THAK

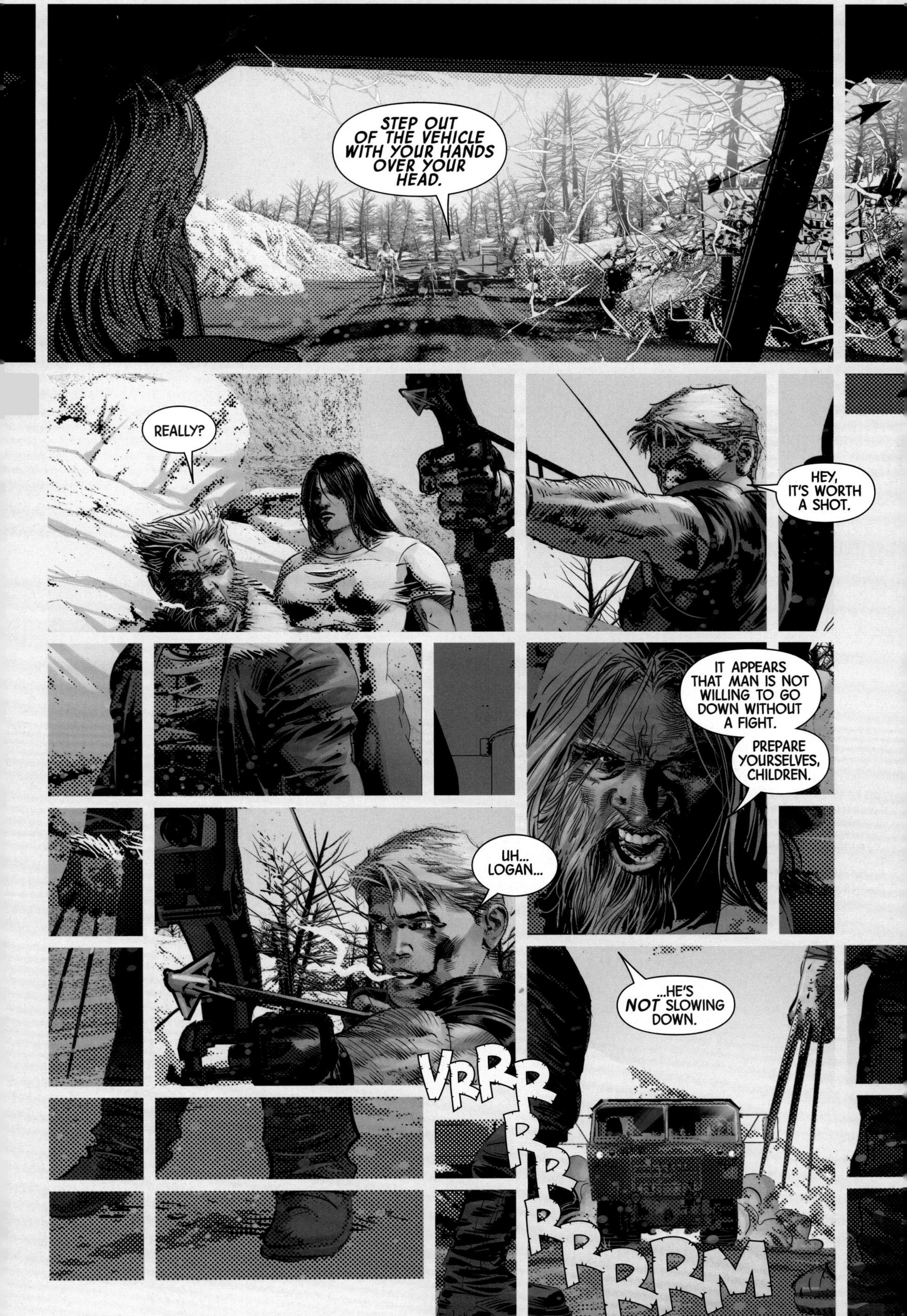
STEP OUT OF THE VEHICLE WITH YOUR HANDS OVER YOUR HEAD.
REALLY?
HEY, IT'S WORTH A SHOT.
IT APPEARS THAT MAN IS NOT WILLING TO GO DOWN WITHOUT A FIGHT.
PREPARE YOURSELVES, CHILDREN.
UH... LOGAN...
...HE'S NOT SLOWING DOWN.
VRRRRRRRRRRRM

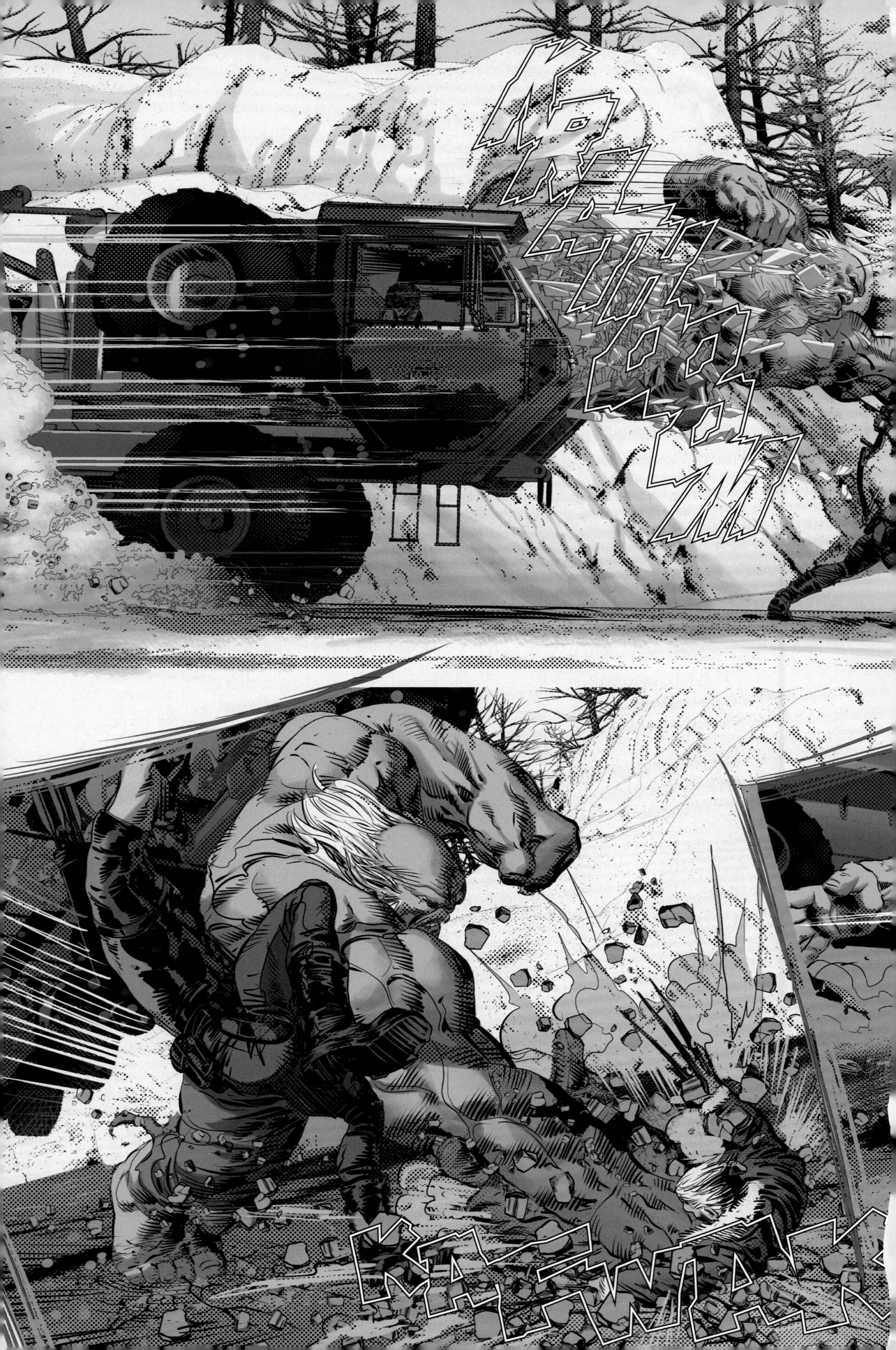
KA-TWAK

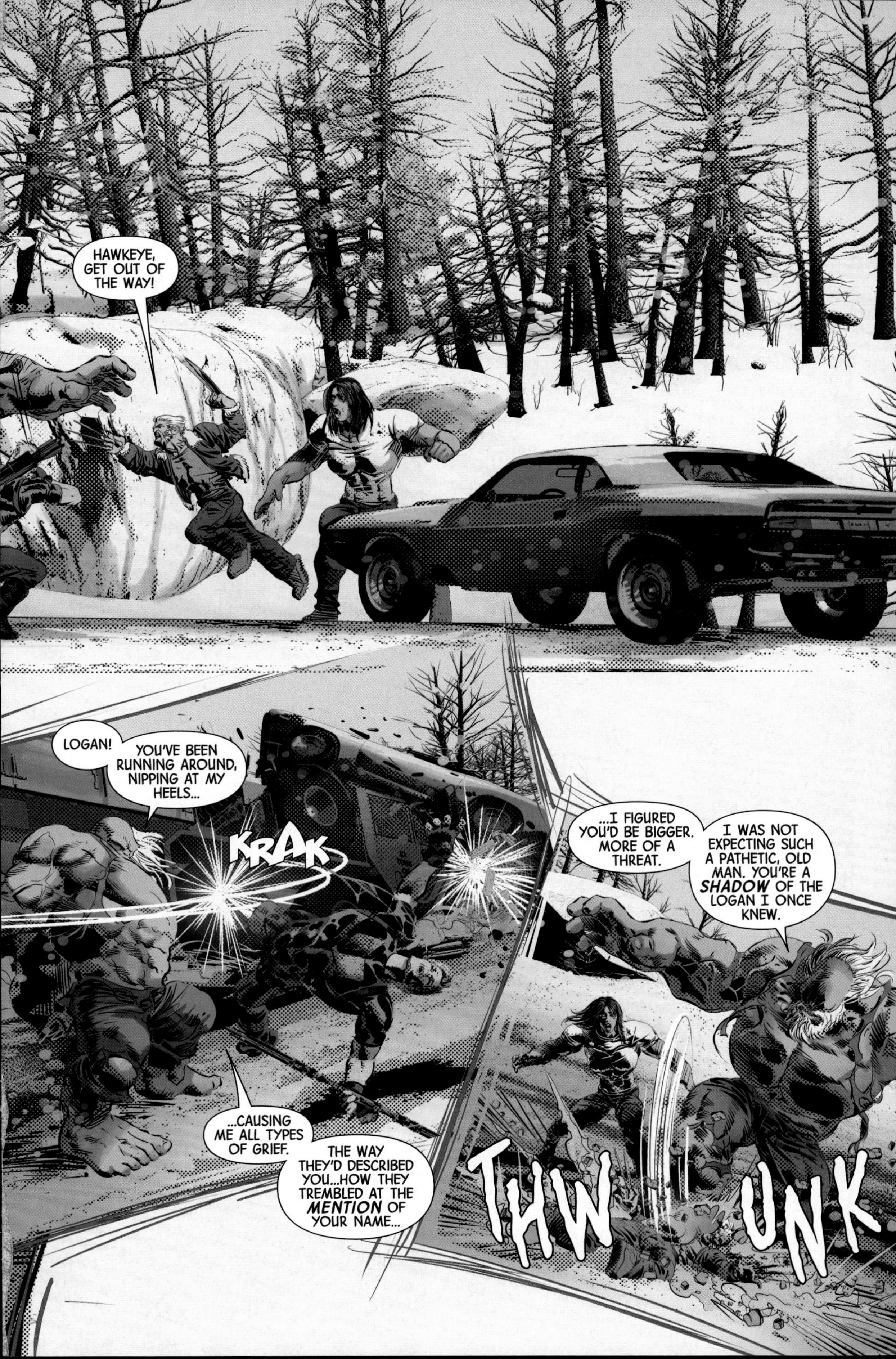
HAWKEYE, GET OUT OF THE WAY!
LOGAN!
YOU'VE BEEN RUNNING AROUND, NIPPING AT MY HEELS...
KRAK
...CAUSING ME ALL TYPES OF GRIEF.
THE WAY THEY'D DESCRIBED YOU...HOW THEY TREMBLED AT THE MENTION OF YOUR NAME...
...I FIGURED YOU'D BE BIGGER. MORE OF A THREAT.
I WAS NOT EXPECTING SUCH A PATHETIC, OLD MAN. YOU'RE A SHADOW OF THE LOGAN I ONCE KNEW.
THW UNK

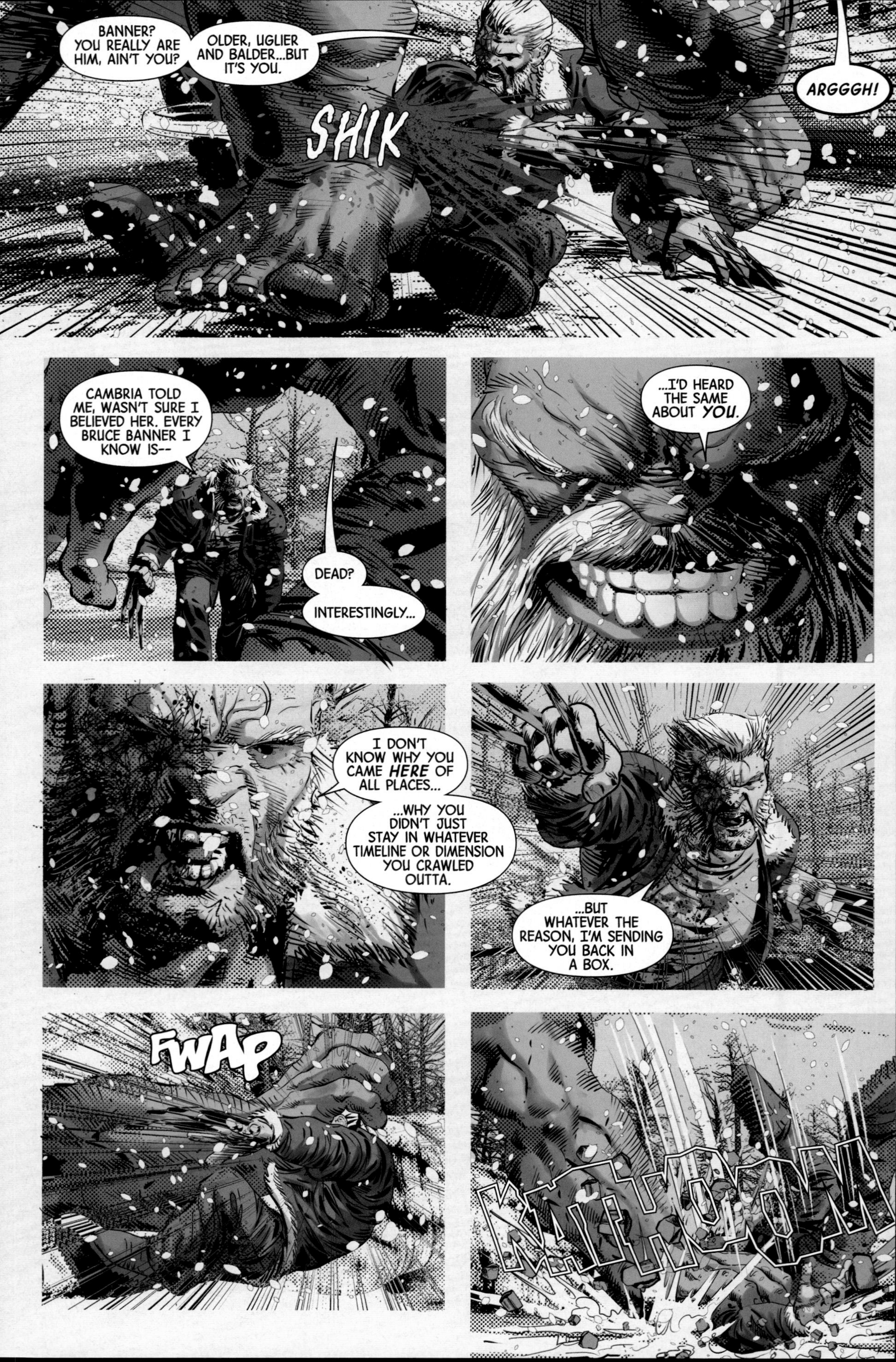
BANNER? YOU REALLY ARE HIM, AIN'T YOU?
OLDER, UGLIER AND BALDER...BUT IT'S YOU.
SHIK
ARGGGH!
CAMBRIA TOLD ME, WASN'T SURE I BELIEVED HER. EVERY BRUCE BANNER I KNOW IS--
DEAD?
INTERESTINGLY...
...I'D HEARD THE SAME ABOUT *YOU*.
I DON'T KNOW WHY YOU CAME *HERE* OF ALL PLACES...
...WHY YOU DIDN'T JUST STAY IN WHATEVER TIMELINE OR DIMENSION YOU CRAWLED OUTTA.
...BUT WHATEVER THE REASON, I'M SENDING YOU BACK IN A BOX.
FWAP

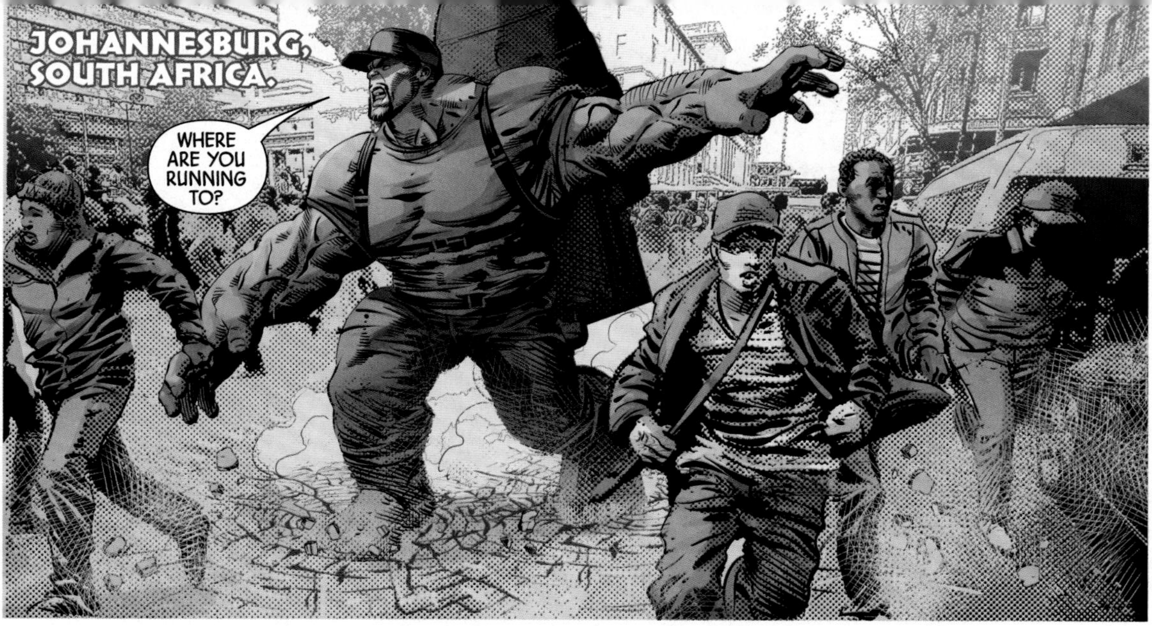
JOHANNESBURG, SOUTH AFRICA.
WHERE ARE YOU RUNNING TO?

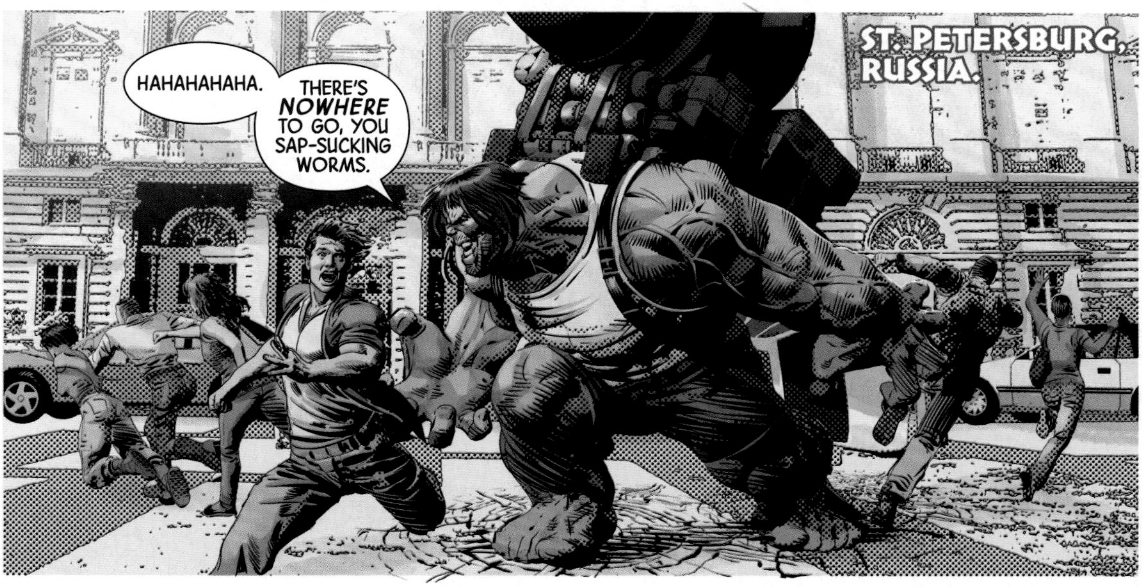
ST. PETERSBURG, RUSSIA.
HAHAHAHAHA.
THERE'S NOWHERE TO GO, YOU SAP-SUCKING WORMS.

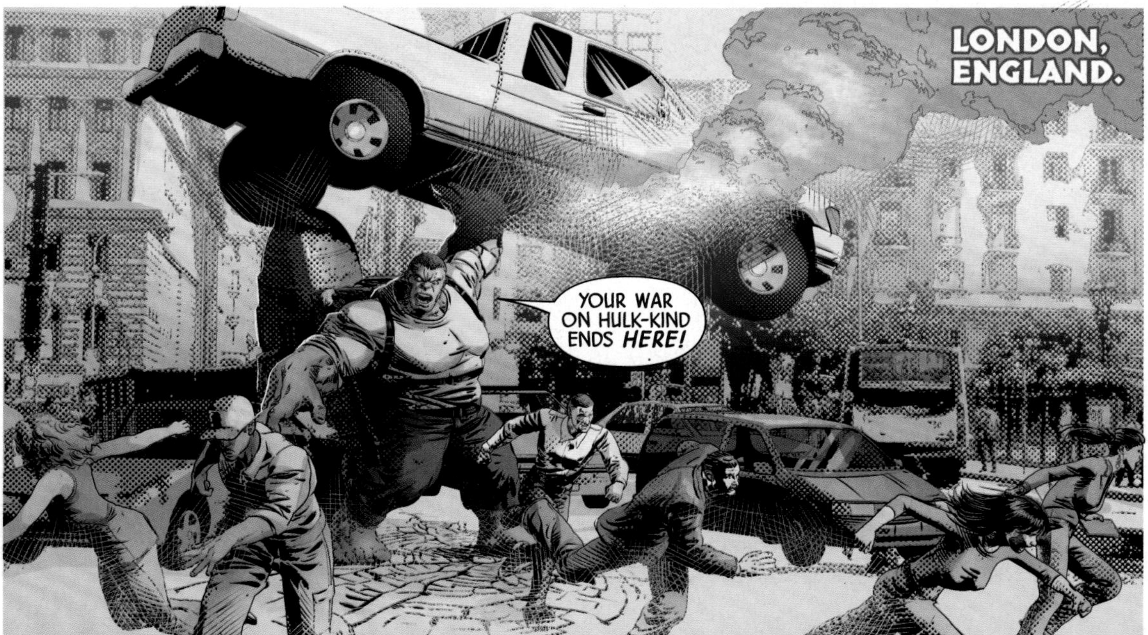
LONDON, ENGLAND.
YOUR WAR ON HULK-KIND ENDS HERE!

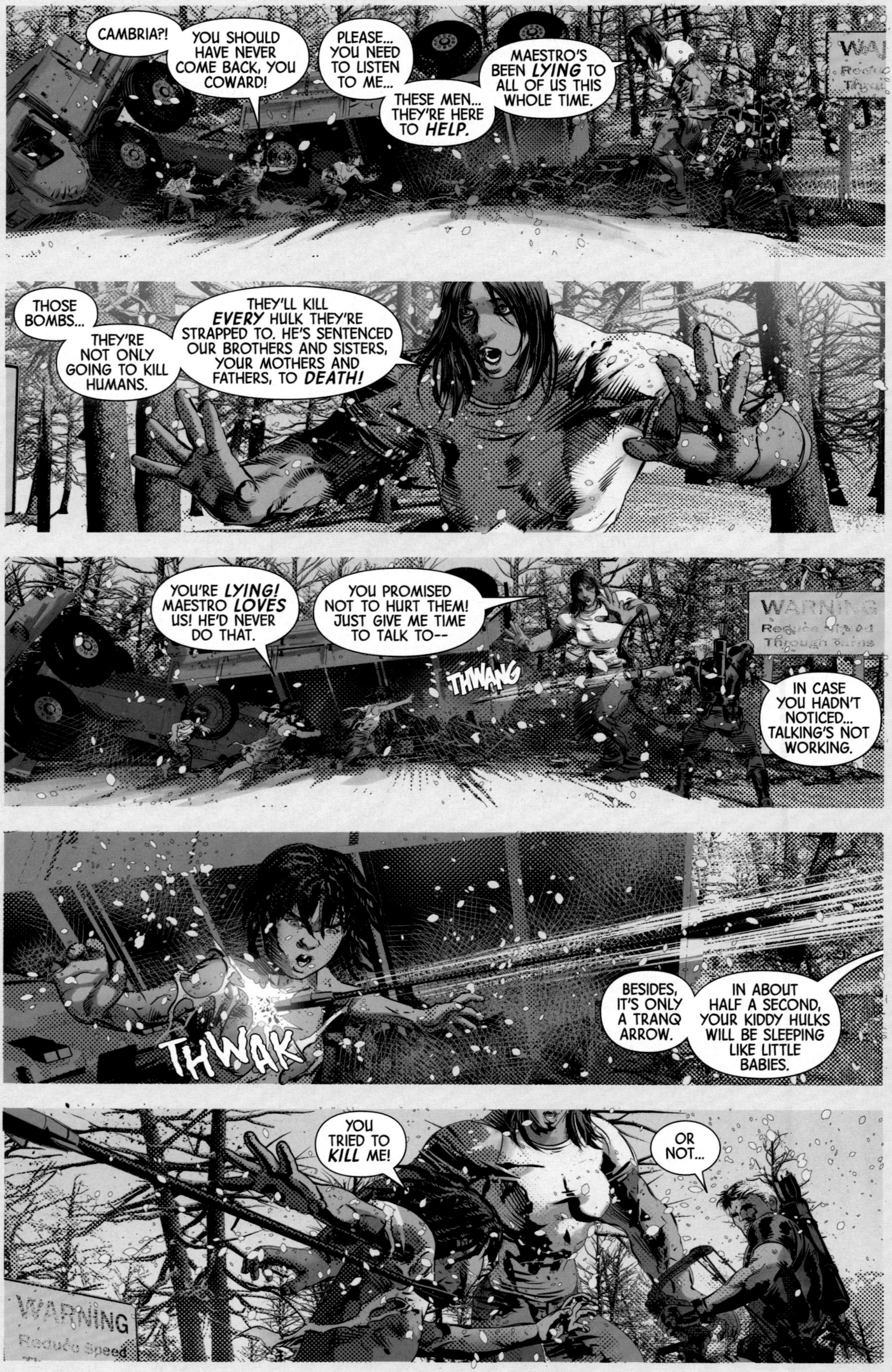
CAMBRIA?!
YOU SHOULD HAVE NEVER COME BACK, YOU COWARD!
PLEASE... YOU NEED TO LISTEN TO ME...
THESE MEN... THEY'RE HERE TO HELP.
MAESTRO'S BEEN LYING TO ALL OF US THIS WHOLE TIME.
THOSE BOMBS...
THEY'RE NOT ONLY GOING TO KILL HUMANS.
THEY'LL KILL EVERY HULK THEY'RE STRAPPED TO. HE'S SENTENCED OUR BROTHERS AND SISTERS, YOUR MOTHERS AND FATHERS, TO DEATH!
YOU'RE LYING! MAESTRO LOVES US! HE'D NEVER DO THAT.
YOU PROMISED NOT TO HURT THEM! JUST GIVE ME TIME TO TALK TO--
WARNING
THWANG
IN CASE YOU HADN'T NOTICED... TALKING'S NOT WORKING.
THWAK
BESIDES, IT'S ONLY A TRANQ ARROW.
IN ABOUT HALF A SECOND, YOUR KIDDY HULKS WILL BE SLEEPING LIKE LITTLE BABIES.
YOU TRIED TO KILL ME!
OR NOT...
WARNING
Reduce Speed

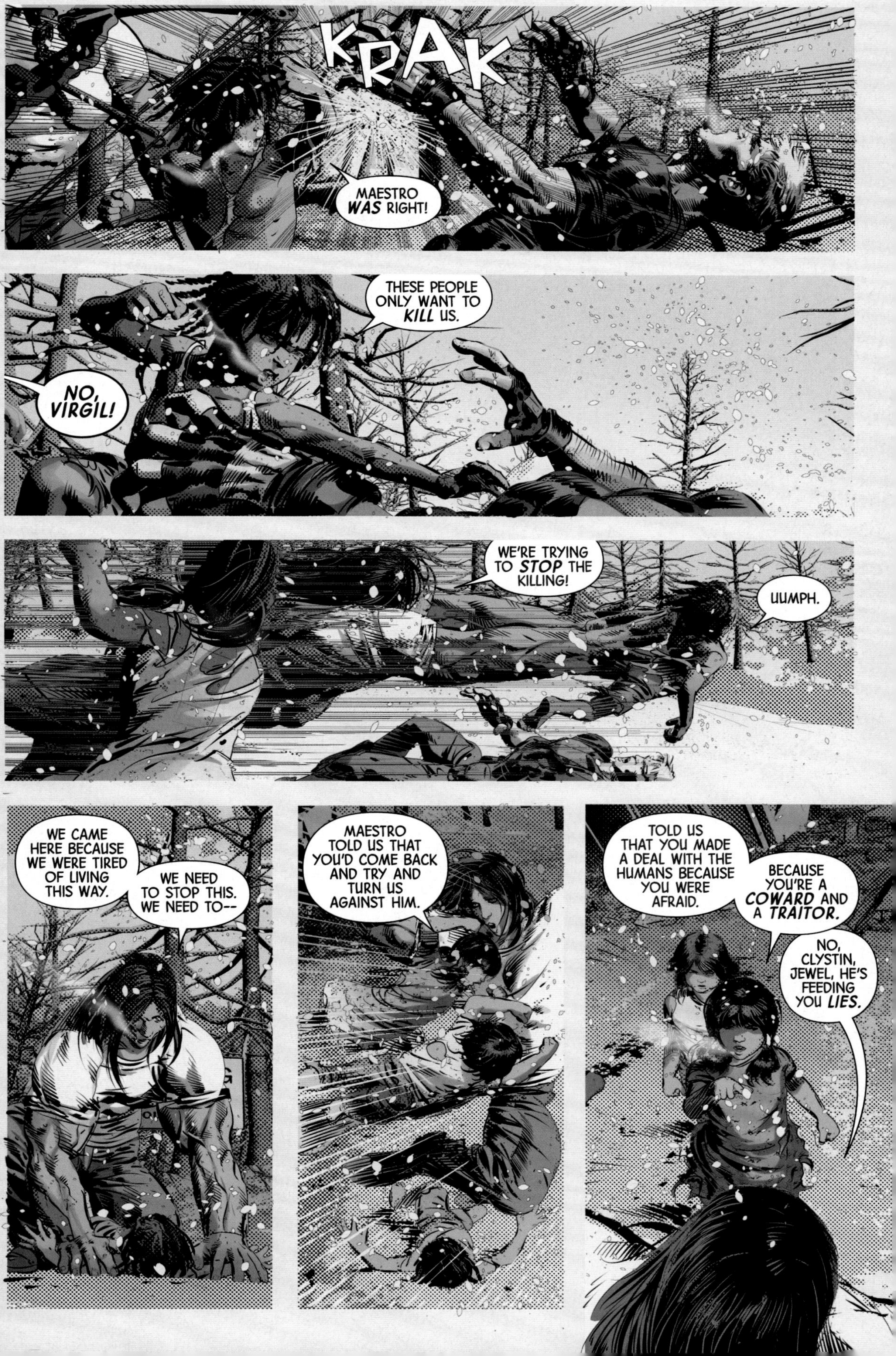
KRAK
MAESTRO WAS RIGHT!
THESE PEOPLE ONLY WANT TO KILL US.
NO, VIRGIL!
WE'RE TRYING TO STOP THE KILLING!
UUMPH.
WE CAME HERE BECAUSE WE WERE TIRED OF LIVING THIS WAY.
WE NEED TO STOP THIS. WE NEED TO--
MAESTRO TOLD US THAT YOU'D COME BACK AND TRY AND TURN US AGAINST HIM.
TOLD US THAT YOU MADE A DEAL WITH THE HUMANS BECAUSE YOU WERE AFRAID.
BECAUSE YOU'RE A COWARD AND A TRAITOR.
NO, CLYSTIN, JEWEL, HE'S FEEDING YOU LIES.

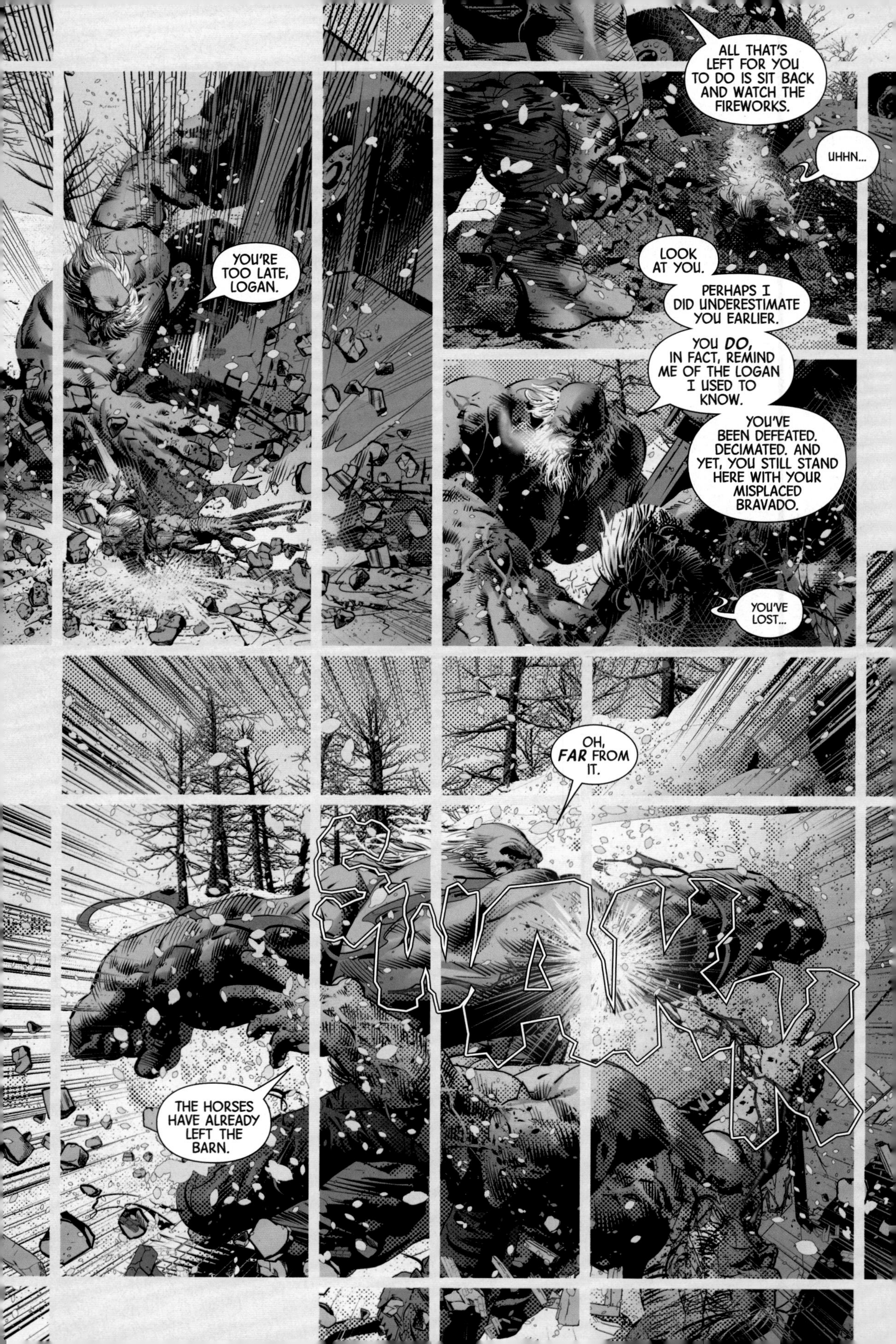
YOU'RE TOO LATE, LOGAN.
ALL THAT'S LEFT FOR YOU TO DO IS SIT BACK AND WATCH THE FIREWORKS.
UHHN...
LOOK AT YOU.
PERHAPS I DID UNDERESTIMATE YOU EARLIER.
YOU DO, IN FACT, REMIND ME OF THE LOGAN I USED TO KNOW.
YOU'VE BEEN DEFEATED. DECIMATED. AND YET, YOU STILL STAND HERE WITH YOUR MISPLACED BRAVADO.
YOU'VE LOST...
THE HORSES HAVE ALREADY LEFT THE BARN.
OH, FAR FROM IT.
SWACK

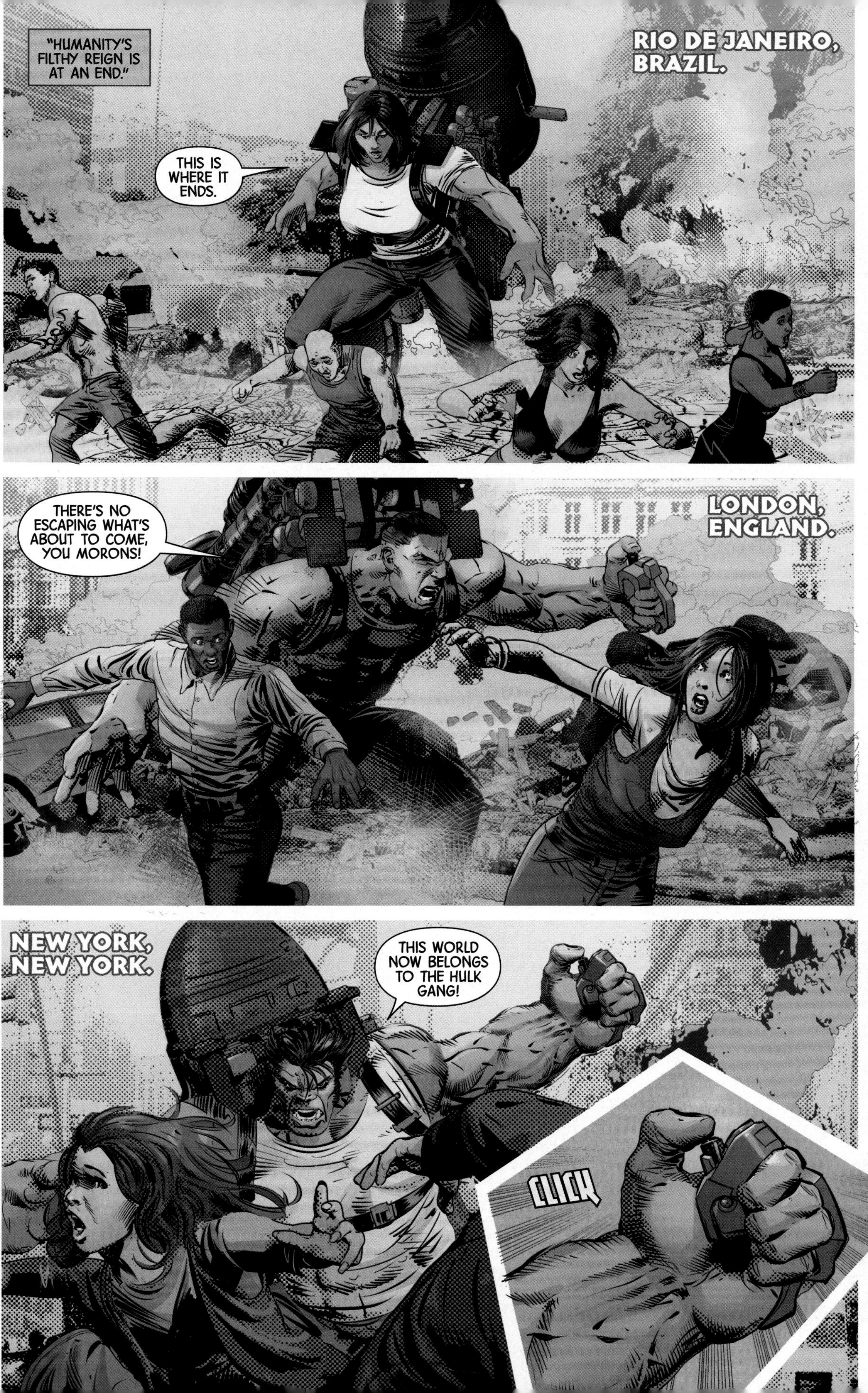
"HUMANITY'S FILTHY REIGN IS AT AN END."
RIO DE JANEIRO, BRAZIL.
THIS IS WHERE IT ENDS.
LONDON, ENGLAND.
THERE'S NO ESCAPING WHAT'S ABOUT TO COME, YOU MORONS!
NEW YORK, NEW YORK.
THIS WORLD NOW BELONGS TO THE HULK GANG!
CLICK

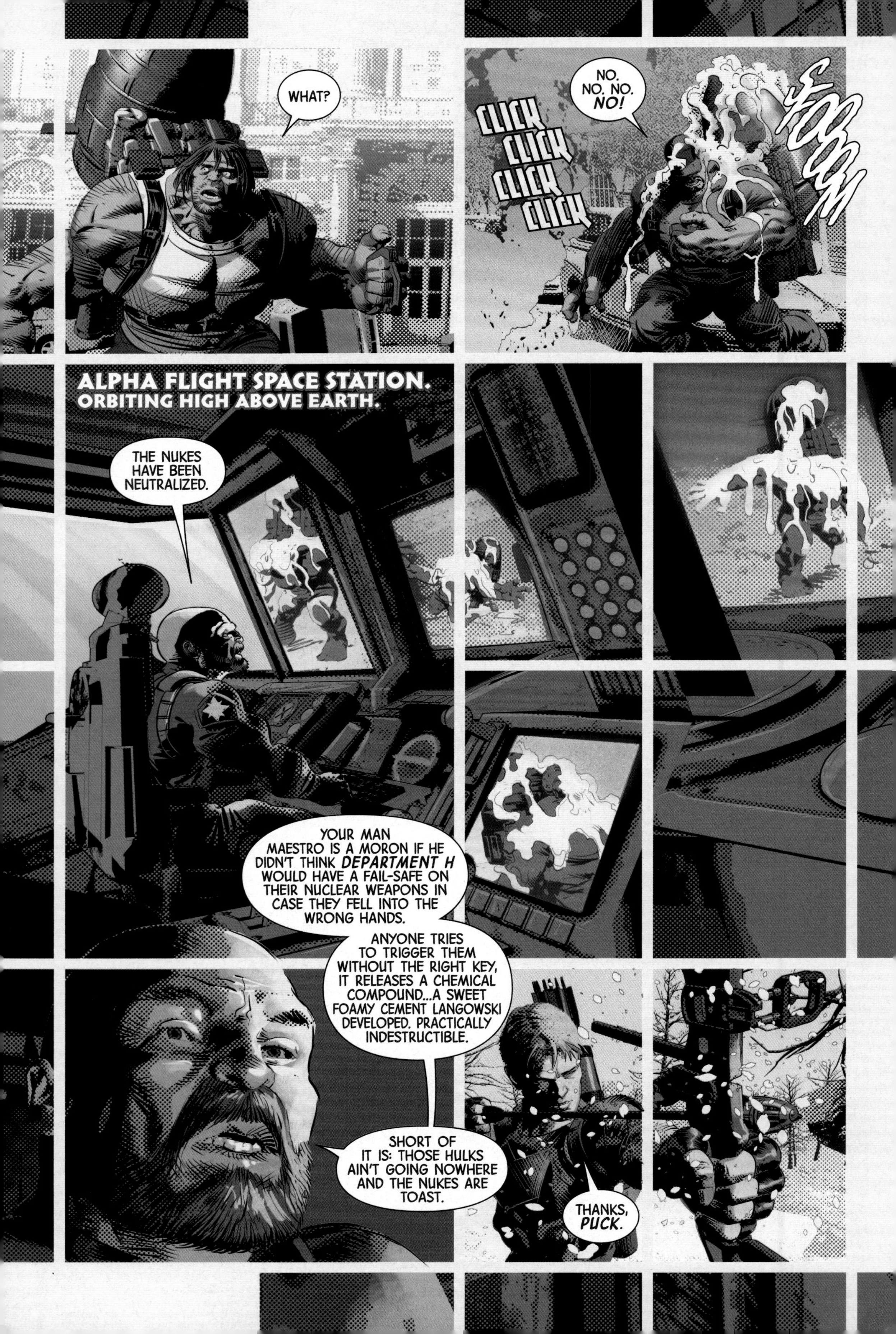
WHAT?
CLICK CLICK CLICK CLICK
NO. NO. NO. NO!
FOOOOM
ALPHA FLIGHT SPACE STATION. ORBITING HIGH ABOVE EARTH.
THE NUKES HAVE BEEN NEUTRALIZED.
YOUR MAN MAESTRO IS A MORON IF HE DIDN'T THINK DEPARTMENT H WOULD HAVE A FAIL-SAFE ON THEIR NUCLEAR WEAPONS IN CASE THEY FELL INTO THE WRONG HANDS.
ANYONE TRIES TO TRIGGER THEM WITHOUT THE RIGHT KEY, IT RELEASES A CHEMICAL COMPOUND...A SWEET FOAMY CEMENT LANGOWSKI DEVELOPED. PRACTICALLY INDESTRUCTIBLE.
SHORT OF IT IS: THOSE HULKS AIN'T GOING NOWHERE AND THE NUKES ARE TOAST.
THANKS, PUCK.

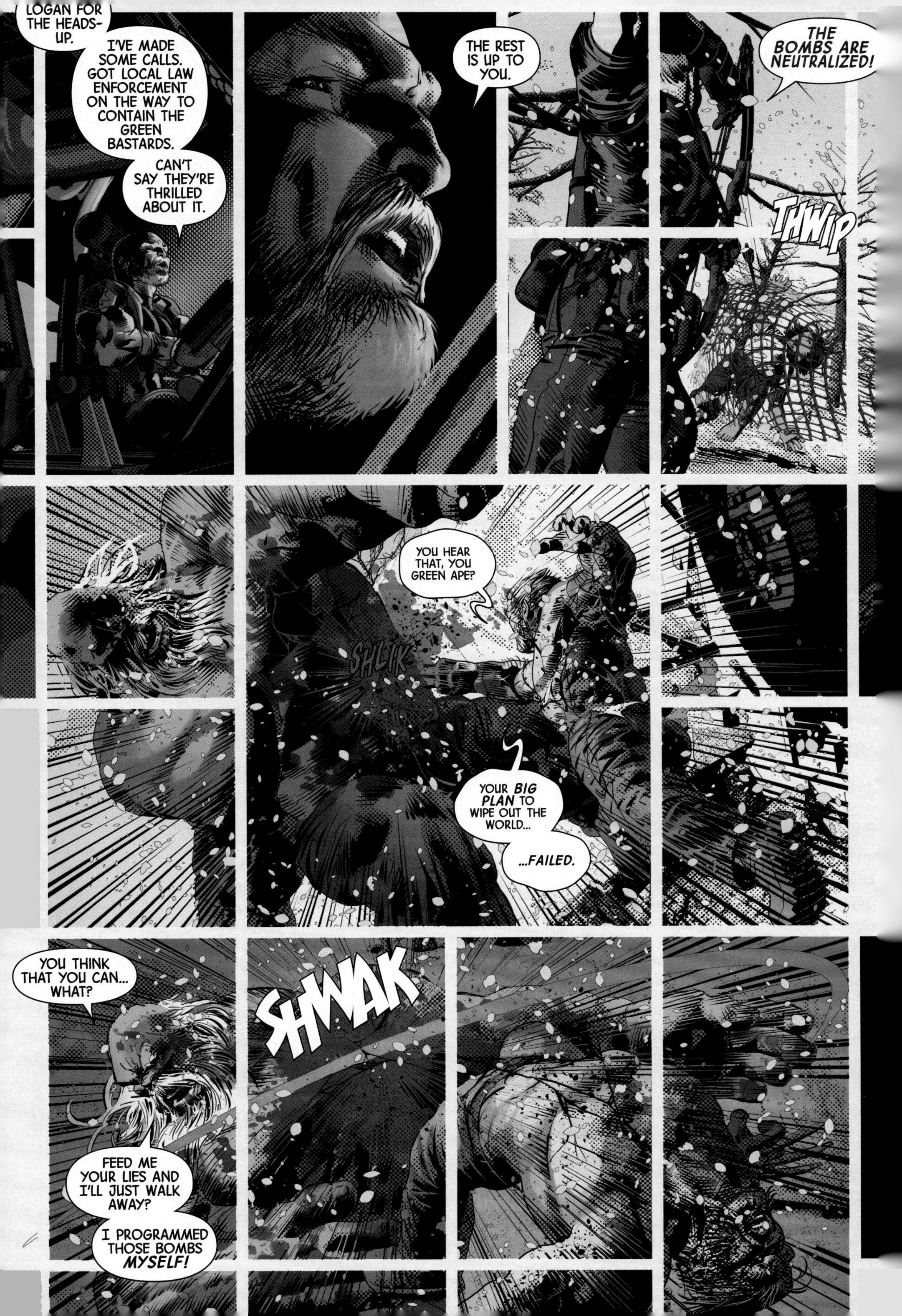
LOGAN FOR THE HEADS-UP.
I'VE MADE SOME CALLS. GOT LOCAL LAW ENFORCEMENT ON THE WAY TO CONTAIN THE GREEN BASTARDS.
CAN'T SAY THEY'RE THRILLED ABOUT IT.
THE REST IS UP TO YOU.
THE BOMBS ARE NEUTRALIZED!
THWIP
YOU HEAR THAT, YOU GREEN APE?
SHLIK
YOUR BIG PLAN TO WIPE OUT THE WORLD...
...FAILED.
YOU THINK THAT YOU CAN... WHAT?
SHWAK
FEED ME YOUR LIES AND I'LL JUST WALK AWAY?
I PROGRAMMED THOSE BOMBS MYSELF!

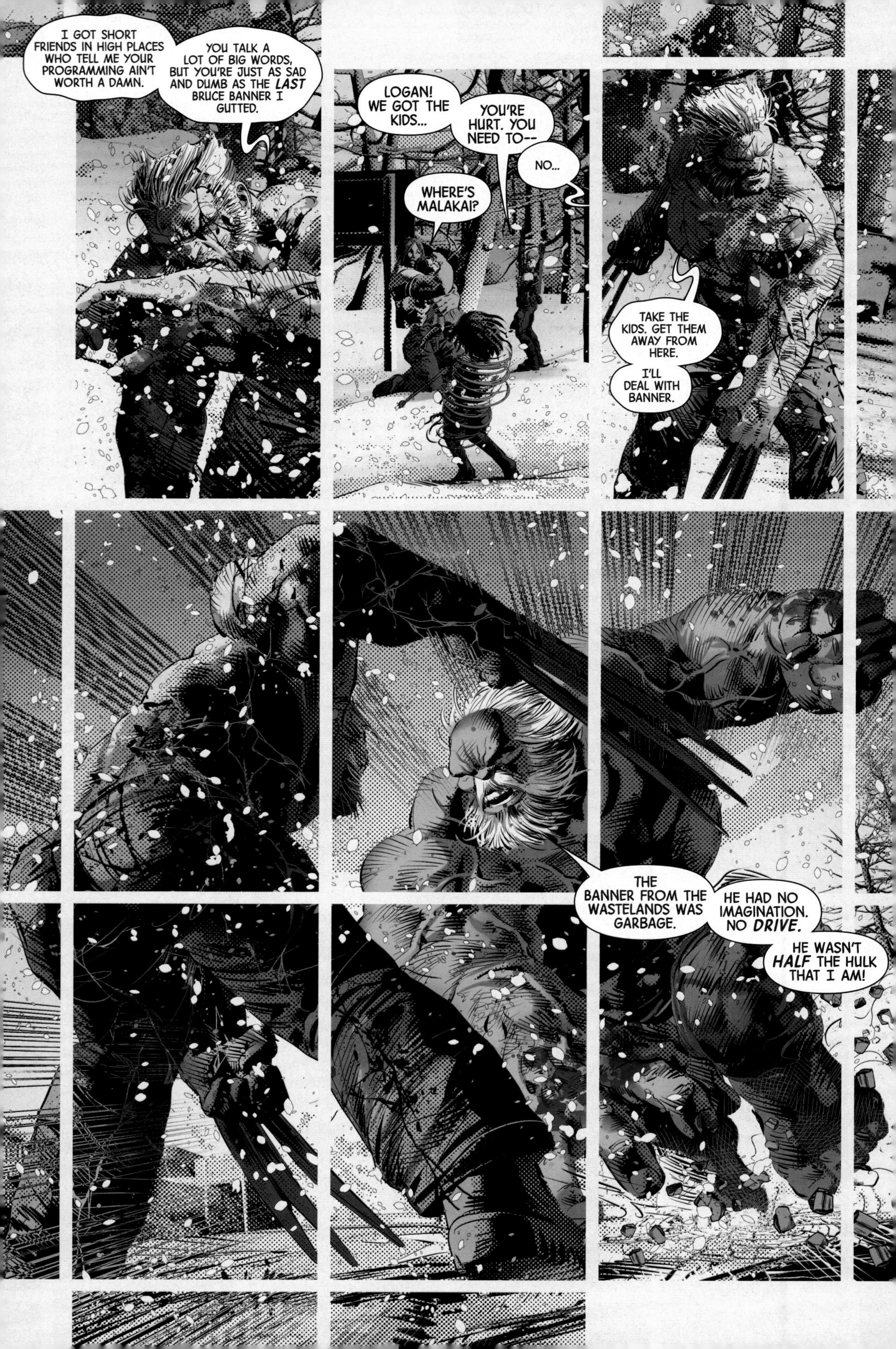
I GOT SHORT FRIENDS IN HIGH PLACES WHO TELL ME YOUR PROGRAMMING AIN'T WORTH A DAMN.
YOU TALK A LOT OF BIG WORDS, BUT YOU'RE JUST AS SAD AND DUMB AS THE *LAST* BRUCE BANNER I GUTTED.
LOGAN! WE GOT THE KIDS...
YOU'RE HURT. YOU NEED TO--
NO...
WHERE'S MALAKAI?
TAKE THE KIDS. GET THEM AWAY FROM HERE.
I'LL DEAL WITH BANNER.
THE BANNER FROM THE WASTELANDS WAS GARBAGE.
HE HAD NO IMAGINATION. NO *DRIVE.*
HE WASN'T *HALF* THE HULK THAT I AM!

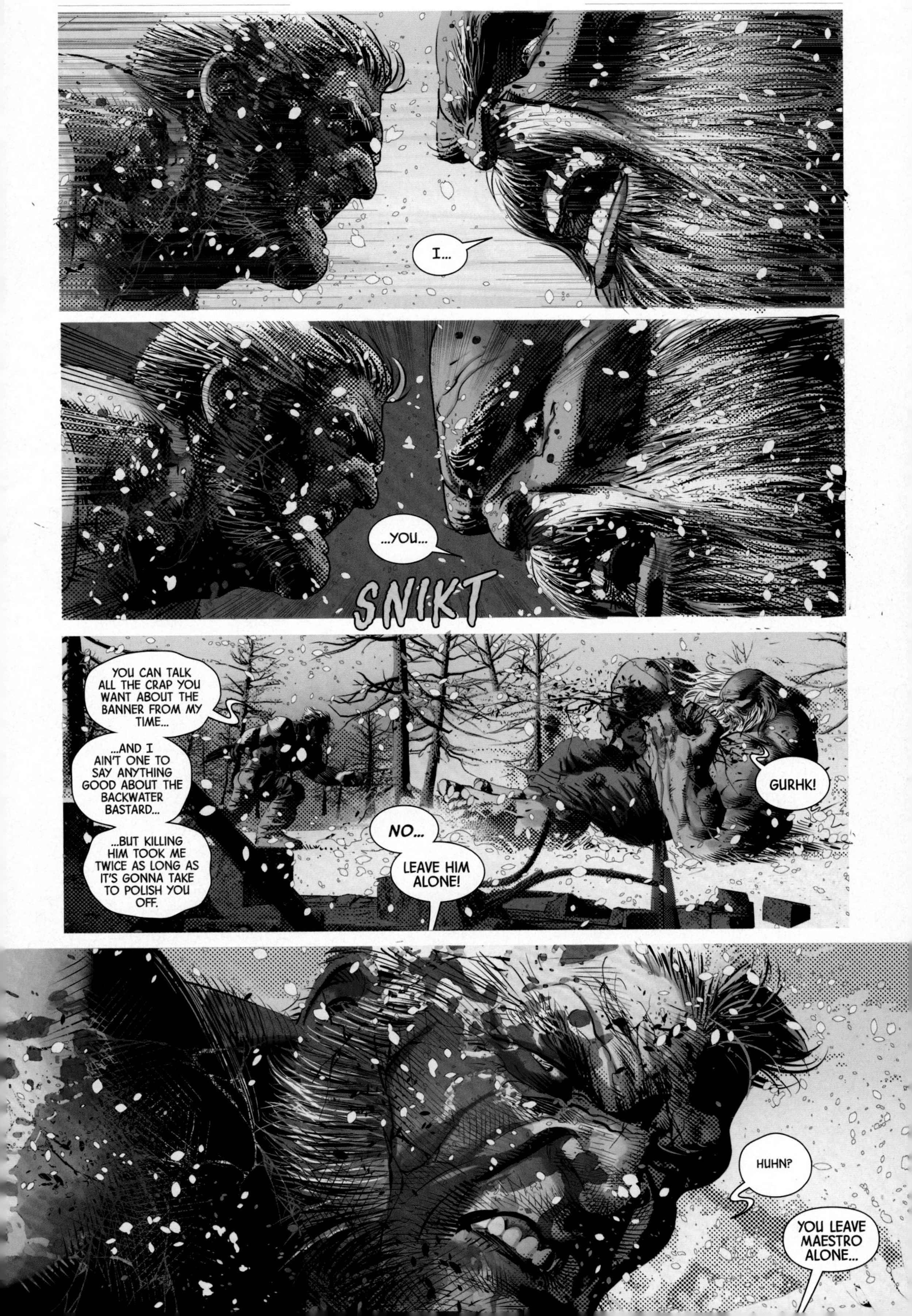
I...
...YOU...
SNIKT
YOU CAN TALK ALL THE CRAP YOU WANT ABOUT THE BANNER FROM MY TIME...
...AND I AIN'T ONE TO SAY ANYTHING GOOD ABOUT THE BACKWATER BASTARD...
...BUT KILLING HIM TOOK ME TWICE AS LONG AS IT'S GONNA TAKE TO POLISH YOU OFF.
GURHK!
NO...
LEAVE HIM ALONE!
HUHN?
YOU LEAVE MAESTRO ALONE...

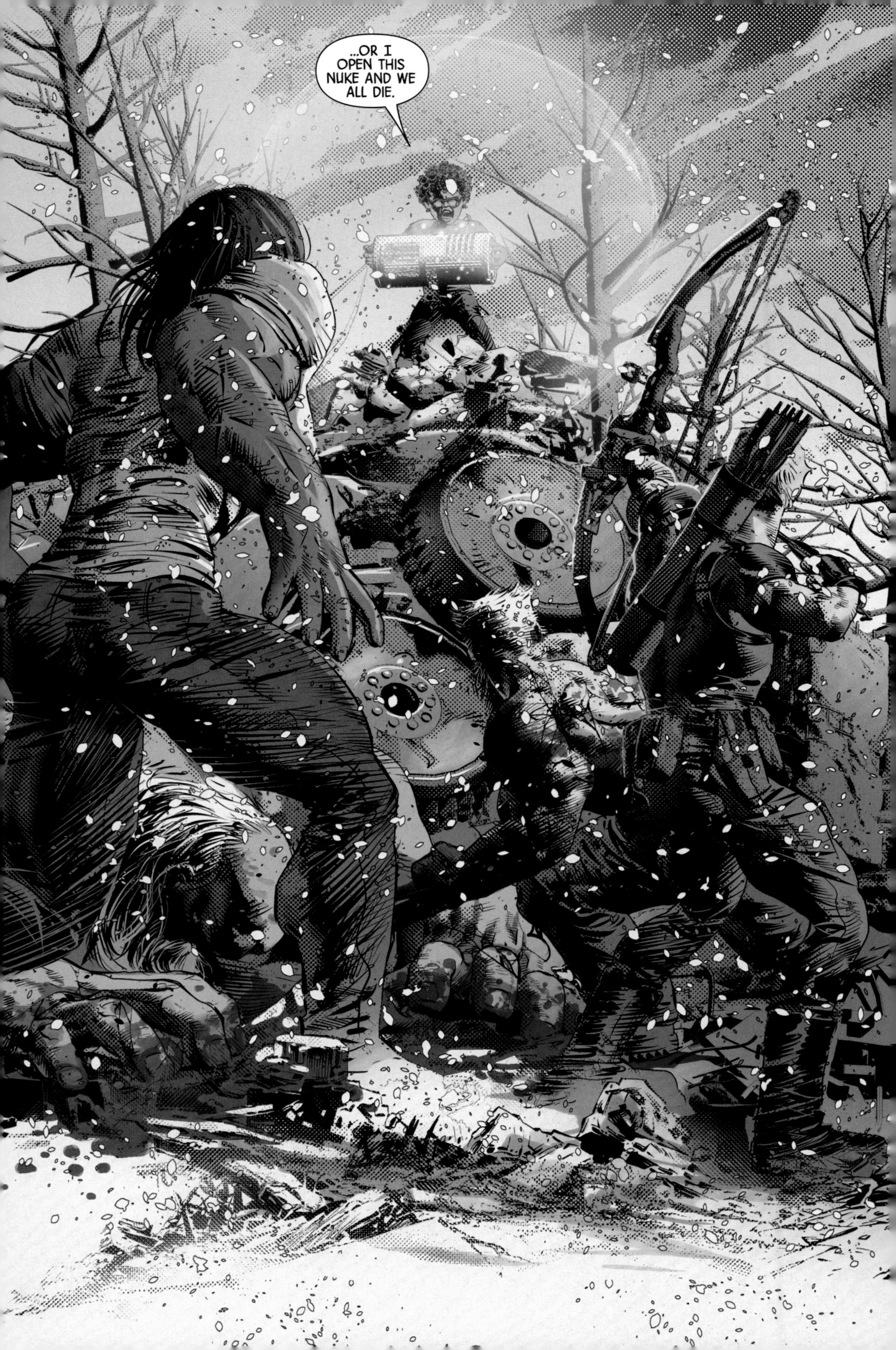
...OR I OPEN THIS NUKE AND WE ALL DIE.

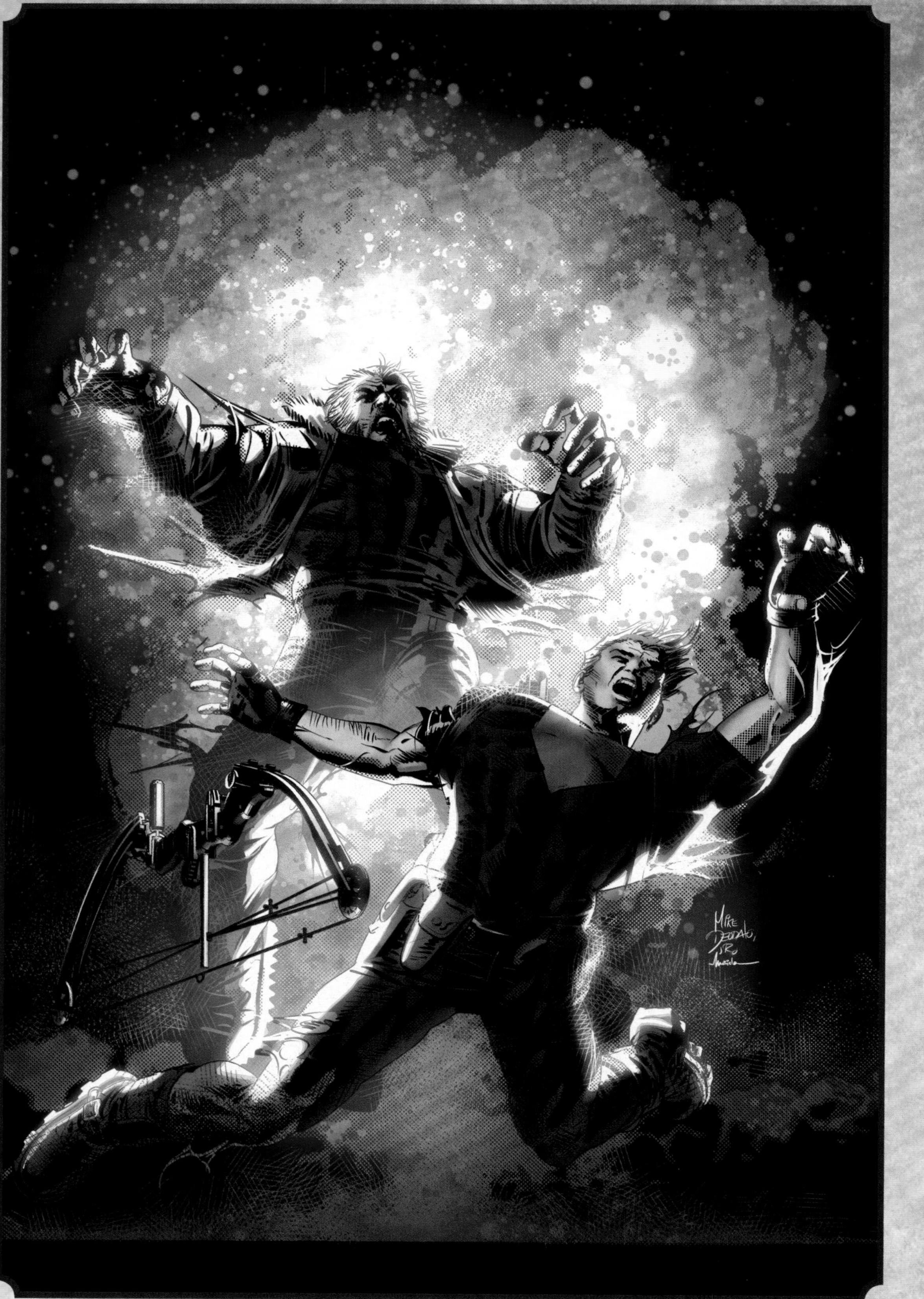

30

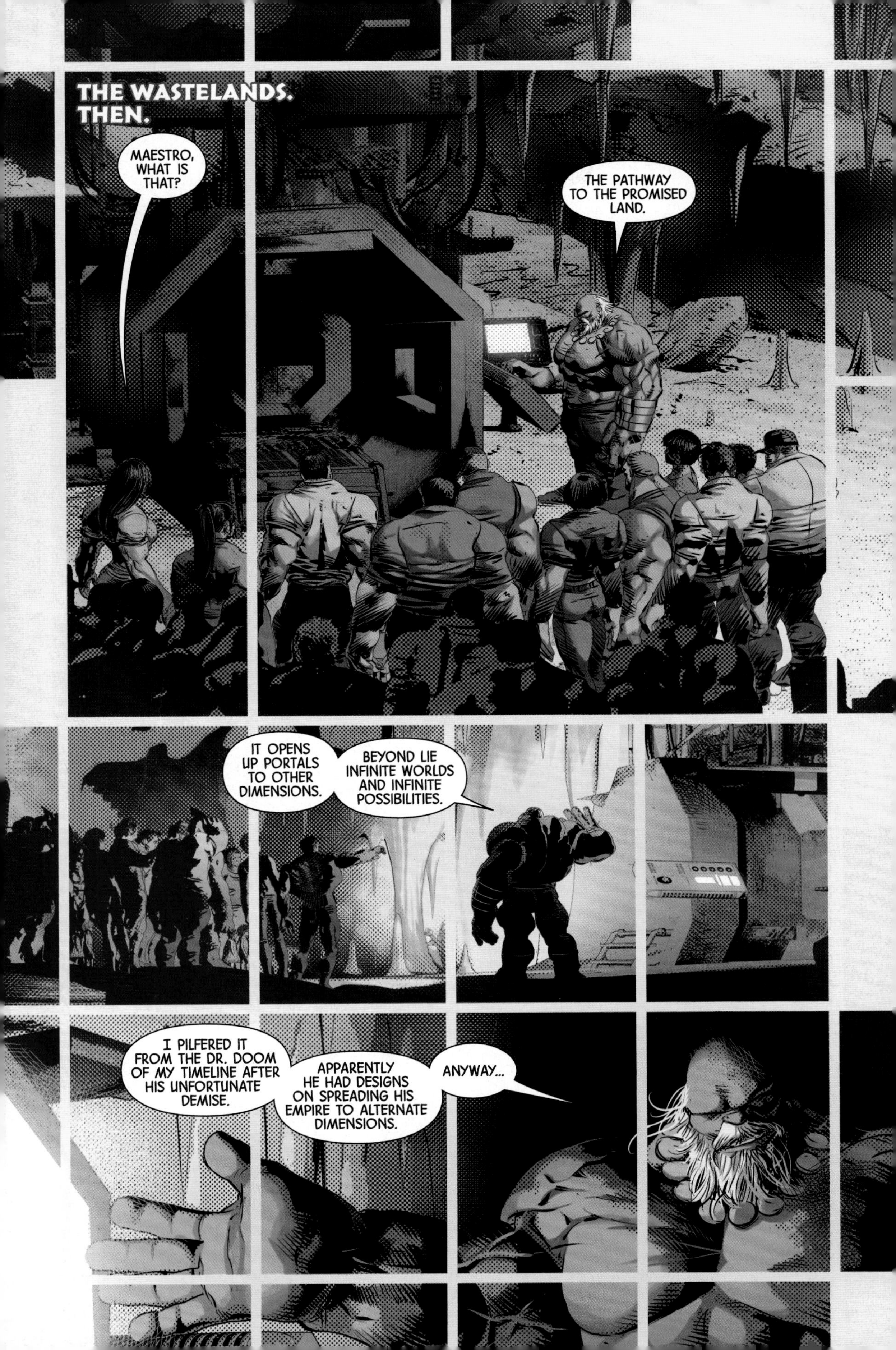
THE WASTELANDS. THEN.
MAESTRO, WHAT IS THAT?
THE PATHWAY TO THE PROMISED LAND.
IT OPENS UP PORTALS TO OTHER DIMENSIONS.
BEYOND LIE INFINITE WORLDS AND INFINITE POSSIBILITIES.
I PILFERED IT FROM THE DR. DOOM OF MY TIMELINE AFTER HIS UNFORTUNATE DEMISE.
APPARENTLY HE HAD DESIGNS ON SPREADING HIS EMPIRE TO ALTERNATE DIMENSIONS.
ANYWAY...

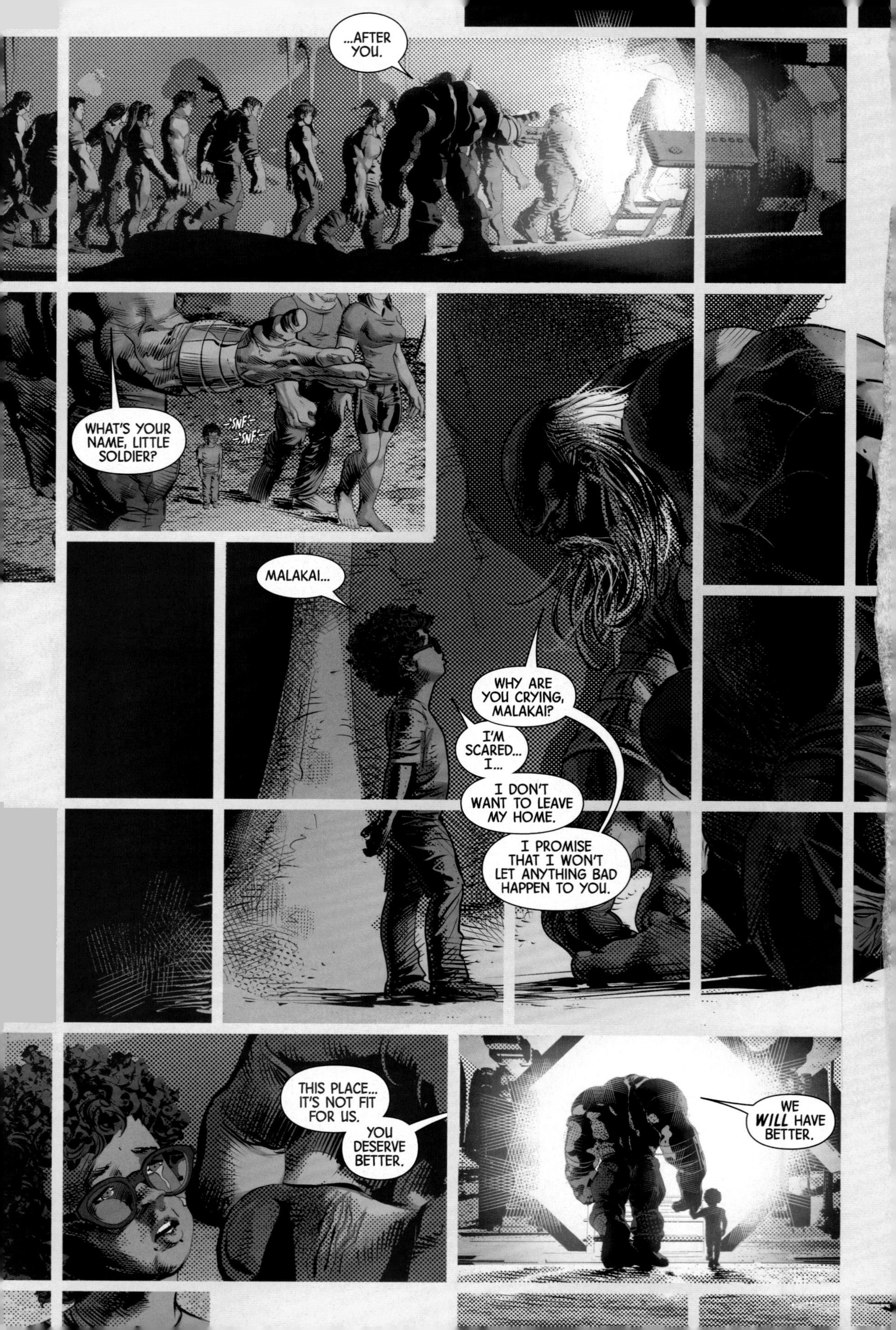

...AFTER YOU.
WHAT'S YOUR NAME, LITTLE SOLDIER?
SNF
SNF
MALAKAI...
WHY ARE YOU CRYING, MALAKAI?
I'M SCARED... I...
I DON'T WANT TO LEAVE MY HOME.
I PROMISE THAT I WON'T LET ANYTHING BAD HAPPEN TO YOU.
THIS PLACE... IT'S NOT FIT FOR US.
YOU DESERVE BETTER.
WE *WILL* HAVE BETTER.

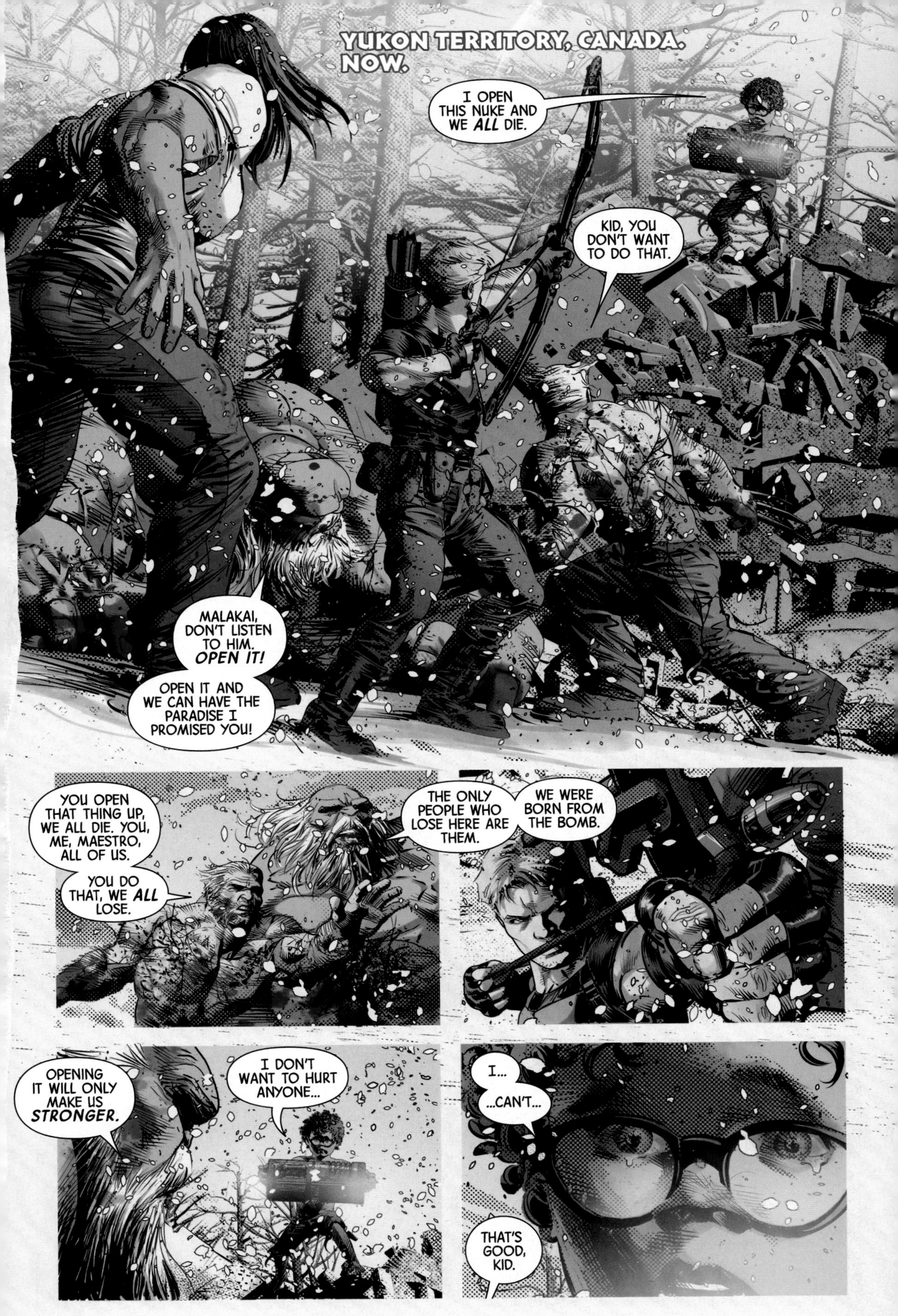
YUKON TERRITORY, CANADA. NOW.
I OPEN THIS NUKE AND WE *ALL* DIE.
KID, YOU DON'T WANT TO DO THAT.
MALAKAI, DON'T LISTEN TO HIM. *OPEN IT!*
OPEN IT AND WE CAN HAVE THE PARADISE I PROMISED YOU!
YOU OPEN THAT THING UP, WE ALL DIE. YOU, ME, MAESTRO, ALL OF US.
YOU DO THAT, WE *ALL* LOSE.
THE ONLY PEOPLE WHO LOSE HERE ARE THEM.
WE WERE BORN FROM THE BOMB.
OPENING IT WILL ONLY MAKE US *STRONGER.*
I DON'T WANT TO HURT ANYONE...
I...
...CAN'T...
THAT'S GOOD, KID.

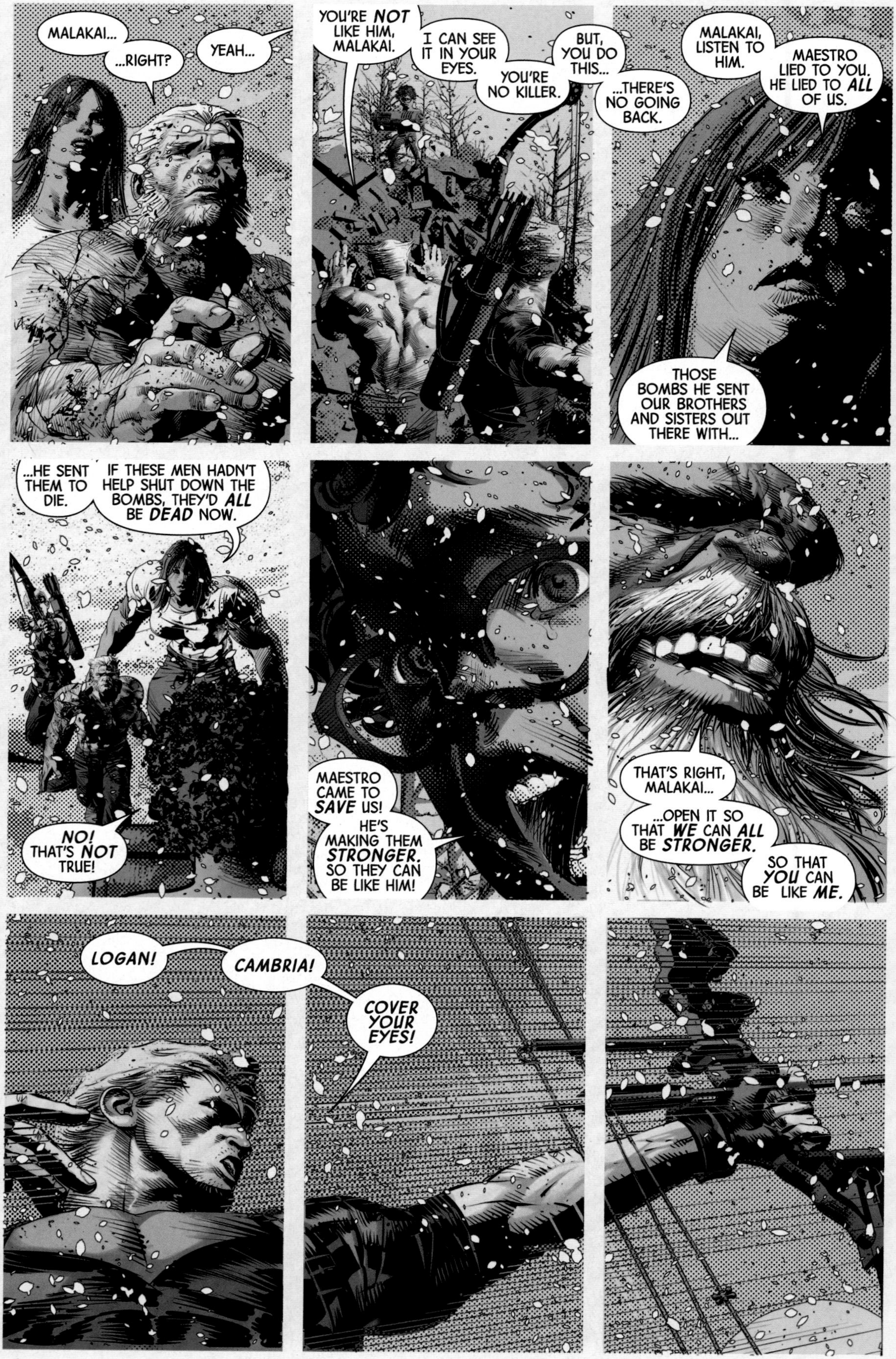
MALAKAI...
...RIGHT?
YEAH...
YOU'RE NOT LIKE HIM, MALAKAI.
I CAN SEE IT IN YOUR EYES.
YOU'RE NO KILLER.
BUT, YOU DO THIS...
...THERE'S NO GOING BACK.
MALAKAI, LISTEN TO HIM.
MAESTRO LIED TO YOU. HE LIED TO ALL OF US.
THOSE BOMBS HE SENT OUR BROTHERS AND SISTERS OUT THERE WITH...
...HE SENT THEM TO DIE.
IF THESE MEN HADN'T HELP SHUT DOWN THE BOMBS, THEY'D ALL BE DEAD NOW.
NO! THAT'S NOT TRUE!
MAESTRO CAME TO SAVE US!
HE'S MAKING THEM STRONGER, SO THEY CAN BE LIKE HIM!
THAT'S RIGHT, MALAKAI...
...OPEN IT SO THAT WE CAN ALL BE STRONGER.
SO THAT YOU CAN BE LIKE ME.
LOGAN!
CAMBRIA!
COVER YOUR EYES!

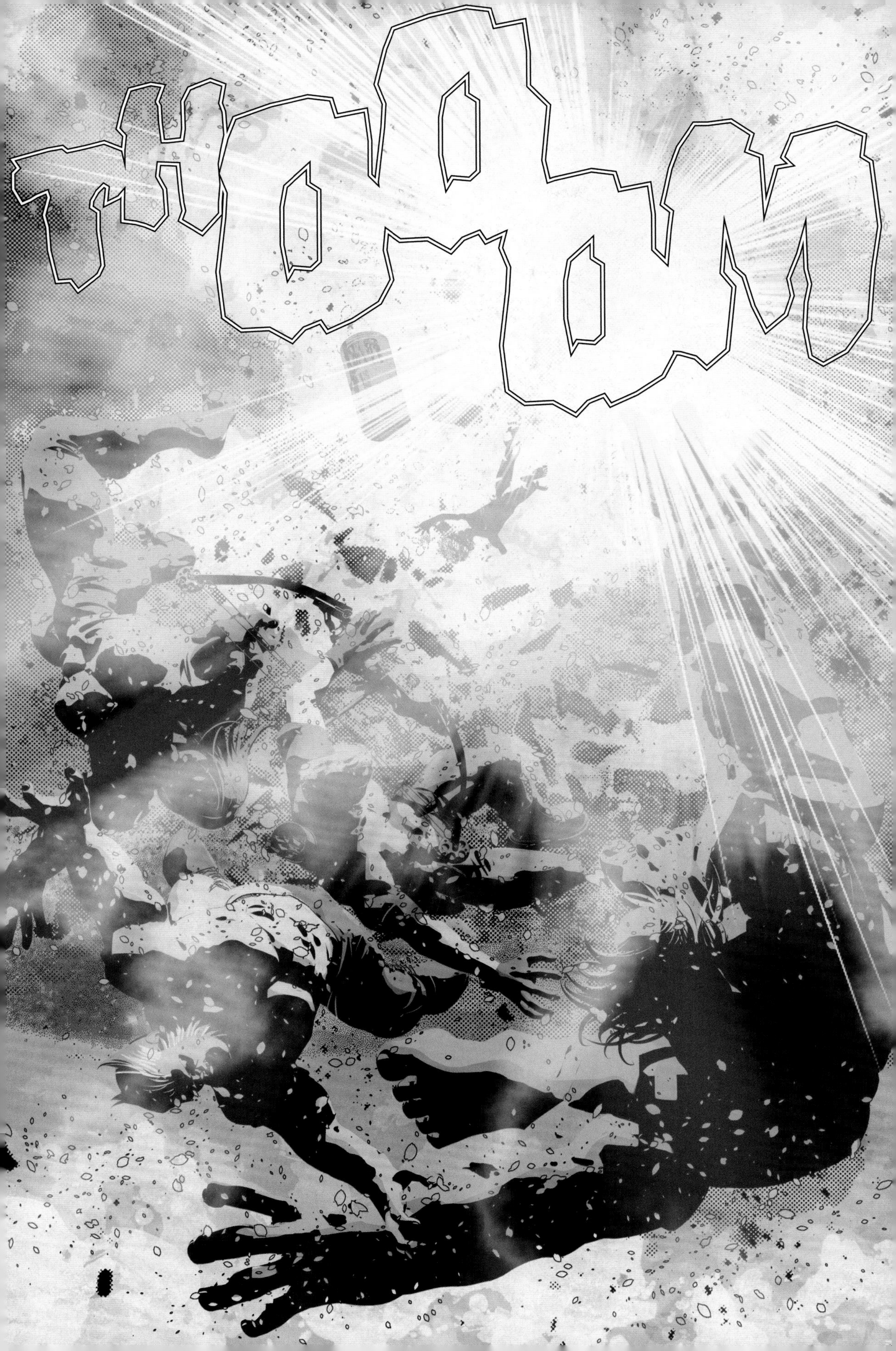
THOOOOM

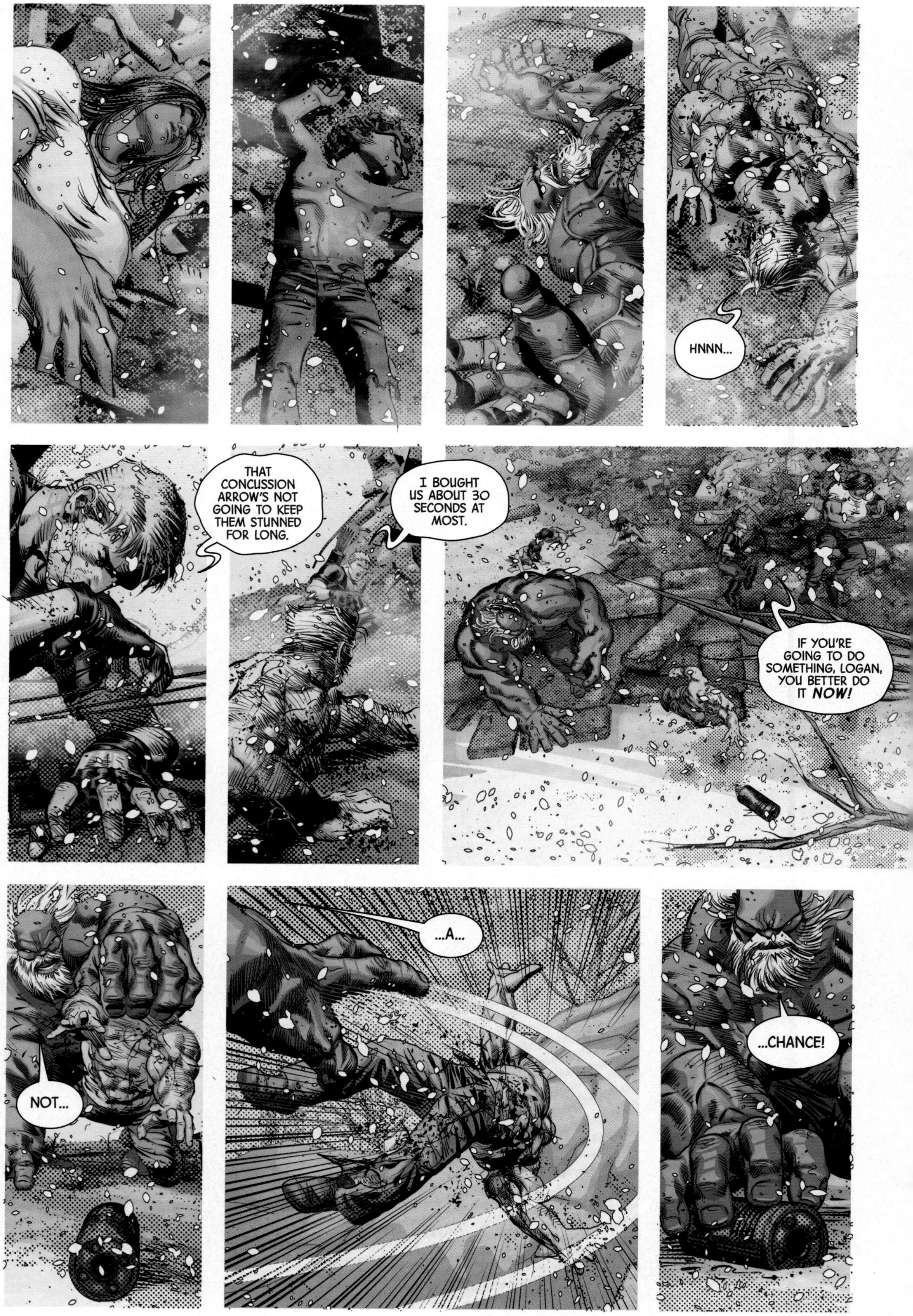
HNNN...
THAT CONCUSSION ARROW'S NOT GOING TO KEEP THEM STUNNED FOR LONG.
I BOUGHT US ABOUT 30 SECONDS AT MOST.
IF YOU'RE GOING TO DO SOMETHING, LOGAN, YOU BETTER DO IT *NOW!*
NOT...
...A...
...CHANCE!

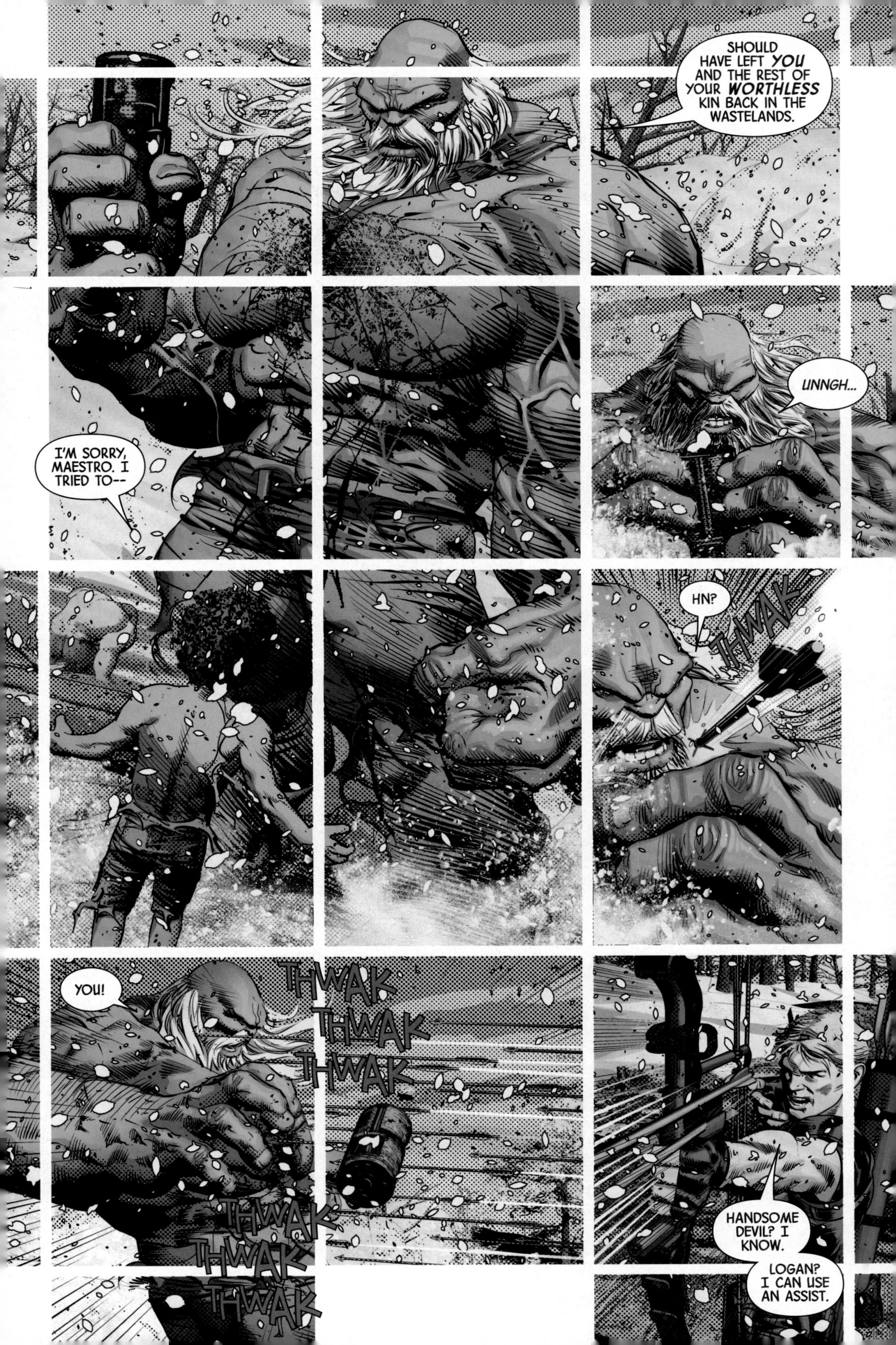
SHOULD HAVE LEFT YOU AND THE REST OF YOUR WORTHLESS KIN BACK IN THE WASTELANDS.
I'M SORRY, MAESTRO. I TRIED TO--
UNNGH...
HN?
THWAK
YOU!
THWAK
THWAK
THWAK
THWAK
THWAK
THWAK
HANDSOME DEVIL? I KNOW.
LOGAN? I CAN USE AN ASSIST.

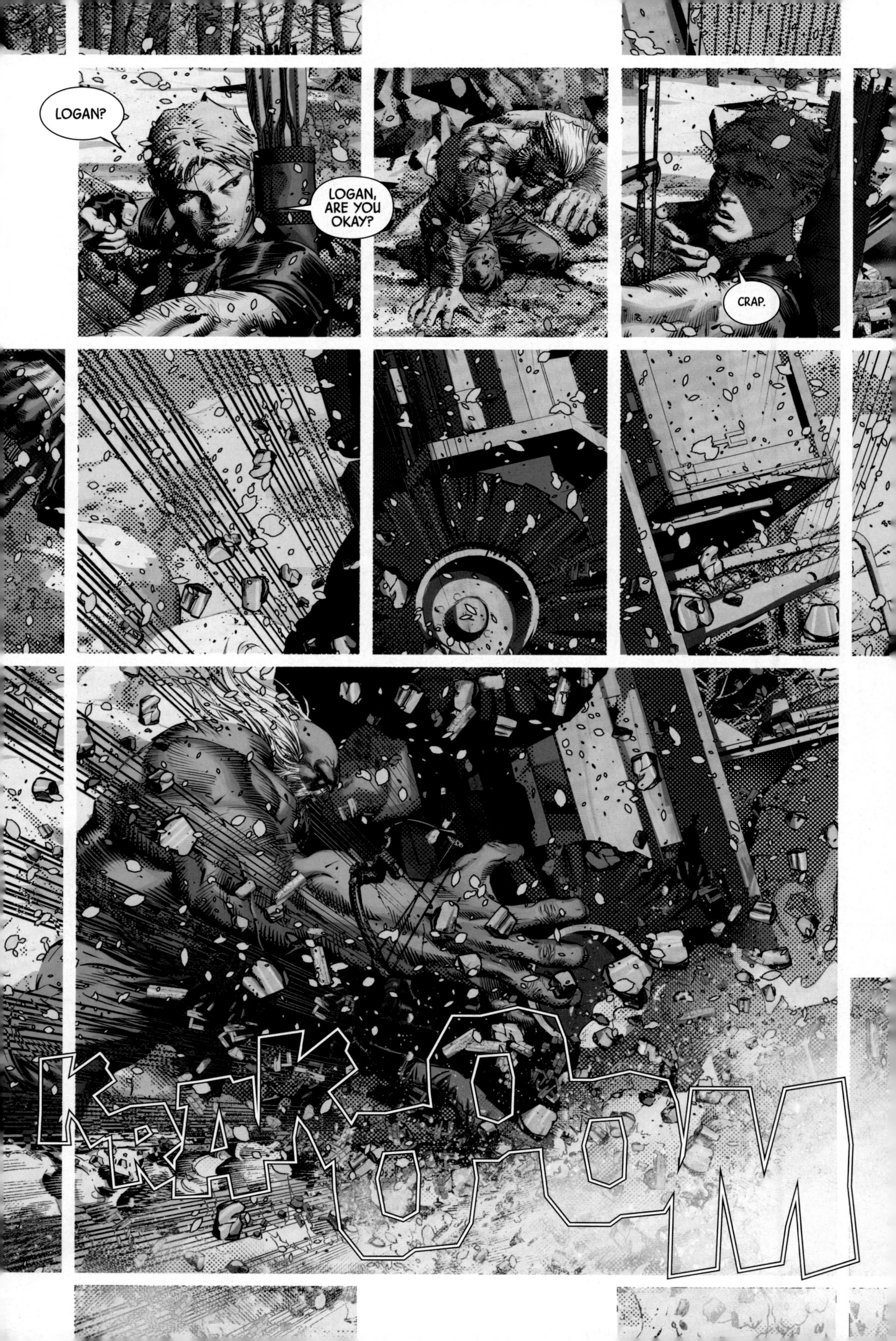
LOGAN?
LOGAN, ARE YOU OKAY?
CRAP.
KRAKOOOM

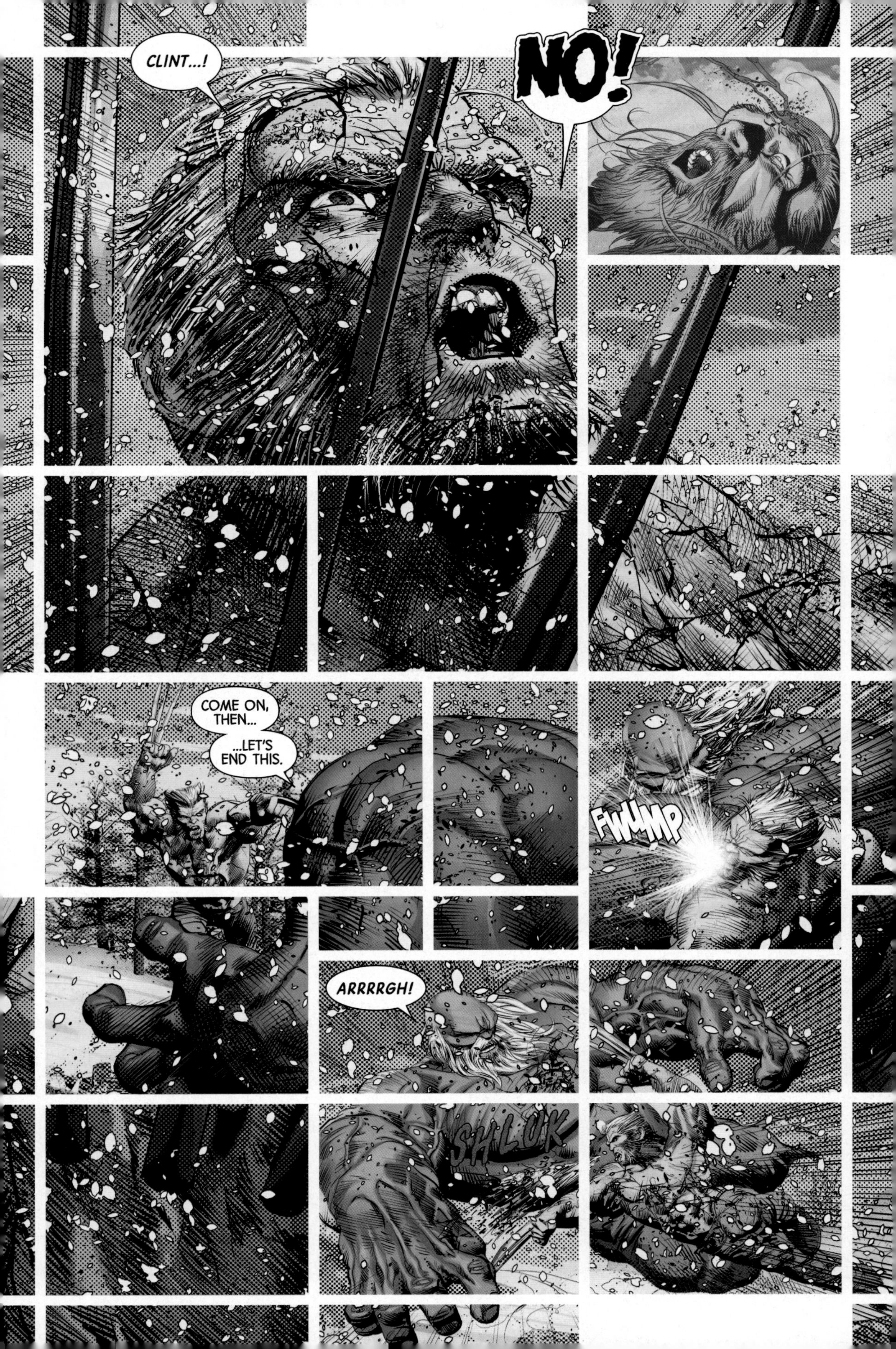
CLINT...!
NO!
COME ON, THEN...
...LET'S END THIS.
FWUMP
ARRRRGH!
SHLUK

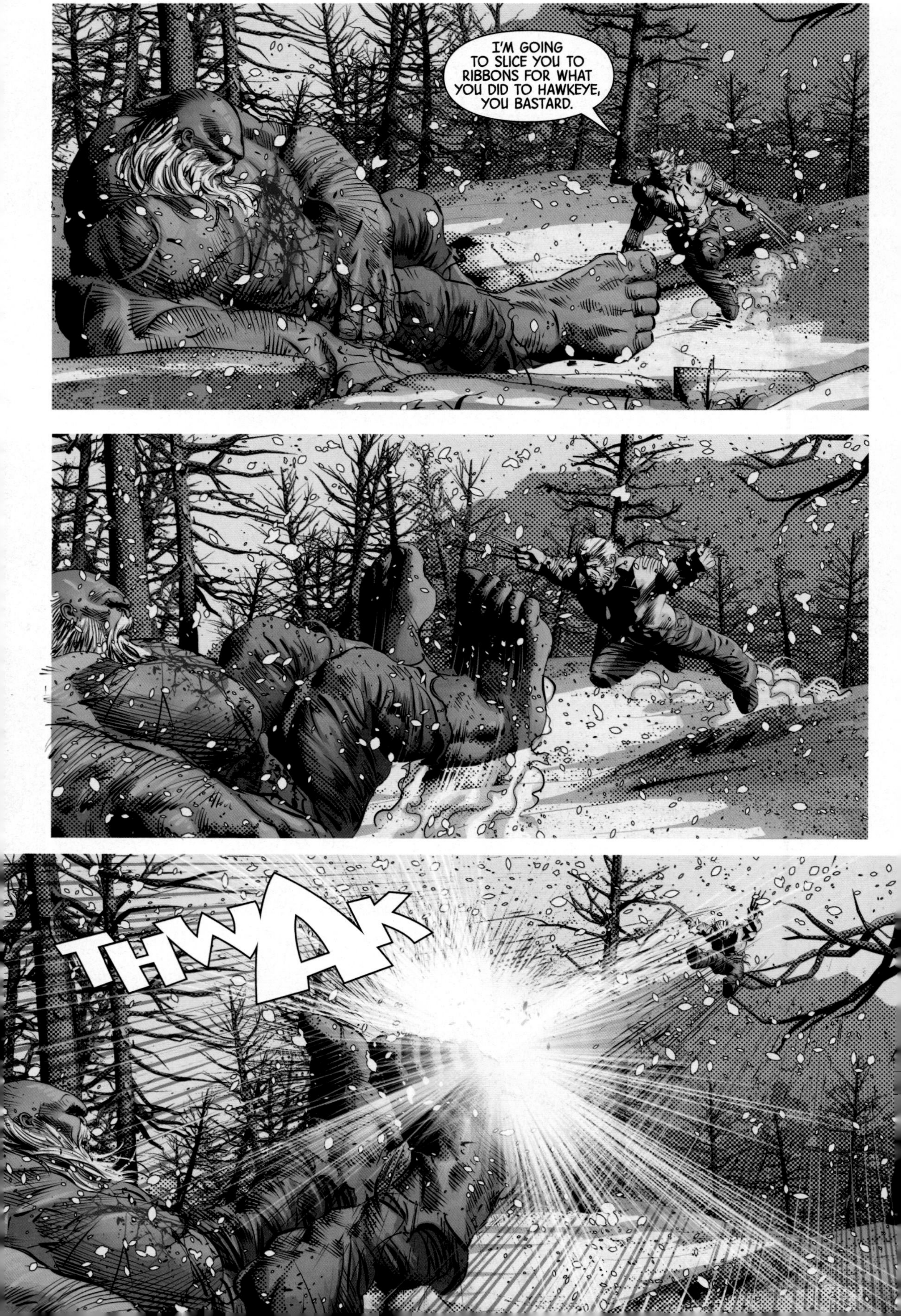
I'M GOING TO SLICE YOU TO RIBBONS FOR WHAT YOU DID TO HAWKEYE, YOU BASTARD.
THWAK

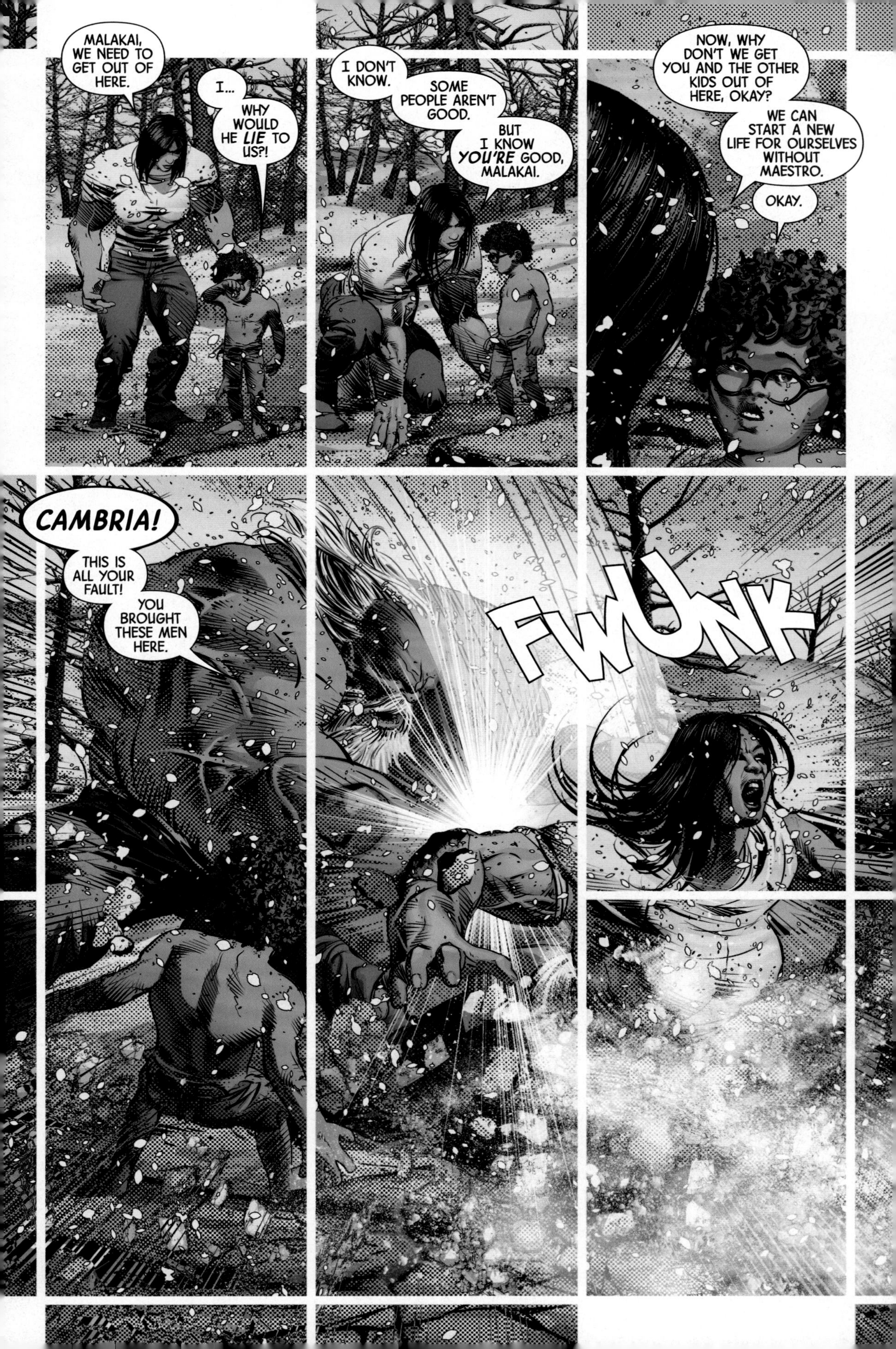

MALAKAI, WE NEED TO GET OUT OF HERE.
I...
WHY WOULD HE LIE TO US?!
I DON'T KNOW.
SOME PEOPLE AREN'T GOOD.
BUT I KNOW YOU'RE GOOD, MALAKAI.
NOW, WHY DON'T WE GET YOU AND THE OTHER KIDS OUT OF HERE, OKAY?
WE CAN START A NEW LIFE FOR OURSELVES WITHOUT MAESTRO.
OKAY.
CAMBRIA!
THIS IS ALL YOUR FAULT!
YOU BROUGHT THESE MEN HERE.
FWUNK

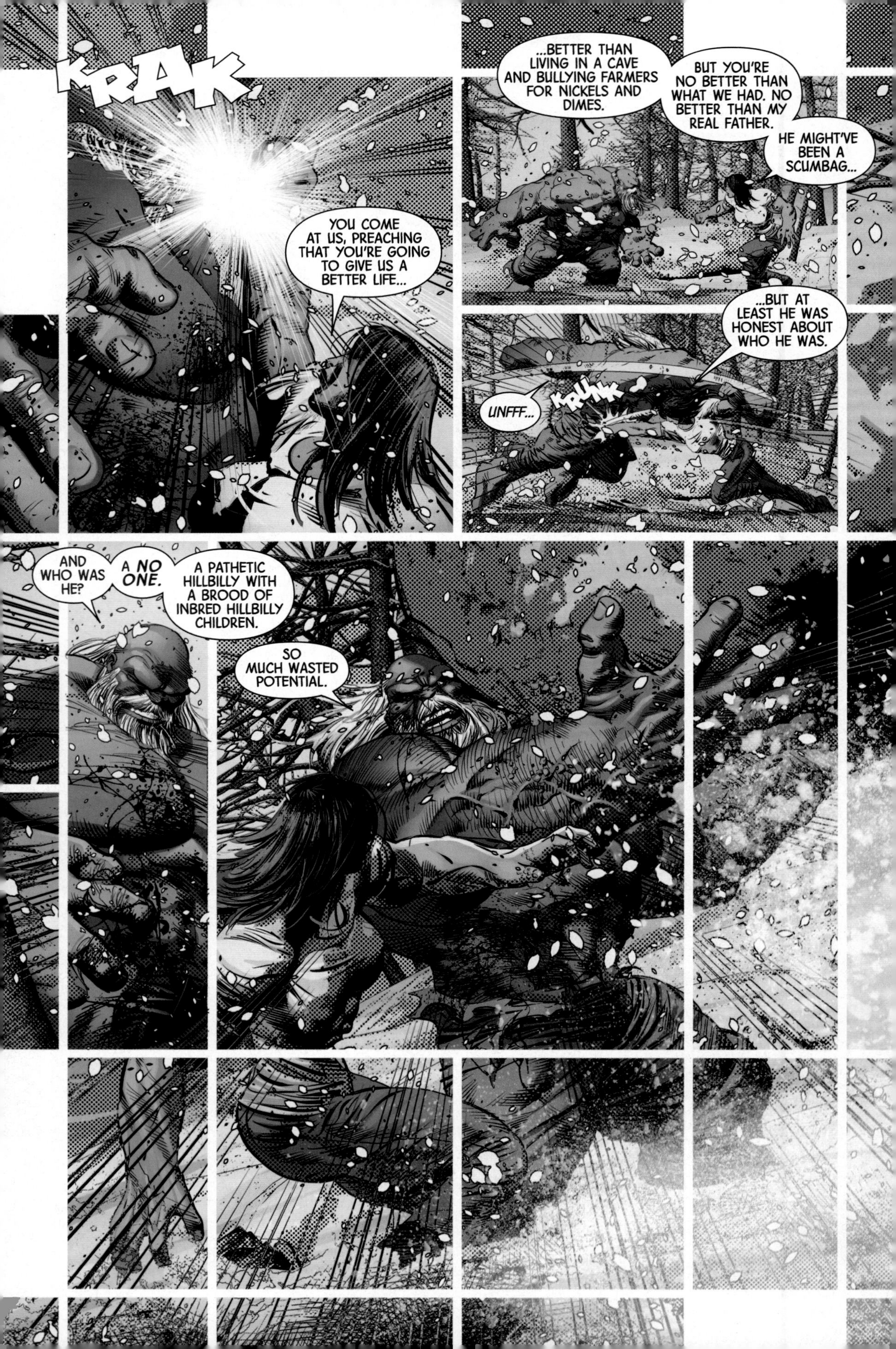
KRAK
YOU COME AT US, PREACHING THAT YOU'RE GOING TO GIVE US A BETTER LIFE...
...BETTER THAN LIVING IN A CAVE AND BULLYING FARMERS FOR NICKELS AND DIMES.
BUT YOU'RE NO BETTER THAN WHAT WE HAD. NO BETTER THAN MY REAL FATHER.
HE MIGHT'VE BEEN A SCUMBAG...
...BUT AT LEAST HE WAS HONEST ABOUT WHO HE WAS.
UNFFF...
KRUNK
AND WHO WAS HE?
A NO ONE.
A PATHETIC HILLBILLY WITH A BROOD OF INBRED HILLBILLY CHILDREN.
SO MUCH WASTED POTENTIAL.

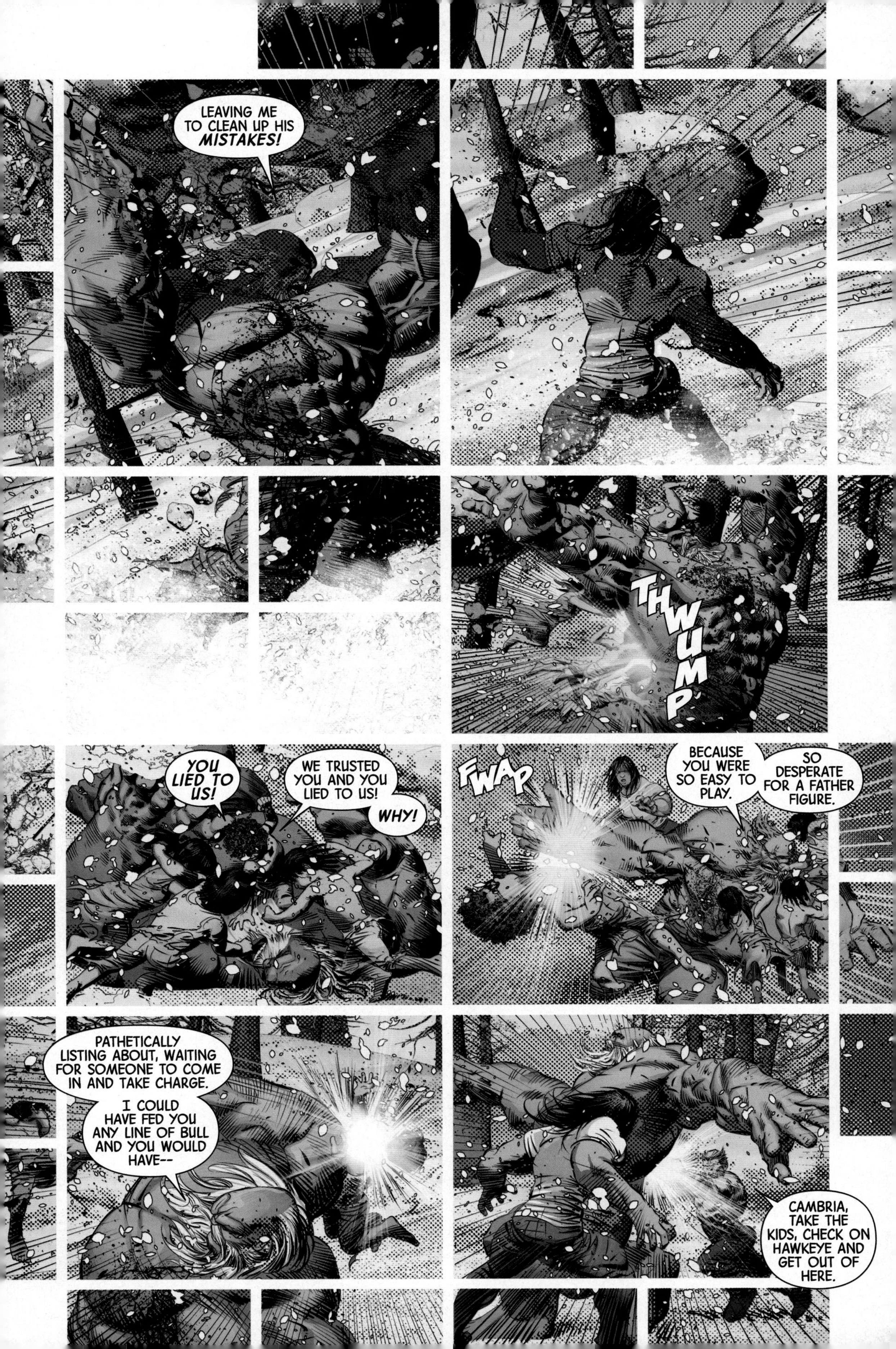
LEAVING ME TO CLEAN UP HIS MISTAKES!
THWUMP
YOU LIED TO US!
WE TRUSTED YOU AND YOU LIED TO US!
WHY!
FWAP
BECAUSE YOU WERE SO EASY TO PLAY.
SO DESPERATE FOR A FATHER FIGURE.
PATHETICALLY LISTING ABOUT, WAITING FOR SOMEONE TO COME IN AND TAKE CHARGE.
I COULD HAVE FED YOU ANY LINE OF BULL AND YOU WOULD HAVE--
CAMBRIA, TAKE THE KIDS, CHECK ON HAWKEYE AND GET OUT OF HERE.

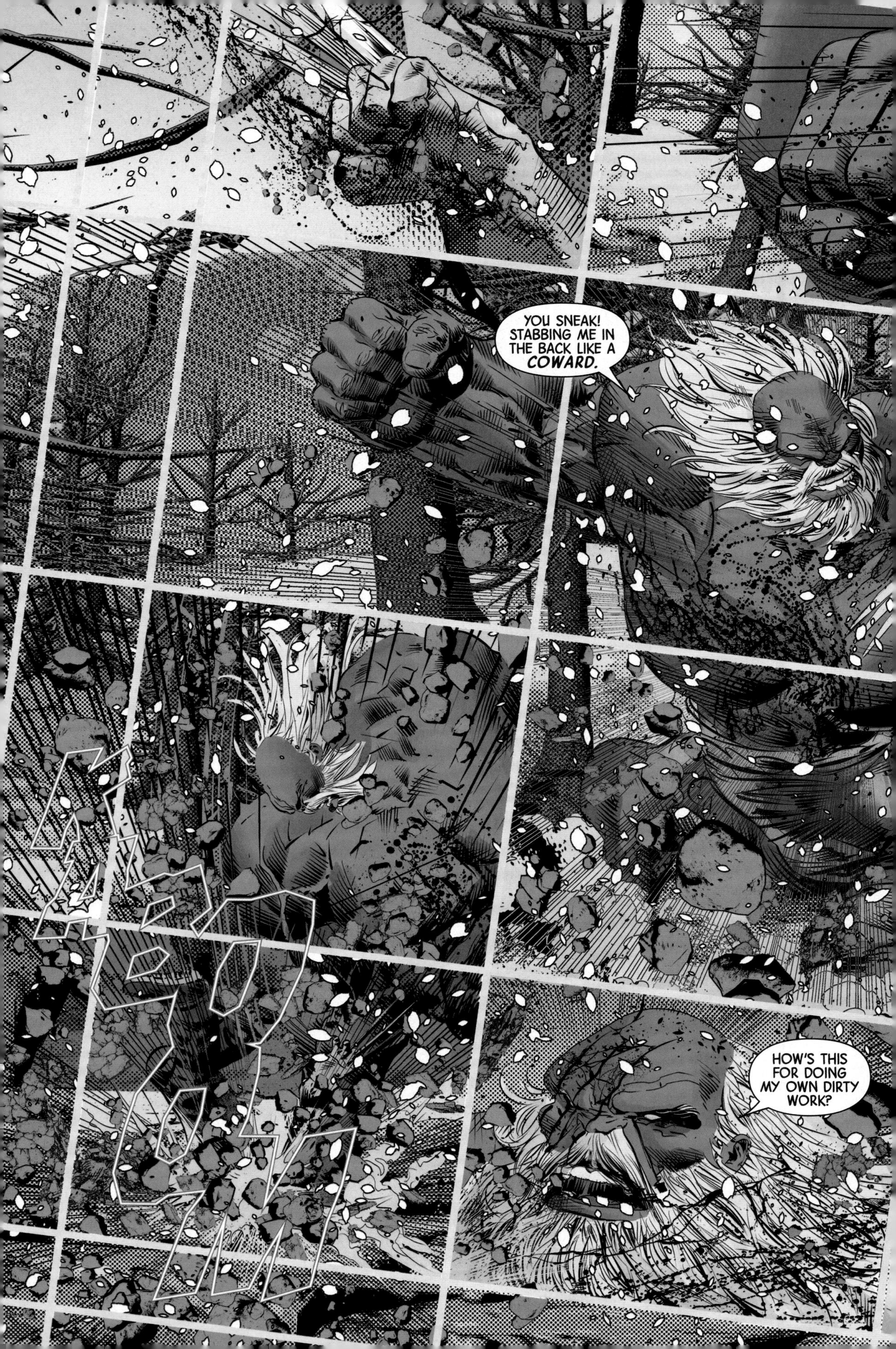
YOU SNEAK! STABBING ME IN THE BACK LIKE A COWARD.
KRAKOOM
HOW'S THIS FOR DOING MY OWN DIRTY WORK?

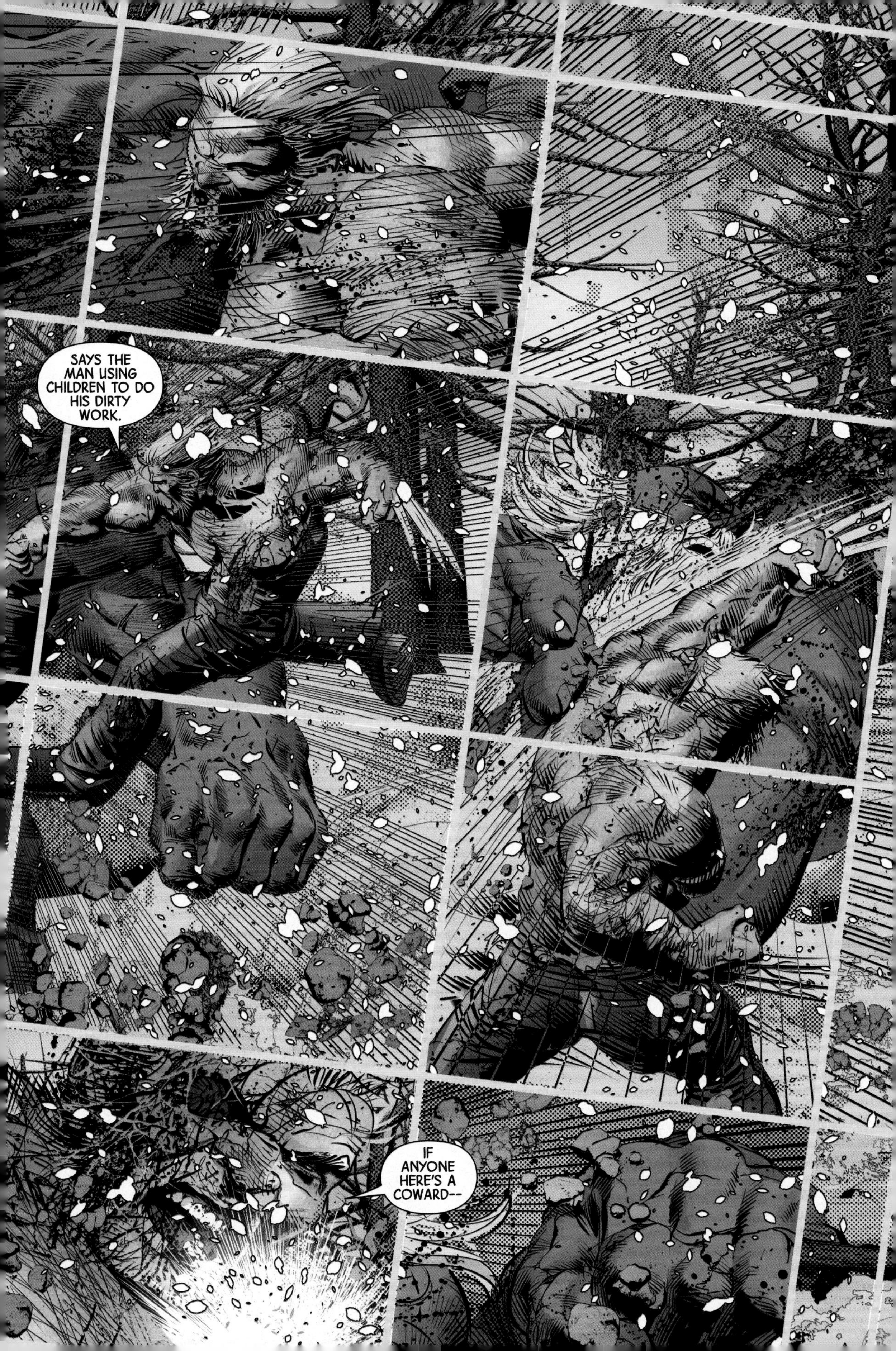
SAYS THE MAN USING CHILDREN TO DO HIS DIRTY WORK.
IF ANYONE HERE'S A COWARD--

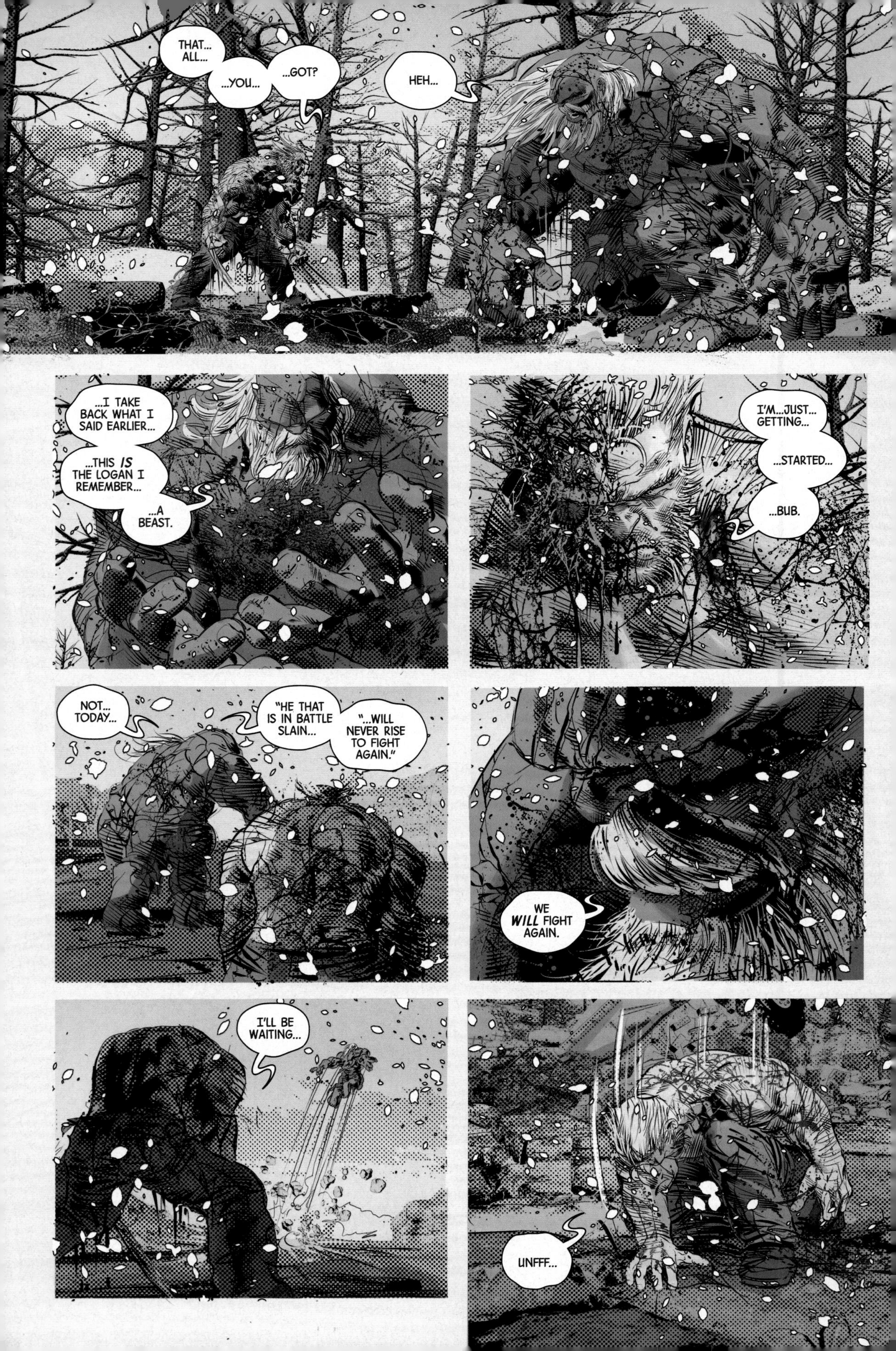
THAT... ALL...
...YOU...
...GOT?
HEH...
...I TAKE BACK WHAT I SAID EARLIER...
...THIS IS THE LOGAN I REMEMBER...
...A BEAST.
I'M...JUST... GETTING...
...STARTED...
...BUB.
NOT... TODAY...
"HE THAT IS IN BATTLE SLAIN...
"...WILL NEVER RISE TO FIGHT AGAIN."
WE WILL FIGHT AGAIN.
I'LL BE WAITING...
UNFFF...

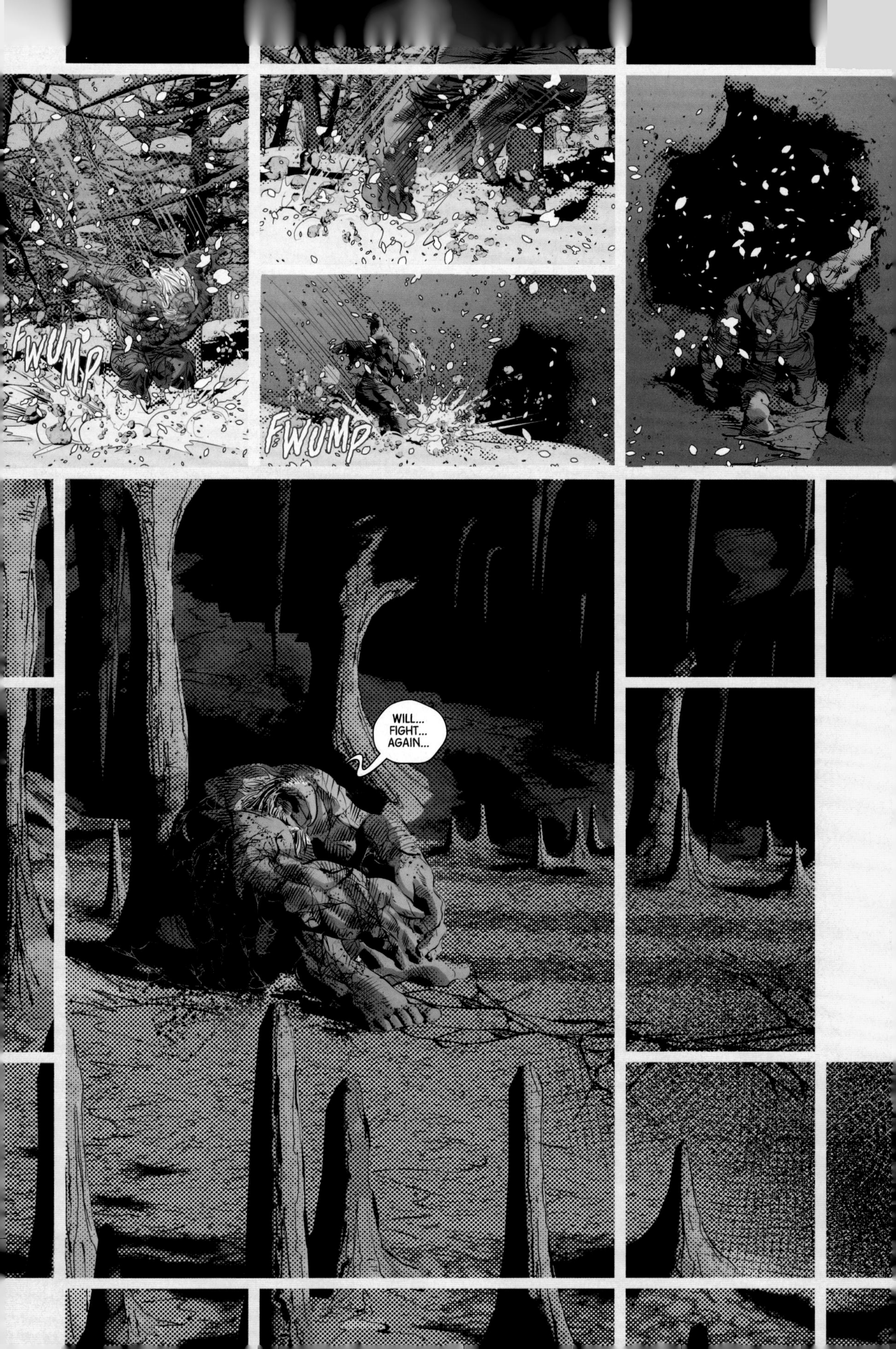
FWUMP
FWUMP
WILL... FIGHT... AGAIN...

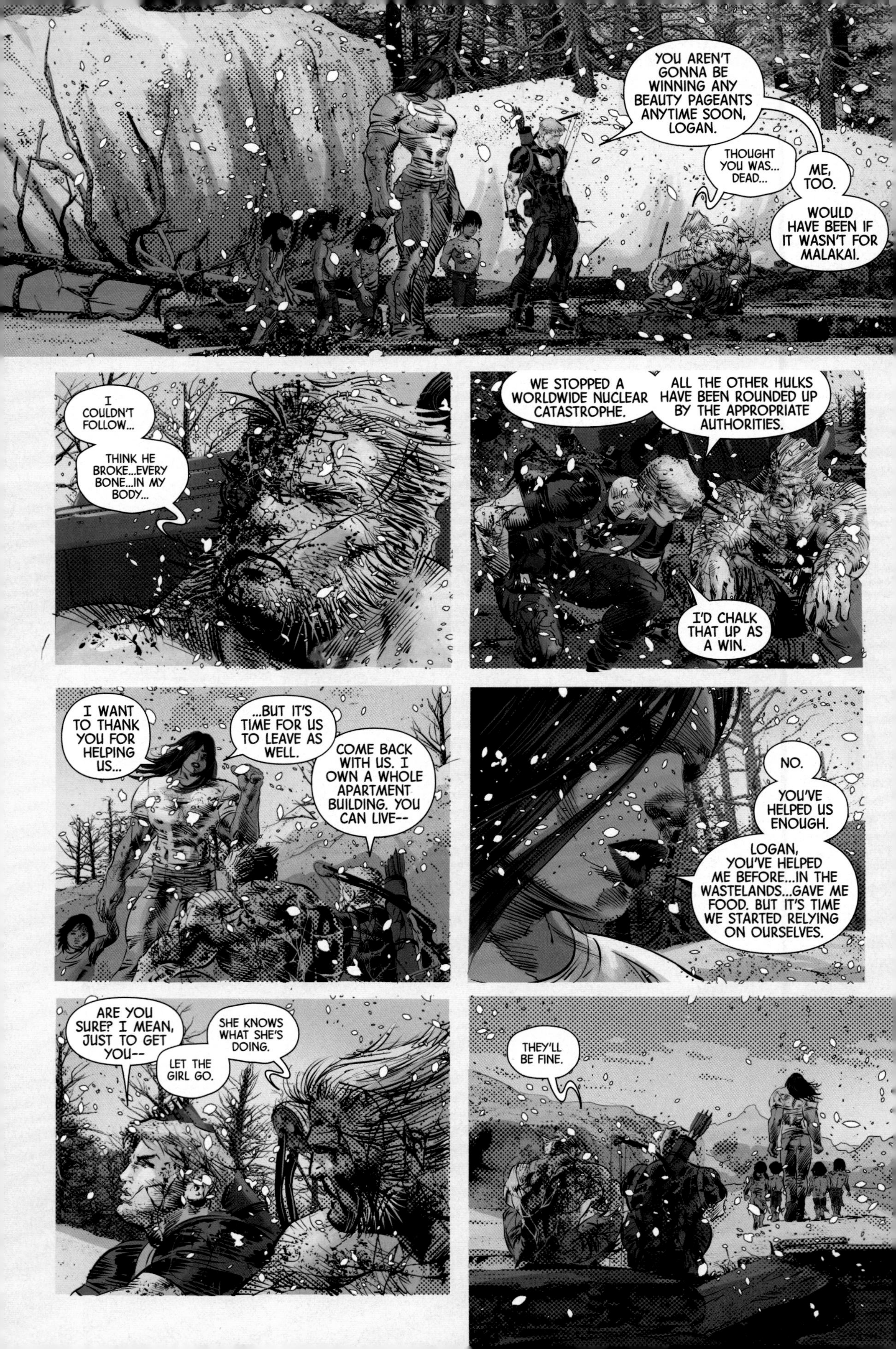
YOU AREN'T GONNA BE WINNING ANY BEAUTY PAGEANTS ANYTIME SOON, LOGAN.
THOUGHT YOU WAS... DEAD...
ME, TOO.
WOULD HAVE BEEN IF IT WASN'T FOR MALAKAI.
I COULDN'T FOLLOW...
THINK HE BROKE...EVERY BONE...IN MY BODY...
WE STOPPED A WORLDWIDE NUCLEAR CATASTROPHE.
ALL THE OTHER HULKS HAVE BEEN ROUNDED UP BY THE APPROPRIATE AUTHORITIES.
I'D CHALK THAT UP AS A WIN.
I WANT TO THANK YOU FOR HELPING US...
...BUT IT'S TIME FOR US TO LEAVE AS WELL.
COME BACK WITH US. I OWN A WHOLE APARTMENT BUILDING. YOU CAN LIVE--
NO.
YOU'VE HELPED US ENOUGH.
LOGAN, YOU'VE HELPED ME BEFORE...IN THE WASTELANDS...GAVE ME FOOD. BUT IT'S TIME WE STARTED RELYING ON OURSELVES.
ARE YOU SURE? I MEAN, JUST TO GET YOU--
LET THE GIRL GO.
SHE KNOWS WHAT SHE'S DOING.
THEY'LL BE FINE.

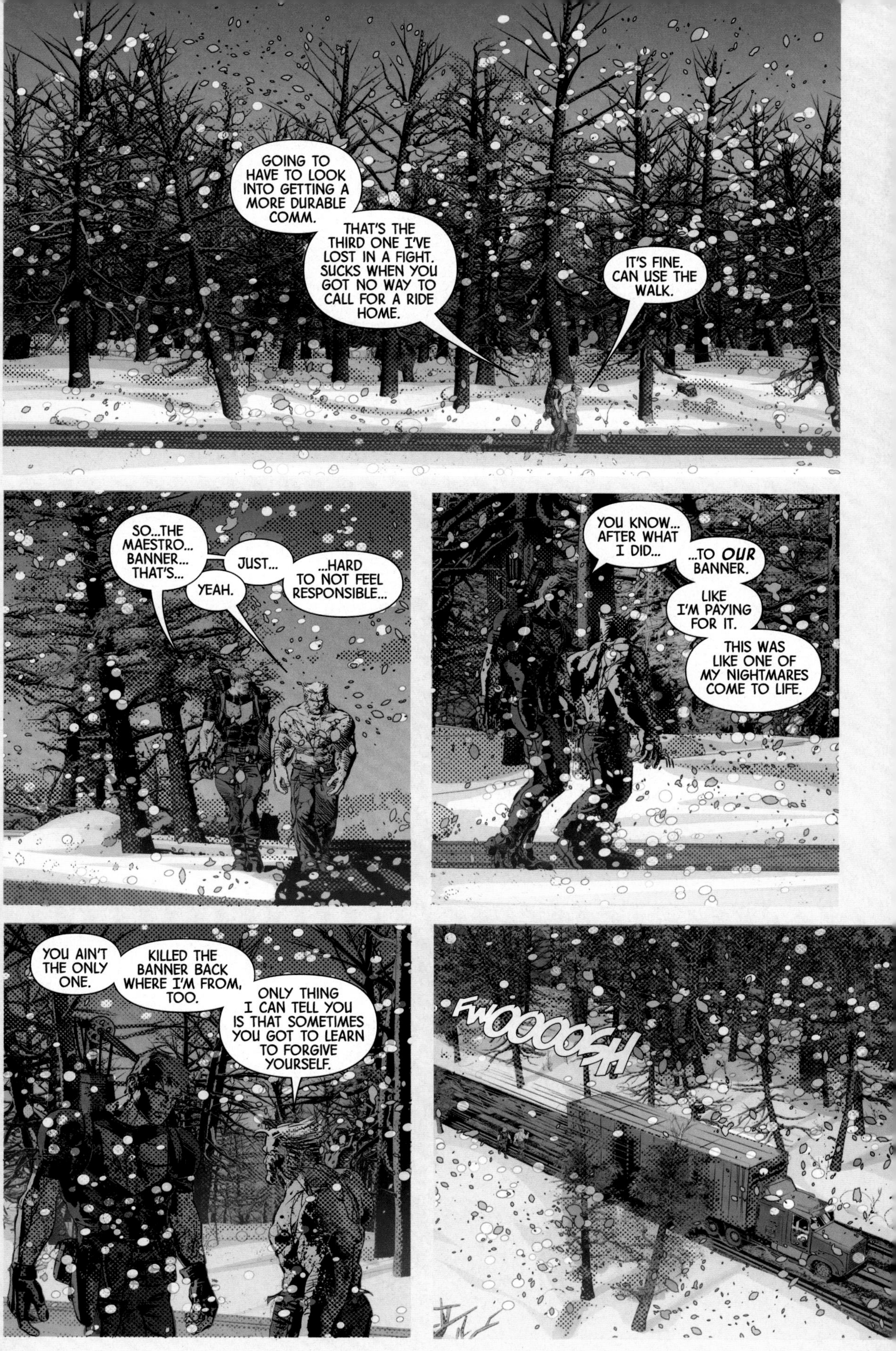
GOING TO HAVE TO LOOK INTO GETTING A MORE DURABLE COMM.
THAT'S THE THIRD ONE I'VE LOST IN A FIGHT. SUCKS WHEN YOU GOT NO WAY TO CALL FOR A RIDE HOME.
IT'S FINE. CAN USE THE WALK.
SO...THE MAESTRO... BANNER... THAT'S...
YEAH.
JUST...
...HARD TO NOT FEEL RESPONSIBLE...
YOU KNOW... AFTER WHAT I DID...
...TO OUR BANNER.
LIKE I'M PAYING FOR IT.
THIS WAS LIKE ONE OF MY NIGHTMARES COME TO LIFE.
YOU AIN'T THE ONLY ONE.
KILLED THE BANNER BACK WHERE I'M FROM, TOO.
ONLY THING I CAN TELL YOU IS THAT SOMETIMES YOU GOT TO LEARN TO FORGIVE YOURSELF.
FWOOOOOSH

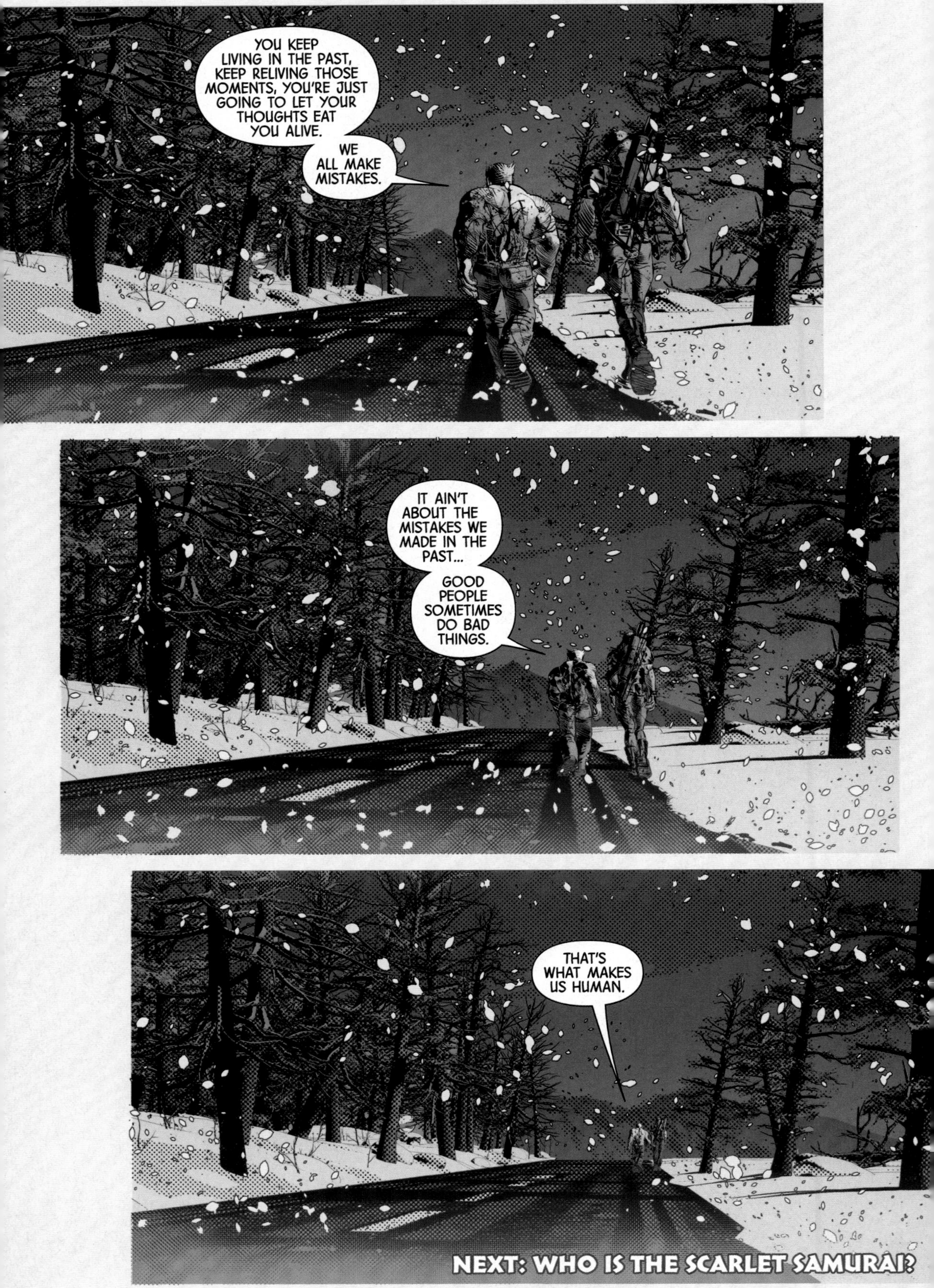
YOU KEEP LIVING IN THE PAST, KEEP RELIVING THOSE MOMENTS, YOU'RE JUST GOING TO LET YOUR THOUGHTS EAT YOU ALIVE.
WE ALL MAKE MISTAKES.
IT AIN'T ABOUT THE MISTAKES WE MADE IN THE PAST...
GOOD PEOPLE SOMETIMES DO BAD THINGS.
THAT'S WHAT MAKES US HUMAN.
NEXT: WHO IS THE SCARLET SAMURAI?

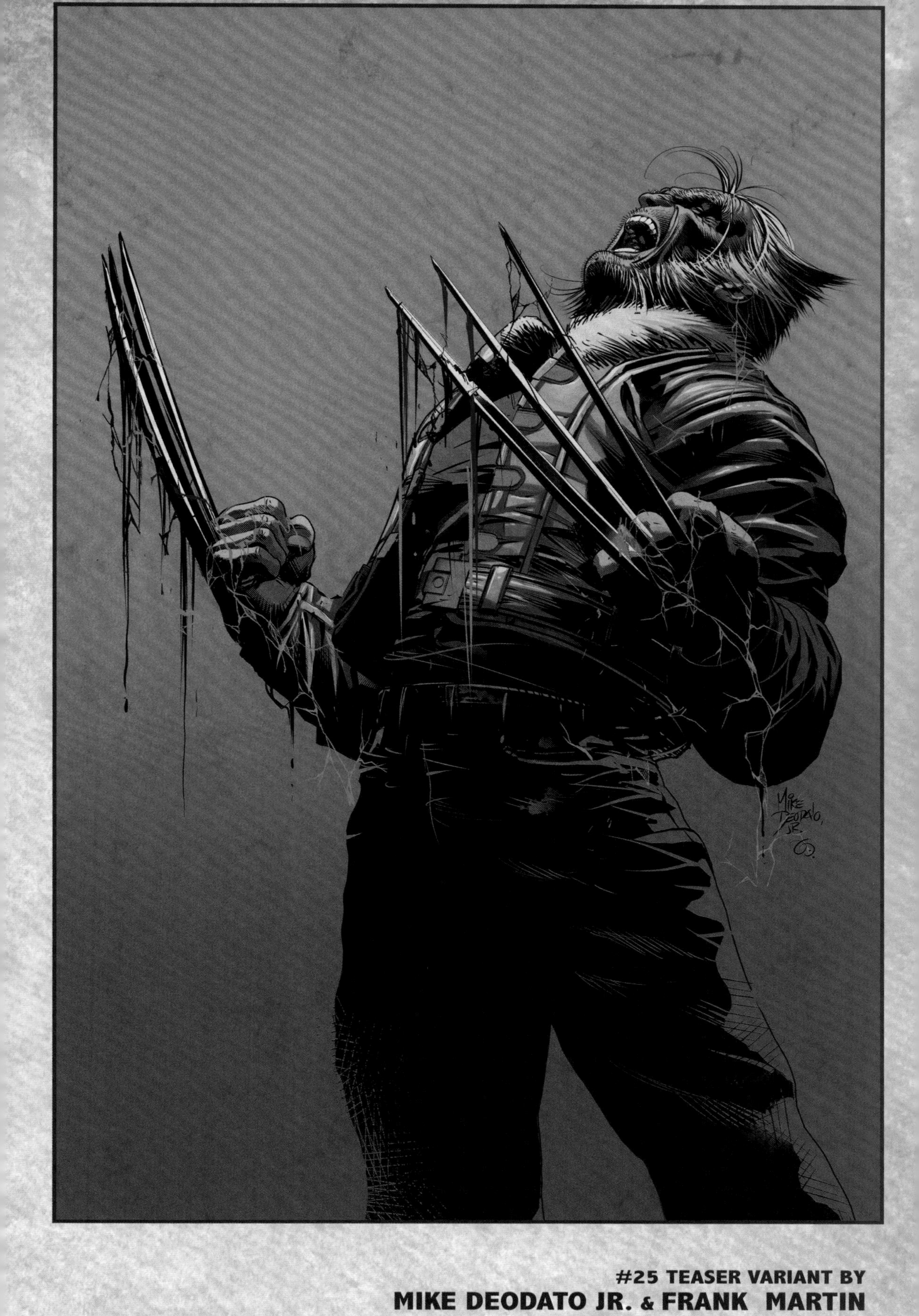

#25 TEASER VARIANT BY
**MIKE DEODATO JR. & FRANK MARTIN**

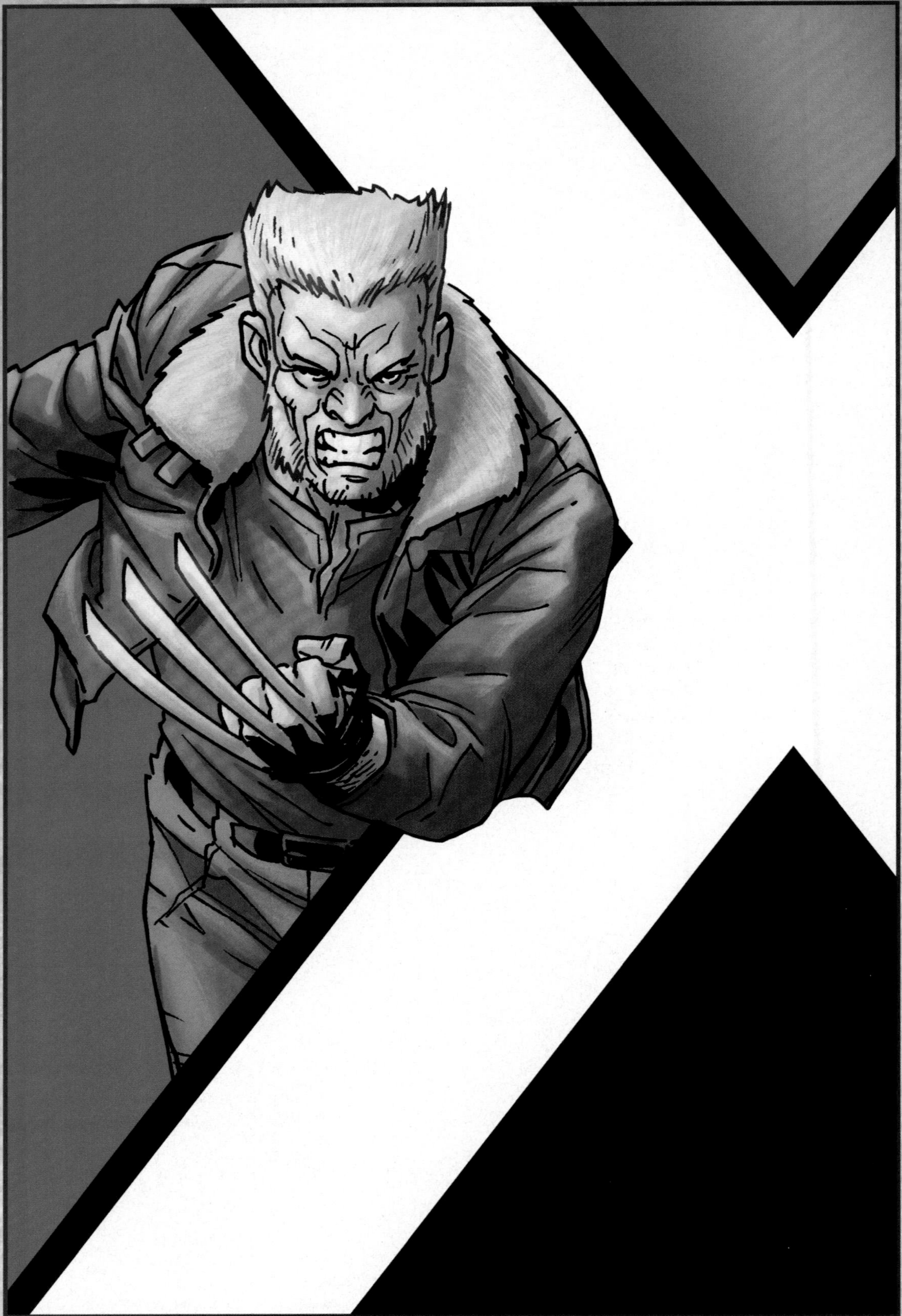

#25 CORNER BOX VARIANT BY
**LEONARD KIRK & MICHAEL GARLAND**

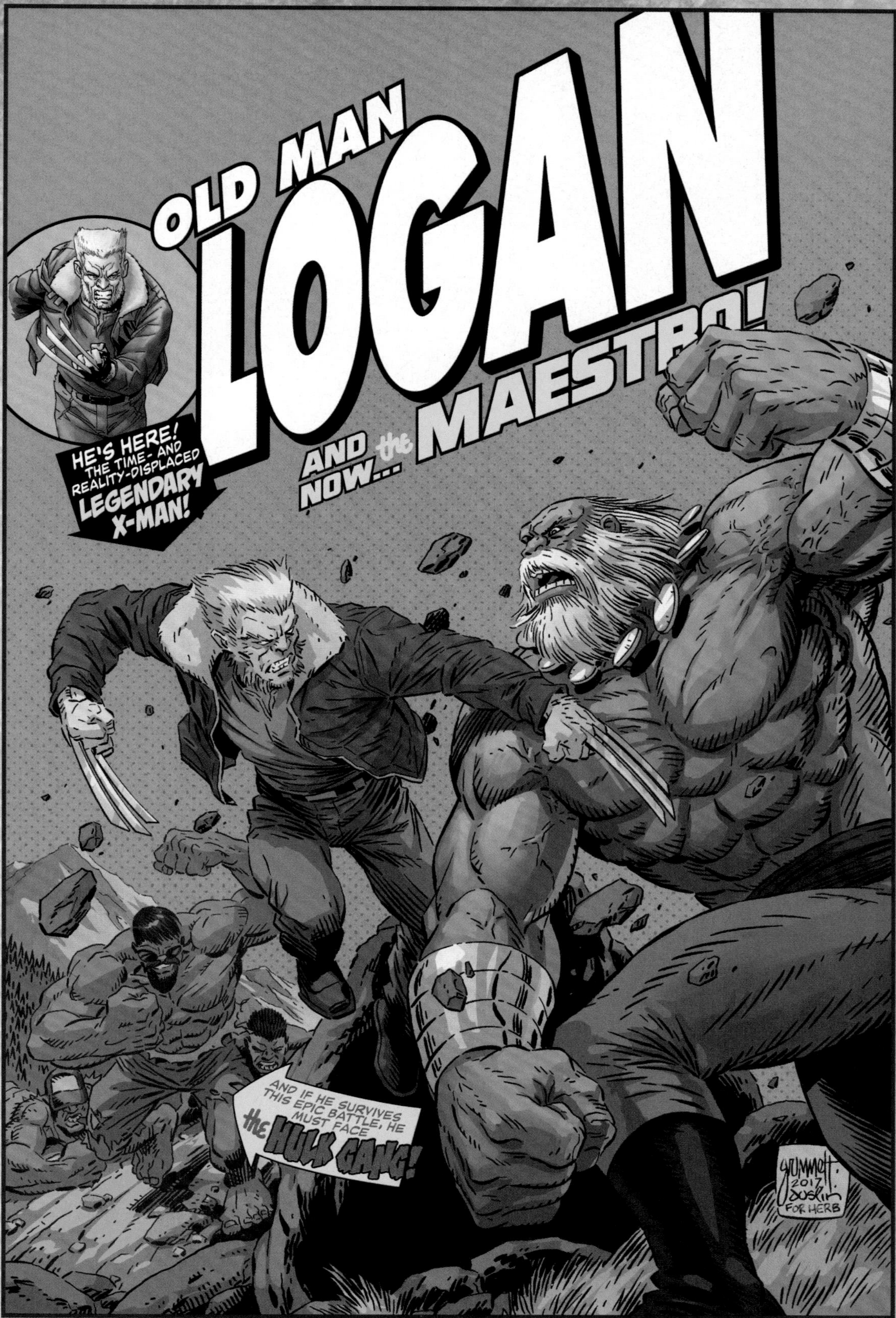
OLD MAN
LOGAN
AND NOW... the MAESTRO!
HE'S HERE! THE TIME- AND REALITY-DISPLACED LEGENDARY X-MAN!
AND IF HE SURVIVES THIS EPIC BATTLE, HE MUST FACE the HULK GANG!
GRUMMETT 2017 AUSTIN FOR HERB

#25 VARIANT BY
TOM GRUMMETT, TERRY AUSTIN & JIM CHARALAMPIDIS

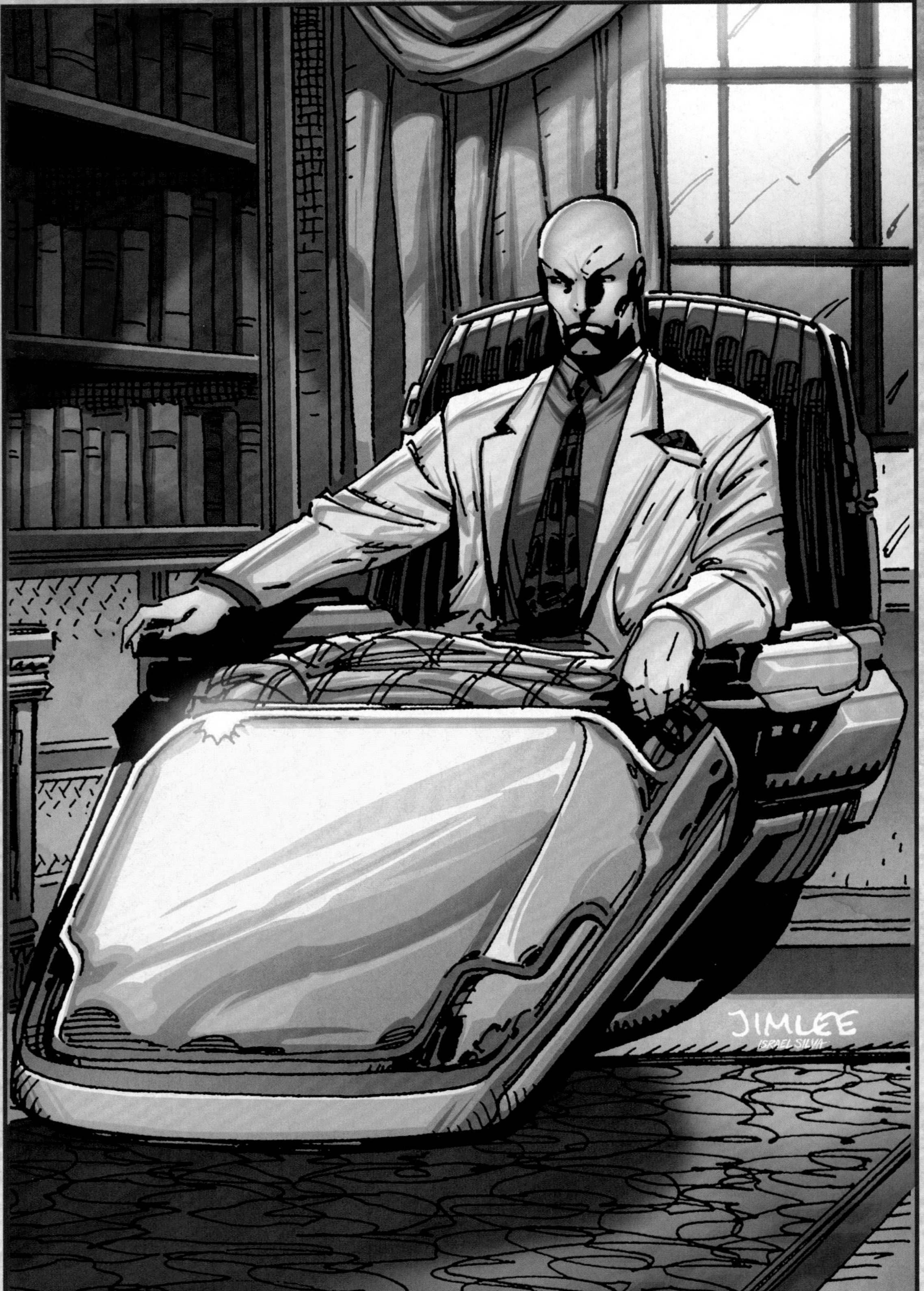
JIMLEE
ISRAEL SILVA

**#26 VARIANT BY**
**JIM LEE & ISRAEL SILVA WITH MICHAEL KELLEHER**